Comparative Education

Comparative and International Education

A DIVERSITY OF VOICES

Series Editors

Allan Pitman (*University of Western Ontario, Canada*)
Miguel A. Pereyra (*University of Granada, Spain*)
Suzanne Majhanovich (*University of Western Ontario, Canada*)

Editorial Board

Ali Abdi (*University of Alberta, Canada*)
Clementina Acedo (*Webster University Geneva, Switzerland*)
Mark Bray (*University of Hong Kong, China*)
Christina Fox (*University of Wollongong, Australia*)
Steven Klees (*University of Maryland, USA*)
Nagwa Megahed (*Ain Shams University, Egypt*)
Crain Soudien (*University of Cape Town, South Africa*)
David Turner (*University of Glamorgan, England*)
Medardo Tapia Uribe (*Universidad Nacional Autónoma de Mexico*)

VOLUME 54

The titles published in this series are listed at *brill.com/caie*

Comparative Education

A Field in Discussion

By

David A. Turner

BRILL

LEIDEN | BOSTON

Cover illustration: Photographs by Guadalupe González Turner & Instituto Bilingüe Ovidio Decroly

All chapters in this book have undergone peer review.

The Library of Congress Cataloging-in-Publication Data is available online at https://catalog.loc.gov

Typeface for the Latin, Greek, and Cyrillic scripts: "Brill". See and download: brill.com/brill-typeface.

ISSN 2214-9880
ISBN 978-90-04-51806-3 (paperback)
ISBN 978-90-04-51807-0 (hardback)
ISBN 978-90-04-51808-7 (e-book)

Copyright 2022 by Koninklijke Brill NV, Leiden, The Netherlands.
Koninklijke Brill NV incorporates the imprints Brill, Brill Nijhoff, Brill Hotei, Brill Schöningh, Brill Fink, Brill mentis, Vandenhoeck & Ruprecht, Böhlau and V&R unipress.
All rights reserved. No part of this publication may be reproduced, translated, stored in a retrieval system, or transmitted in any form or by any means, electronic, mechanical, photocopying, recording or otherwise, without prior written permission from the publisher. Requests for re-use and/or translations must be addressed to Koninklijke Brill NV via brill.com or copyright.com.

This book is printed on acid-free paper and produced in a sustainable manner.

Contents

List of Figures   VII

1 **What Is Comparative Education?**   1
    1   In Search of a Definition   1
    2   Culture Shaping Perception   8
    3   Our Field Is about People   10
    4   A Field in Discussion   12

2 **Models and Multi-Centred Studies of Education**   19
    1   Introduction   19
    2   The Detail of Macro Level Patterns   24
    3   The Game of Life as Metaphor   26
    4   An Area of Special Interest   28
    5   The Next Step   32
    6   Life Is Not the Game of Life   34
    7   A Thought Experiment   39
    8   Games against Nature   45

3 **Understanding Comparison**   51
    1   Introduction   51
    2   An Educational Computer Programme   54
    3   An Historical Approach   57
    4   A Dynamic of Diversity   60
    5   More Models   63

4 **Mapping the Field**   86
    1   The Field as Context   86
    2   Weaving the Personal and the Professional   101
    3   Toward a Science of Comparative Education   106

5 **National Character**   118
    1   Introduction   118
    2   Forming a National Character   134
    3   Essentialism   144
    4   Encyclopaedism   146
    5   Pragmatism   150

		6	Polytechnicalism 155
		7	Other Ideal Typical Models 161
		8	Confucianism 170

6   Nicholas Hans Revisited 179
    1   Hans' Factors 179
    2   The Way Forward 192

7   Holmes' Problem Solving Approach 201
    1   Holmes' Taxonomy 201
    2   Sociological Laws 218

8   Revisiting the Field 244
    1   The Field in Conversation 244
    2   Conclusions 256

References 263

Figures

1.1 Flag (a) in white light, (b) in red light, (c) in blue light, and (d) "ideal" representation.   5
1.2 Colour illusion.   7
2.1 Static patterns.   24
2.2 An oscillator from one generation to the next.   25
2.3 Five generations of a glider.   25
2.4 The cross/box through two generations.   28
2.5 The Kanizsa triangle.   29
2.6 Precursors of cross/boxes.   31
2.7 Pay-off matrix for A's winnings in scissors, paper, stone.   40
2.8 Modified pay-off matrix for A's winnings in scissors, paper, stone.   42
2.9 Reduced pay-off matrix for A's winnings in scissors, paper, stone.   42
3.1 Stafford Beer's viable system model (adapted from https://en.wikipedia.org/wiki/Stafford_Beer).   81
5.1 The price of shares over time.   167
7.1 Holmes' diagram of critical dualism.   202
7.2 Path of particle in Brownian motion (from Lee & Hoon, 1995).   221
7.3 Normal distribution with percentage of cases in each standard deviation (Mean = μ, Standard Deviation = σ).   222

CHAPTER 1

What Is Comparative Education?

1   In Search of a Definition

I have thought of myself as a comparative educationist for a long time now, but I have never tried to write a book specifically about comparative education before. Instead, I have mostly written about education in general. In one way, comparative education is not at all special. One encounters the same epistemological and ontological issues as any scholar of sociology, or history or education. How much of what I am seeing is shaped by the eyes that I see it through? How would this look different if I had been exposed to different cultural experiences before I came to this situation? But comparative education is rather special in the sense that these questions are unavoidable, inescapable. It may be possible to bracket out some of these questions, and get on and study sociology, or history, or education in general. But in comparative education we confront the difficulties of being an insider or an outsider in particularly acute form. It strikes me as significant that Archer (1979) chose to test her ideas in the field of comparative education, before going on to make more general statements about the field of sociology (Archer, 1995).

So, this is not a textbook. First of all, there is the difficulty over the concept of a textbook; having a textbook suggests that the ideas of the discipline or field have been settled, that there is an agreed way of looking at things. And frankly, in comparative education, that is not the case. We each have a different idea of what comparative education is, and what it should be. So this is a rather personal statement about what I think comparative education is and should be. And that includes the notion that comparative education is a very special proving ground; the prejudices and perceptions of the author become an inescapable part of the study itself.

But having said that, for the scholar who comes to comparative education for the first time, probably the first question that will come to mind is, What is comparative education? And it is not necessarily a question that can be answered once and for all. Scholars who have been in the field come back to that question again and again, and offer different answers, either explicitly or implicitly. Huge amounts of ink have been spent on answering the question, and yet it still seems to be unresolved. What is comparative education? What is international education? Are they the same thing, or different? And so on.

Certainly, we will all have a vague idea of what constitutes comparative education. It must involve comparison, and normally that would be a comparison of educational systems in different countries. But it could be comparison between the education of two different sub-populations in a single country, or comparison of different countries with some kind of international standard. And then what should we count as an "educational system"? Will it include social groupings that come together without official support? Will it include libraries, and the informal advice and recommendations that librarians give to readers? At what age do children enter the educational system? At age seven? Or five? Or three? Or at birth? And the more that we try to pin down exactly what comparative education is, the further we seem to move from having a clear idea of what makes up the subject. Comparative education, as an idea, seems to be slipping through our fingers.

That may explain why the two main types of answers that are given to this question are unsatisfactory. The first type of answer to the question of what is comparative education involves specifying the content, the subject matter that we are going to look at. Fairly obviously, the content matter is education, what happens when a society passes on its culture to a new generation. But that could be almost anything, from how a society manages childbirth, to how it funds universities. It might include studies that we recognise as anthropology, sociology or psychology, so it leaves untouched the question of what is distinctive about comparative education.

More specific answers have been given along these lines. Harold Noah (1974) famously used the metaphor of whaling; comparative education is any topic that comparative educationists have stuck a harpoon into, and the etiquette of academia requires that one should recognise the prior claim of any sociologist, anthropologist or psychologist who has already harpooned a topic, and leave it alone. This amounts to the suggestion that comparative education is what comparative educationists do. And that is true, but not very helpful.

Alternatively, we might argue that comparative education is what appears between the covers of *Comparative Education Review*, *Compare* and *Comparative Education*, or similar journals, handbooks and encyclopaedias. And that is also true, and is not a bad starting point for the new student of comparative education. Reading those journals and handbooks will provide a wealth of valuable information about the concerns that have motivated comparative educationists. But it is less helpful for the editors of journals and book series who have to try to decide whether a study belongs in their publication, or whether it might not better be published as a study in economics or politics. So, unfortunately, defining comparative education in terms of its content turns out to be unsatisfactory.

The second type of answer to the question of what constitutes comparative education is to try to provide a method that comparative educationists employ, or should employ. For example, comparative educationists study education by applying methods that they have drawn from another discipline, such as history or economics. That is also true, but will not serve very well to distinguish comparative eduction from history of education or economics of education. Perhaps comparative educationists are distinctive for using methods that they have drawn from two or more parent disciplines. But even if true, that would still make it difficult to claim that they were very different from social psychologists, or behavioural economists, who also seek to combine insights from cognate fields of study.

So perhaps comparative educationists can lay claim to some distinctively comparative method, can raise the art of comparison to some kind of scientific method that is distinct and all their own. I have come to the conclusion, for reasons that I shall come back to below, that such a definition of the field is impossible. It is a search for a chimera, or the holy grail of method, and it always ends in disappointment. On the other hand, I think that it can be helpful to look at the life work of many comparative educationists, and see it in terms of just such a search. Many of the leading authors in our field have given us a text that sets out the method of a scientific comparative education, although they did not necessarily agree about what would count as "scientific." Even those who agreed that the goal of study was to develop a science could not agree over the best method to attain it, and those who thought that a science of human effort was an abomination dismissed the whole project.

The fact of the matter is that most comparative educationists will use whatever method is at hand, whatever method they think will produce results, in order to illuminate the subject that they are examining. In the end, trying to define comparative education in terms of methods fails in much the same way as the attempt to define it in terms of content; there is no agreement, and a definition that includes everything is probably accurate, but does not help to distinguish between comparative education and other fields of study.

So if we cannot offer a succinct definition of what comparative education is, why is the question so difficult? Why are other disciplines and fields of study not plagued with the same kind of identity crisis? Why do sociologists, economists, historians, physicists and biologists not seem to spend time agonising over the identity crisis of their chosen field of study?

Actually, if we tried to define any of those other disciplines, rather than comparative education, we might find ourselves in exactly the same difficulties as we have in the paragraphs above. Physics is the study of all the material and energy in the universe. Chemistry is the study of all the material and energy in the universe. And biology is the study of all the material and energy in the universe that might at some time contribute to or support life, which is not very much of a limitation. Defining a discipline in terms of content seems to have the problem that, to be realistic, it has to be inclusive, and that makes it very difficult to distinguish it from other disciplines. And that applies just as much to sociology, economics and history as it does to the physical sciences.

The situation is not much better in terms of method, since scholars in any field seem willing to beg, borrow and steal methods from other areas, and engage in what Derrida (2001) describes a "bricolage," a philosophy of make do and mend, and do anything that gets the job done and produces a valuable insight. Methods in physics have changed over the centuries; in the seventeenth century the great scientist was an experimentalist, but in the nineteenth and twentieth century the great scientist was a theorist. Newton saw the universe as made up entirely of physical particles that bumped into each other, each collision producing an effect. He regarded the idea that objects might interact without coming into contact as the worst nonsense. Faraday saw the universe entirely in terms of interacting fields and action at a distance. The objects that were at the centre of such influence, if there were such objects, were of little interest. Such changes in methods and viewpoints are part of the history of every field or discipline. Kuhn (1962) has offered an account of such shifts between incommensurate viewpoints, distinct views that revolutionise disciplines, and yet the disciplines survive seemingly intact.

And so, perhaps, at last I come to what is truly distinctive about comparative education. All disciplines suffer from such crises of identity. They change and morph as new content is included, new methods predominate or new theoretical frameworks replace old ones. All subjects seem to slip though our fingers when we get up close to them, in much the same way as a beautiful lawn turns out to be made up of mud and struggling blades of grass when you get up close. The difference is that most disciplines seem to be able to put this on one side, to bracket it out, most of the time and just get on with doing economics, or history, or whatever. For comparative education, the sense of identity crisis seems to be continuous and inescapable. And it is worth devoting some thought to why that might be the case.

We each see the world through the filter of our culture and our language. That may not be a very good metaphor, because it implies there is a real world beyond our filter, and we can never know that, because the world cannot be known without some filter or other. Our particular rose coloured spectacles, our language and our culture, are part of how we see the world and interpret it. If I tell you what the world is like for me, I am telling you about the world, but I am also telling you something about myself. If I tell you that our meeting starts at ten o'clock tomorrow morning, then what that means is tied up with all sorts of cultural overtones about what it means to make an appointment, what it means to be punctual, what it means to show respect to the important guests who are coming to the meeting, and so on. It is not just a meeting; it is a meeting that has a cultural context.

Now if comparative education is about anything, it is about acknowledging that there are these different perspectives on everything. A meeting, a school, a doctor or a school principal all have a social context which shapes how we interpret them. Once we get up close, the apparent solidity of the concept tends to evaporate, to slip through our fingers.

It is in addressing that lack of consensus about what each of the terms that we use to describe education that comparative education becomes practical philosophy. Philosophy, either famously or notoriously, never finally resolves any question or settles any debate. Philosophers have, for centuries, been adding footnotes to the work of Plato, and returning endlessly to the same old discussions. That should not be confused with the idea that they have not moved on, or have not found anything out. The debates now are richer and more textured than before. But nothing is ever finally resolved. In much the same way, comparative education seeks to clarify, or make more precise, the concepts we use in education, taking into account the different perspectives implied by the fact that different scholars have different cultural perspectives.

Let me start now by looking at one of the simpler and more persistent problems of philosophy. How do our descriptions of objects and events manage to represent those objects and events? How does what we say manage to represent what we see?

Consider the flag shown in Figure 1.1. The flag is quartered diagonally, and has a white, a blue, a red and a yellow quarter. And that is how we see it if we

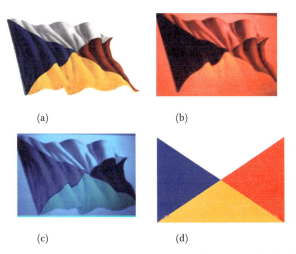

FIGURE 1.1   Flag (a) in white light, (b) in red light, (c) in blue light, and (d) "ideal" representation

look at it in white light. But if we look at it in red light, or through a red filter, it appears quite different; it appears to have a black quarter, a dark red and a light red quarter, and a white quarter. And in blue light it appears to have a black quarter (but a different black quarter from before), a dark blue and a light blue quarter, and a white quarter.

I want to say something like, "The flag is really blue, yellow, red and white as it appears in Figure 1.1a, but in special conditions it looks different." The sensation of redness, blueness and so on is something that does not really belong to the flag, but it happens in my eye when I perceive the flag. Kant suggested that objects, like the flag, have primary and secondary properties, and colour is a secondary property. The particular colours are not essential for the object's flagness.

I think that we can see what he meant. I see a metal object in the street, painted a distinctive colour and decorated with the logo of the mail service, alongside a list of times when mail is collected. I think that I have just offered a general description of a mail box. And where I come from, such mail boxes are usually red. I am used to red mail boxes. But if you say to me, "Imagine a yellow mail box," I will not have any real difficulty. I would say that it being red is not essential for it to be a mail box; it is contingent. But if you said, "Imagine a mail box with no slot where you could put the letters in," then I might respond by saying that it could not really be a mail box. Colour is not really intrinsic to it being a mail box, but the ability to receive and retain letters is.

Kant went on to suggest that, although colour is a secondary characteristic, there are primary characteristics that are essential to objects, among which, for him, the most important was extension in space, or what we might call "shape." We look at Figures 1.1a–c, and we think that we are looking at a flag that has the shape shown in Figure 1.1d. Really, the flag is rectangular. We know that the very large majority of flags in the world are rectangles of material. But how do we know such a thing? We never see flags as rectangles. Even when we see them neatly spread out on a flat table, what we see is a trapezium, or a rhombus, or some other shape, as we normally look at the flag from an oblique angle, and it does not appear as the regular rectangle that we have in mind. Why should shape be any different from colour?

But perhaps more importantly, and more generally, what is the connection between the various, specific instances of us looking at objects (in this case flags) and the idealised image of them that we have in our minds? Philosophers have come to a wide variety of different conclusions when they have considered this question. From Plato and Aristotle, through Descartes and Hume, to Kant and Hegel, not to mention modern philosophers, a wide variety of answers have been given to the question of how we know about the world that is around us. And we are acutely aware that looking at events from a different theoretical perspective will produce different results. We say of an optimist that she is looking at the world through rose-coloured spectacles. This is the metaphorical version of looking at flags in different lighting conditions. What the observer brings to the situation will affect her conclusions about what is in front of her.

The realist thinks that the world exists in its own right, and imposes certain constraints on how we see it. The idealist, like the story of the Chinese emperor who dreamed he was a butterfly, and on waking could not decide whether he was now a butterfly dreaming that he was emperor, believes that everything exists only in our imagination. Between those two extremes, different philosophers have thought of bringing our experiences of the world together with our concepts of the world in every imaginable way. Most try to strike some sort of balance between what we sense in the world and how we conceive it. We come to think there are objects like flags, even though we never experience them directly, but only sense patches of colour that change in different conditions, and shapes that change as we move. Perhaps concepts like "flag" are merely shorthand summaries for a wide range of experiences of colours and shapes. But were we born with the ability to produce those summaries, or did we learn?

Figure 1.2 shows a famous optical illusion. It represents a cube. The square in the middle of the top surface appears brown, while the square in the middle of the front surface appears yellow. In fact, in reality, they are the same colour. The eye makes automatic adjustments to one's perception, to take into account such things as shade and tone. That suggests (if the fact that you understood what I meant by "top surface" and "front surface" were not enough) that we do not simply respond to patches of colour in front of us, but that we integrate our senses to form a sense of the world. But how do we do that, since there seems to be no firm starting point?

FIGURE 1.2
Colour illusion

Some philosophers have sought ways to find such a firm foundation to build their understanding upon, while others have denied the possibility of any such firm foundation. Yet others have tried to strike a balance between having firm foundations and having no idea about where to start reasoning from. But the trouble with maintaining balance is that there is always the risk of falling off the high wire, and the need to constantly readjust between the extremes. On the other hand, extreme positions are tempting, as they may be easier to make logically consistent.

So where does comparative education come in to the picture? The point is that a number of important problems have dogged philosophy throughout millennia. One of those problems, how we bring concepts and perceptions together to produce knowledge of the world, and whether some characteristics of objects are essential and others are secondary, have been introduced here. The fascination of comparative education is that it foregrounds and emphasises those problems in a very practical way. Far from producing answers to those questions, it provides a context for understanding that the problems associated with knowledge are inescapable, and creates the need to live with the ensuing ambiguity.

2 Culture Shaping Perception

To take the example above, although mail boxes are red in the United Kingdom, and I have come to see red mail boxes as "natural," mailboxes in Spain are yellow, in the United States of America are blue, and if there are such things in China, they are probably green. Experience of how things are done in different countries is an antidote to certainty, and de-centres the observer in a way that creates the possibility of understanding that competing interpretations are possible, and that there may not be one best way of interpreting phenomena.

Of course, it also makes life more difficult, since one can hardly open one's mouth to say anything, without pausing to question whether somebody else might understand something quite different by the words one uses. Comparative education becomes a question of how different people, from different countries, different cultural backgrounds and using different languages, interpret the world, and by implication, how each generation passes its interpretation on to the next generation. And we do not have the luxury of being able to take off our rose-coloured glasses to see the world in its true colours; the world can only be interpreted through one kind of filter or another.

This can be linked to the idea that we should not "reify" abstract concepts; some concepts, like colours in the above examples, are brought about by the observer, rather than being in the objects observed, and we should be wary of thinking they exist in the real world, like flags and mail boxes. Actually, we should be careful of reifying any concepts, and thinking they have an existence outside the way that we think about them. We should be careful about saying anything is "really" like this or that. With colours, we seem to have a natural condition (of white light) where we can see how objects really are. But in other senses, there is no obvious way of seeing things as they really are, without seeing them through a particular filter.

It has become commonplace to talk of theories as "lenses"; I shall present this study through the lens of structuralism, for example, or functionalism. But this is not quite correct, as we have no way of viewing the world without a lens. A lens may be seen to distort our normal picture, by making things appear closer, for example. But when it comes to viewing the world without concepts, or a theoretical framework, there is no corresponding undistorted representation, and we should be automatically wary of anybody who claims to be able to identify "reality." It is that wariness that is central to an understanding of comparative education.

People see the world through the lens of their language and their culture. So being English is like seeing the world through a blue filter, while being French is like seeing the world through a red filter. Different features will be highlighted, or will disappear, depending on the filter that is used. Colour vision is a metaphor for seeing the world though different cultures. But not an exact metaphor, because there is nobody who can stand outside all culture and view the world without a filter. Comparative education should make us aware that different people view education differently, because they have been inducted into a particular cultural approach to education. But it should do something else as well. It should undermine our own sense of certainty, our own sense that what we have viewed as "natural," the obvious way to approach things, is the only way to view things. As we come to see the world as others see it, we should also become less certain about how we see it.

This, in the end, for me, is the thing that makes comparative education endlessly fascinating; as you learn more about the ways in which other cultures approach questions, you also learn about yourself.

But the cultural issues relating to colour vision are more than just metaphorical; different cultures literally see colours differently. When I go to Japan, people might tell me that a temple, such as the temple at Miyajima, is painted red, because red is the colour of holiness. But I always am given pause by the colour, because it does not really look red to me; vermilion is more the colour that comes to mind. On the other hand, the Chinese might tell me that red is the colour of good luck, while the Russians named Red Square because red is the colour of beauty. The colour red has different associations and is seen in slightly different ways in different cultures.

I think of this as an issue for comparative education because, although the link between what is in the world, and what we bring to it when we perceive it, has been a perennial issue for philosophy, for most people it will probably seem esoteric, and not something that needs worrying about very much. Most people can probably get by with a fairly common sense notion that there is a real world, and we can test our ideas out by holding them up in some way against the real world. This is what Wilfrid Sellars (1953) has called, "the myth of the given"; "the given" because it presupposes the existence of a real world out there that can stand as the court in which our theories are tested, and "the myth" because, as we have seen, there is no way to get to the world except through the use of theories and concepts. In the words of John McDowell (1994), there is nowhere that is beyond the conceptual.

Each comparative educationist will have to form his or her own idea of how it is possible to know what exists in the world, and what exists, like beauty, in the eye of the beholder. And then, having decided his or her own position, they will have to cope with the fact that every other comparative educationist has made up their own mind, and none of them agree. This makes it very difficult to begin, as it is impossible to find any safe starting point from which one can develop a simple approach to comparative education.

These questions of what is in the world, and how we know about it (which may be described as the questions of ontology and epistemology, respectively) are not the only philosophical questions that run through the study of comparative education. Equally important is the question of what people are like, or rather what is the nature of a person? Again, when we look at this question we are likely to find ourselves torn between incompatible answers.

3   Our Field Is about People

People are unlike any other objects of study. When we examine the physical world, we expect to see causal links; if we do this, then that will follow. And although people may respond to external stimuli, their responses are always qualitatively different, because people do not merely react. They act. Except in the case of physical reflexes, the stimulus must first enter consciousness and they must then decide to act. The connection between stimulus and response is not automatic. Or to put it another way, people have scope for being spontaneous. Unlikely though it is, I might wake up tomorrow and realise that my existence has been futile, and I should spend the rest of my life meditating in a cave. That, as a human being, there is scope for such radical spontaneity is a feature of humanity, as is our need to see everything through the lens of making meaning out of our actions.

And one obvious area where we express that spontaneity is in choosing the lens through which we view the world. I see an incident in the street, and I may choose to interpret it through a lens of sociology, or through a lens of psychology. And as far as anybody involved in education is concerned, this question is unavoidable, because education is precisely about helping people to see the world through a different lens. After an educational experience, it should be possible to see the world in a different light. Recognising that extreme volatility or spontaneity is part of respecting the individuality of the people that we live and work with.

On the other hand, if we actually lived in a world where every individual was radically unpredictable, life would be impossible. For the most part people behave in a way that more or less conforms to the pattern that they have set previously. People turn up for work, go home to their family, follow certain routines, and, generally speaking, exercise their spontaneity in a fairly constrained way. Especially when we come to considering large numbers of people, it is possible to make certain predictions. The population of a city, for example, will, without conscious coordination, create traffic jams in the morning and evening rush hour. If we increase the price of something, other things being equal, we expect people to buy less of it. For many purposes, people behave in ways that follow fairly simple rules, such as, "If we do this, that will follow."

At the extreme end of this spectrum are cyberneticists such as Stafford Beer (2009) and Norbert Wiener (1954), who think that people are just another example of an information processing machine, and that there is no sharp division between machines and people. Thus we have a range of views of how to deal with people, from an extreme humanism that recognises only the spontaneity of individuals, through to a scientific approach that concentrates only on regularities in understanding human behaviour. Somewhere in between those extremes each observer of education will try to find some acceptable position, although, again, it is probably easier to be logically consistent at one extreme or the other. But we are unlikely to meet an individual who accepts that he or she is a "mere" machine, any more than we would wish to continue long acquaintance with somebody who was completely unpredictable. (How could you arrange to meet them?)

But even thinking about larger groups of people, as they come together in social groupings and society at large, people will differ as to whether they think that social groups move as a result of choices that individuals make, or individuals make choices because they are part of a group. An extreme example of this difference in perspective can be found in *War and Peace*, where Tolstoy (2007), who opposes the idea that history is shaped by the decisions of individuals, and especially Napoleon, argues that, during the march on Moscow, the French people were moving toward the east, and Napoleon happened to be the personification of that geographical tendency.

As with the other questions, it seems to be easiest to be logically consistent at one end of the spectrum or the other, but maintaining such a position generally appears to be in conflict with common sense. So Tolstoy's account of history strikes us as bizarre. But we have each been inducted into a language community, with all that implies for our worldview, and we might find it less strange to hear sociologists describing us as shaped by the language that we use to characterise the world: "the language speaks through us" or "the language speaks us" (Heidegger, 1971).

So I come back to the basic tenets of comparative education that I was taught by Brian Holmes, that each comparative educationist must decide his or her position on these key questions: what constitutes knowledge, what kind of creature is a person, and how does society function. I would perhaps only add the question of ontology; what kind of objects exist in the world?

4 A Field in Discussion

Actually, if what we seek before we start is a firm foundation, like the Cartesian starting point for reasoning, things are rather worse than that. As comparative educationists we have each of us to make up our own minds on these questions, but we also have to recognise that any account that another comparative educationist offers is filtered through his or her own position on these questions. And, in addition to that, each individual in each different education system will also have had to come to a position on these questions at one level or another.

Fortunately, for most of our lives, we can bracket out those difficult questions and treat the concepts that we use as simple. If I say I am going to visit a school tomorrow, you do not normally need to ask me a lot of questions about what I mean by a "school"; is that just the buildings, or do people have to be present? Do all the people have to be present, or just some? Do they have to do anything special for you to call it a school? No, in everyday life we know what we mean by a school, and we can treat it as an uncontested concept. This turning of amorphous, ambiguous concepts into uncomplicated objects of study is called "reification." And by and large, although we know that reification is an illusion, and that it is a bad thing, we do it and we can get along very well. We can deal with love and enthusiasm and uncles and radishes as though they were uncontested, clear ideas, that everyone will understand when we use the words. We may have to stop and recognise some of the difficulties occasionally – "He is not a real uncle. He is a long term friend of my father's, but I call him 'uncle'" – but for the most part we do not need to keep interrupting the flow of our conversation with such qualifications. And we might sometimes step back and reflect on what we really mean by "love," or "wisdom" but those are special moments in our lives, and will not prevent us from saying, "I love you," or "She is a wise woman."

And in most disciplines the situation is the same. Most of the concepts can be bracketed out and treated as solid objects most of the time. There will be moments when the concepts are questioned, but those are special moments. I can go into my chemistry class and learn that atoms are made up of electrons circling a nucleus, and use the number of electrons to understand and explain the chemical properties of different elements. On another day I may have to study quantum mechanics and learn that what electrons do is not exactly "circling" as I normally understand the expression, but something rather mysterious. Everything can be questioned sometimes, but not necessarily all at once.

In comparative education the situation is rather different. At any moment what I thought of as a concrete, uncomplicated concept can be called into question. This can range from the simplest, wondering whether Japanese people mean the same by the word "radish" as I do, through to the most complicated, wondering whether "education" is an adequate translation of the German "Bildung." This is partly because the content of comparative education is explicitly about recognising differences in culture, for example between different nations. But it is also a question of attitude. Long involvement in the study of comparative education should stimulate a concern over the dangers of reification; treating concepts as given, as uncontested can lead to all sorts of misunderstandings.

For example, Waldow and Steiner-Khamsi (2019) use the metaphor of projection to account for a range of phenomena linked to interpretations of PISA results. Scholars in one country project their concerns and debates onto another country that has done well or badly in PISA, in order to make sense. As Waldow puts it, "The ensuing image is mostly determined by the 'slide' and not by the 'screen'" (Waldow & Steiner-Khamsi, 2019, p. 5). What we see when we look at the good results of Finland, China or Singapore has less to do with what is going on in those countries than on what we want to understand, the filter that we look through. That double vision, understanding our own understanding, is integral to comparative education.

So one reason for the difficulties in answering the question, What is comparative education? arises from a refusal to reify "comparative education," an academic orientation or inclination to treat disciplines and fields of study as problematic. Now I am not arguing that comparative education is unique. I actually believe that we do a huge amount of damage when we reify other disciplines. Our students are faced with choices in their educational development and have to choose subjects. And because we reify those subjects, the question is put as one of matching; Do you think you will fit better in history or in languages? And as a result, when they get to university, or upper secondary school, and find they are not enjoying the subject that they chose, they tend to see it as a failing. They did not fit in the subject. I would much prefer to see disciplines and fields as something as a background against which one could do something, study something. Not, Do you want to study history? But, What do you want to do with history? What will you contribute to make history your own?

Now clearly, over centuries and decades a lot of scholars have decided to change what history is. They were disillusioned by the study of dead, white men, and wanted to include social history, minority history, economic history and other elements that would not have been considered history before their intervention. And the same with every other discipline. Literary criticism today is not what it was a hundred years ago. Economics is not what Adam Smith wrote, and sociology is not what Max Weber wrote. Disciplines change as a result of determined efforts of individuals who have decided that they have a contribution to make that shifts the focus of study. But generally speaking, this activity is seen as distinct, as revolutionary practice rather than "normal."

With the possible exceptions of art and music, where what is to be included in the field is routinely contested, comparative education stands out for not having formed into a solid and agreed shape. The question should not be, What is comparative education? But, What do you want to do with comparative education? What do you want to make out of it? And there can be no general answer to that question. Each of us will be pushing the study in our own particular way, and where it eventually moves will depend on the efforts of all of us, or of none.

For my part, I am interested in how people behave. I want to understand why people do what they do, and why the social world is as it is. I do not particularly want to be active in politics, but I do wish to understand how political decisions are made. And I would quite like to know if there is a better way to organise things. And, yes, I suppose that I must admit to wanting to encourage people to be more thoughtful, more reflective, more questioning, and less reliant on common sense. And I have chosen the field of comparative education to pursue those interests.

Now the choice of comparative education is not, as I hope is by now clear, completely arbitrary. There is a match between how I see the world, or perhaps rather, how I want to see how other people see the world, and the central concerns of comparative education. I have a concern not to reify abstract concepts. I recognise that what one sees is shaped and formed by the conceptual framework through which one views it (for want of a better description). And there is a range of practical issues that arise from this, and which are best illustrated through international and intercultural contexts.

But I also recognise that I bring to these tasks my own personal, unique history, with all the concepts and prejudices I have picked up along the way, so I am not going to offer an answer to the question of what comparative education is, but rather present what comparative education is for me. And that brings me back to the difficulty of presenting a textbook. A textbook typically presents the crystallised, reified body of knowledge that counts as a discipline. For reasons that should be clear by now, there can be no textbook of comparative education. Some scholars have offered what they intended to be textbooks, and I mean them no disrespect. But what they eventually produce is a piece of advocacy that pushes the study of comparative education in one direction or another. And I think that is valuable. In fact, I think it so valuable that I am going to offer here my own version; comparative education as seen through my eyes, using rose coloured spectacles that I have borrowed from other people.

So perhaps I should start with what I intend to make out of comparative education. At the risk of exhibiting hubris, my goal is to understand why people do what they do, and if possible try to anticipate what they are going to do. It is an ambitious goal. I have chosen comparative education as the appropriate approach because, as I have already stated, for me the key to understanding is that we each see situations through our own filter of meaning, and this shapes our actions. As education is the process through which we learn to see the world through the eyes of our native culture, the study of education seems a good place to start when seking insight into how that cultural filter functions. And comparative education, more than any other study I have come across, emphasises this cultural veil that we cast across the world we encounter. In psychology it is too easy to believe that we all have the same underlying mental mechanisms. In economics it is too easy to believe that people act to maximise their benefits. Most fields of study seek to universalise, to tell us about the way that all people function. But in comparative education it is always at the back of one's mind that this is just another filter through which to understand what people are doing.

Elsewhere, taking an idea from Steve Klees (CIES, 2006), I have argued that comparative education is composed of a number of core debates and that it is the unsettled nature of those debates that characterises comparative education (Turner, 2019). Actually, more than that, it is the fact that those debates are fundamentally insoluble that characterises the study. I will try to keep two of those debates firmly in mind as I work through this exposition.

The first is a seeming paradox, that we approach the people that we are trying to understand with two quite distinct ideas about what it means to be a human agent. On the one hand, people *en masse* seem to be very predictable. In policy terms we treat people as subject to the forces and pressures of life, that an increase in tax can discourage certain actions, or a simple advertisement will have them rushing to the shops. On the other hand, at an individual level people are unpredictable, whimsical and volatile. At that personal level, people are as likely to react against pressure as to acquiesce; well perhaps not as likely, but there is scope for an unpredictable response. Human beings never behave exactly as though effects follow directly from causes.

These two very different insights into the behaviour of people have become embodied in distinct disciplines in humanities and the social sciences. In the humanities of history and philosophy the outstandingly individual is celebrated. The rational being can rethink her or his situation and change direction, opening up the endless possibilities of change. And by seeing things as they have never been seen before, the individual can change history, change the course of intellectual development, or establish new ways of thinking and acting. In contrast with that, the social sciences look for continuity and patterns. They look for forces, sociological and psychological, that shape people in intelligible and predictable ways.

If we are to understand education we need both of these incompatible approaches. If people cannot be changed, cannot break out of the continuity and trends that have shaped them up to now, then there is no point in engaging in education at all. But if people are completely unpredictable and whimsical, the idea of understanding and planning education is impossible. A multidisciplinary approach to education must incorporate both of these insights into the nature of human action, or it is doomed to be incomplete.

In parallel with that distinction between the two views of the people we hope to understand, there is the methodological debate over whether we should conceive a person's action in terms of the concepts she or he actually employs, or whether we can impose our own categories on the actions we see before us. If people are rational, and able to rationalise their own actions, then we have no hope of understanding what they do unless we first understand how they think. My fear of spiders is real, and has real effects on my actions, even if it is whimsical and unpredictable. On the other hand, if people are driven by forces which operate, as it were, behind their back, and in a way of which they are unconscious, then what they think is irrelevant to understanding their actions.

These two debates, which are not so much debates between groups of people or schools of thought, as two perspectives that are in constant tension in each of us, are the ontological basis (what kind of beings exist in the world) and the methodological basis (how we should understand, interpret and study their actions) of everything that follows in comparative education. I am not sure whether we are looking for some kind of middle position or compromise. But at the very least, a person must be able to understand the concepts that are being used to explain their actions. For a tax on sweets to reduce the consumption of sugary snacks it is essential that those who are doing the consuming must understand the concepts of money and the meaning of a transaction (in a way that a child of three, for example, seems not to). On the other hand, that same person may understand the concepts, while denying that they actually explain their actions. Increasing taxation on cigarettes reduces the average level of smoking in society, but that was not the reason that I gave up smoking; I had other, personal reasons that were specific to my case.

In bringing together these disparate views of what people do and why they do it, it is only to be expected that different scholars, at different times, will put the accent in different places. In what follows I will try to develop and present my own approach to those debates, and to produce a coherent view of education as it is observed in different cultural contexts. However, before I start on that properly, I need to make a detour into some further questions of method. In line with the distinction drawn above, between the reasoning individual and the individual who is driven by society's currents, we seem to have two powerful tools to help us understand what is going on in the world: reason and observation. We can, like Descartes, distrust observation and our senses, and rely only on reason to critique what we think we know. Or we can, like Bacon, put aside what we think we understand, and let observation dictate the development of our theories.

I will argue that neither of these approaches is suitable. Observation on its own cannot tell us anything. We need to interpret what we see, and to give it meaning. Although we talk about the "data" of observation, in fact nothing is "given." Meaning is made and not taken. Problems are made and not found. But on the other hand, reason alone is powerless, because we can all too readily let the flights of fancy create complex theoretical structures that turn out to be castles in the air. In the words of Marx, "Practice without theory is blind. Theory without practice is sterile." But that still leaves the question of exactly how the two are to be brought into a coherent whole.

My own answer to that is through a process of modelling. We need first to develop a model, a reasoned ideal, of how we think things are working. As we develop the model in a logical and reasoned way, certain features will become clear about how we might expect the system to work. We then look at experience and observation to see whether the model we have developed helps to understand what is going on, committed to the idea that if the model does not explain anything difficult or interesting, then it will have to be rejected. This is the hypothetico-deductive method, which has been put forward by Popper (1959) as the method of science. Popper insisted that a model or theory should have interesting empirical content; it is easy enough to find true theories that explain very little, or very complicated theories that can expain absolutely everything. A good theory should not only explain something of importance, but should also make clear what it would take to refute the theory. Popper's particular dislike was for psychoanalysis, which, he thought, could, with a few turns of logic, explain any behaviour at all, and therefore really explained nothing. But before I go too far along the line of explaining that approach, I had best explain why I think that is a preferable approach to induction, based on direct observation.

There are good philosophical reasons for rejecting induction, which can be seen in discussions of science since the eighteenth century and the work of David Hume (1739/1969). But notwithstanding those shaky foundations, induction seems to predominate in the study of education, from informal acceptance of the dominance of observations, such as a reliance on PISA results, to a formal adoption of grounded theory, where theory is supposed to be driven by data (Glaser & Strauss, 1967). Rather than revisit that philosophical debate, which in my view has vanquished induction but allowed it back by default, I will start from the practical consideration of educational models, to indicate how they offer a different way of unifying methods in educational concerns.

CHAPTER 2

Models and Multi-Centred Studies of Education

1   Introduction

In the previous chapter, I suggested that one of the key problems we face, as either scholars or philosophers, is how to match up what we learn about the world through our senses, and how we reason about the way in which the world is a reasonable, intelligible place. How much faith do we put in reason? And how much in observation? On the one hand, those who put their faith only in observation and experience seek to look at the world, and to note how patterns and connections reveal themselves to the observer. This is basically the method of induction, of drawing out generalisations from a host of individual observations. In the seventeenth century, David Hume, the Scottish philosopher, demonstrated that there was no logical reason for supposing that induction was well founded, although we might, he suggested, have an in-built psychological tendency to believe that patterns we have observed will persist into the future.

Notwithstanding that rather unpromising start, induction received something of a boost in the eighteenth century with the publication of Bayes' Theorem, and in the twentieth and twenty first centuries seems to go from strength to strength with general embodiments in grounded theory, and specific developments in neuroscience and the "Bayesian brain."

This persistence of methods that depend on induction was, perhaps, understandable, while Newton's cosmology, the best example of successful Renaissance science, was dominant. But when cracks started to show in that body of knowledge at the beginning of the twentieth century, with Einstein's publication of the theory of relativity, people started to take seriously the problems of induction, which had previously been regarded as merely of theoretical importance. The philosopher who did most to re-examine the idea that knowledge became more certain through a process of prolonged observation was Karl Popper (1959). He put forward the idea that, rather than simply observe, one starts with a theory, and the theory guides the process of observation. Moreover, since refutation of a theory is more certain that confirmation, observation was performed until a theory was definitively refuted. That is to say, one can generally tell from a single observation when something has gone very wrong with a theory, while repeated successful observations do not necessarily do much to support confidence in it.

A variation was offered by Thomas Kuhn (1962) who argued that the scientific community works within a "paradigm," a widely accepted theoretical framework. "Normal science" involves fitting different observations and experiments into that framework, while occasionally, in revolutionary periods, the whole paradigm is overturned when too much contrary evidence accumulates. On this model, refuting a theory is not a simple finding of a single contrary observation, but a social process where the community as a whole becomes convinced.

Although Popper and Kuhn are not advocating the same idea about how science is, or should be, conducted, they share the view that a theoretical framework is necessary before worthwhile empirical observation is possible. I take this as an important methodological point, the topic of a decision that each researcher has to make before they can start; to observe in the hope of inducing patterns and sequences, or to develop a fully articulated model beforehand. This idea of developing a hypothesis and setting out to test deductions from that hypothesis is known as the hypothetico-deductive method, and since it depends on deductive logic rather than inductive logic, it is not open to the same logical complaints as induction. My own choice, having been persuaded of the logical reasons for rejecting induction, or theory-free observation, is that I prefer to use theoretical frameworks and models to shape observation. I also take the view that such a framework or model should be fairly well developed, in the sense that it should have all the features that one hopes to study in observation or experiment.

Of course, such a model will be based on, and draw on, previous experience, so it can be argued that this is a hidden kind of induction, and that the gap between the inductive and hypothetico-deductive approaches is not so very wide. But I think that it is worth emphasising that developing a complex hypothesis in this way can make very clear exactly what observations one needs, either to support or to refute it. In this chapter I will present two different hypothetical models of aspects of education, and try to show how they might be used to develop studies.

But if I allow that the gap between induction and hypothetico-deductive reasoning may have been over-estimated from one side, it may also be narrower on the other. That is to say, I simply do not believe that anybody can approach observation with a blank mind, or, in the terms of grounded theory, can "bracket out" previous prejudices. The selection of instances from the wealth of experience that we have, to construct "data," involves a filtering process. And if we do not construct the filter deliberately and consciously, we will do it accidentally and unconsciously. Attempting observation without theory is an invitation to include prejudices, prior assumptions and common sense ideas without examination. And that can hardly lead to any new approaches.

In a fascinating reflection on the methods of comparative education, Max Eckstein (1983) draws attention to the use of metaphor. While the use of metaphor, as Eckstein argues, is not unproblematic, he suggests that metaphorical thinking is an inescapable part of human thinking and communication. So rather than arguing for or against the use of metaphor, his central argument is for the reflective, self-conscious use of metaphor, since 'the unexamined metaphor, like the unexamined life, may be of limited value' (Eckstein, 1983, p. 311).

He also points out that we need to examine metaphors critically, and occasionally consider new metaphors, as 'those we rely on are rather simple, overworked, derivative and limiting' (Eckstein, 1983, p. 321). By way of an indication as to where we might seek such new metaphors, Eckstein highlights the influence that the computer-as-metaphor has exerted in the accounts of psychologists and educators. The new technology of computer-related developments may provide other useful metaphors.

The case I am making here is that metaphors can become so much a way of thinking about an issue that the metaphor effectively disappears, and we take the metaphor for a description of the phenomenon that we are examining, and a project can become no more that a confirmation of common sense. And, as Popper has pointed out, we should prefer bold hypotheses that are likely to be wrong or interesting, over those that are bland and obvious.

In his analysis of viable systems, Stafford Beer (Hilder, 1995) argues that in dealing with variation in our environment, we need to select the information that we need, so that we can adapt to changes in the environment. In order to do that, we need a theory or hypothesis which represents our world and our relationship to it. Such hypotheses can vary in complexity, and will set the level of variability in the environment that we can cope with. For that reason I am suggesting that we need to go beyond simple metaphors, to build hypotheses that can capture and illuminate important aspects of institutions and societies. However, any theory is an abstraction from experience, and is used to isolate certain features for the purpose of study. It is therefore rather important not to confuse a theoretical abstraction with any idea that it represents "reality."

The first complex hypothesis, or extended metaphor, that I wish to introduce in a reflective way, is John Conway's "Game of Life" (Gardner, 1970). For several years now I have been using Conway's "Game of Life" as a metaphor for some of the concepts that are central to, and problematic in, comparative education. The "Game of Life" is a metaphor on several different levels. As a computer programme, it is not alive, and so is already metaphor, indicating that it might offer some insights into the processes of living. At the same time, it is not a game either, as the word is usually understood, and it suggests that life might be understood as a process in which an organism might "win" or "lose." But before I can develop any of those external links, and explain how this metaphor might be used to generate hypotheses, I need to explain exactly what I understand by Conway's Game of Life.

For those who are unfamiliar with the Game of Life, it is a cellular automaton. That is to say, it is a grid pattern of cells, where each cell can be either filled in (alive) or left blank (dead). The pattern of cells that are alive in the next generation depends upon the pattern in the current generation, and only upon the pattern of the current generation.

The rules that govern whether a cell is alive or dead are quite mechanical. The fate of a cell is determined by its eight immediate neighbours. If a living cell has either two or three living neighbours, then it will survive into the next generation. If it has fewer living neighbours it dies of loneliness, while if it has more living neighbours it dies of overcrowding. If a dead cell has exactly three living neighbours, then it will come to life in the next generation. Over a sequence of generations, patterns morph and shift in unpredictable ways which are fascinating in their own way.

This is such a dynamic way of visualising events that it is helpful to have a version of the Game of Life to run and have moving pictures to supplement the static pictures that I can include here. I use a version called Winlife,[1] but other implementations are available on the Internet.

When I use this computer model for teaching, I take a starting position with a grid 1,000 cells by 1,000 cells and fill it with a random pattern in which 50 per cent of the cells are alive in the first generation, and set it running, before explaining the rules that govern the passage from one generation to the next. Over time, a pattern develops in which some areas of the screen are relatively inactive, while other areas are shifting and changing and there appears to be a great deal of activity.

The Game of Life is an explicit, and simplified, model of more complex naturally occurring phenomena. As the name implies, it is supposed to model the process of life, perhaps as we might see the growth and death of colonies of bacteria in a petri dish. But I choose to use it as a metaphor for aspects of another organic process, the process of education, and highlight some features of the model that attract my attention as relevant to education.

The initial stage of explicit modelling, namely setting the rules by which one generation gives rise to the next, is a simplified metaphor for one of the central themes of education: How does the environment shape and/or possibly determine the thoughts and actions of an individual? Since the environment in the model consists only of other individuals, this is a question of how the culture in which one lives shapes the individual. In the model, this influence is settled by fiat; the rules are simple, and as I have explained them above. Cells do not have individual agency. Since cells do not have agency and people do, we must expect that the Game of Life will not be a good model for all aspects of education. But that is the nature of a simplified model and it may nevertheless help to illuminate certain other aspects.

We know (because it is the definition of the Game of Life) that cells are only influenced by their immediate neighbours. And yet this immediately local influence produces patterns that are reliably reproduced over large distances. One can always see the same pattern, of some relatively static areas and other areas that exhibit a great deal of activity. Something similar was shown in the simulation of bird flocks and fish schools by Craig Reynolds (1987), where short range influence nevertheless produces large scale patterns that would not necessarily be expected. This is the second central concern of comparative education, namely, how does the action of many individuals add up to a greater overall pattern? Or, perhaps, more precisely, how is the existence of a culture developed by the actions of a lot of uncoordinated individuals.

In the case of the Game of Life, no linkage between cells that are not directly in contact has been specified, and still the structure of the game produces consistent patterns, time and time again, over large distances. As I emphasise when I use this to teach, I start with a new random pattern, but the outcome is the same result.

This is an opportunity to discuss the questions raised by Archer (1995) in relation to the inter-connectedness between the macro level, the meso level and the micro level. Archer points to the, in her view, errors of upward and downward conflation. Upward conflation is the perspective that everything is determined by the macro level; culture, and the environment that the individual lives in, determines what the individual is, and what he or she can become. Downward conflation is the perspective that only individuals exist, and only individuals make decisions, so anything that appears at the macro level is purely an epiphenomenon created by individual psychologies. I believe that Archer is right in identifying the two key processes as crucial to our understanding: how the micro influences (but does not determine) the macro, and how the macro influences (but does not determine) the micro.

These are, and must be, constant problems in the study of comparative education. We engage in upward conflation when we apply national stereotypes, for example, and suggest that all individuals from a specific country have such and such a characteristic. And we engage in downward conflation when we think that everything can be explained by individual and universal psychology, which is not impacted by culture.

Archer separates, and unites, these two processes by invoking the passage of time. Past generations have created the macro level, which influences the individual. In turn, the individual's actions at the micro level can shape the macro level culture, which will shape future generations. I think that this is a mistake, in the sense that I want to envisage a situation where both influences can operate concurrently and reciprocally, so that what an individual does is shaped buy the culture they wish to create, as much as the culture of the past.

But that is really a topic for another time and place, because the Game of Life models a very clear passage of time, with each generation only influenced by the immediately preceding generation. Cells cannot have hopes, aspirations or anticipation. In addition, since the model has been defined in terms of the behaviour of individual cells, it models downward conflation. Nevertheless, the emergence of large scale patterns which seemingly take on a life of their own raises the problematic question of downward conflation, and opens a space for the discussion of the interpretation of micro, meso and macro level events.

2 The Detail of Macro Level Patterns

The next stage in my discussion of the Game of Life involves focusing on a number of small features that can be seen in the patterns that emerge, and to offer a language to describe them. There are three types of features that I want to draw attention to: static patterns, oscillators and gliders.

There are a number of patterns that remain perfectly static through successive generations, subject only to the condition that no external event occurs to disturb them. The simplest of these is a block of four living cells in a square. Since each cell has three living neighbours, all persist into the next generation. But any pattern that involves a chain of living cells (each cell having two living neighbours, will remain unaltered.

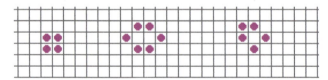

FIGURE 2.1 Static patterns

There are also patterns that oscillate between two states, coming back to their original pattern in the next generation. The simplest of these is a line of three living cells, which in the next generation transforms into another line of three living cells, but perpendicular to its original orientation.

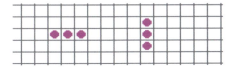

FIGURE 2.2 An oscillator from one generation to the next

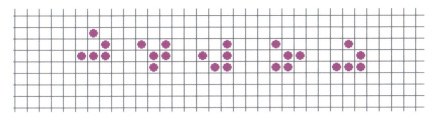

FIGURE 2.3 Five generations of a glider

And the third important shape that has played a major part in the study and development of the Game of Life is the glider. The glider is a pattern that consists of a configuration of five cells. As shown in Figure 2.3, it goes through a number of transformations, so that after each four generations it returns to its original shape and orientation. However, the significance of the glider is that after generations it has moved its position. Gliders move in a characteristic diagonal direction that makes them relatively easy to spot when they occur (and they do occur) randomly in the larger patterns.

Armed with this attention to detail, we can focus on a new random pattern of living cells when the simulation is run once more. The same happens as before, but now we can create a more detailed commentary. There are large parts of the overall pattern where there are only static patterns or oscillators, which is to say that nothing of much interest is happening. But in other areas, activity is obvious as areas of living cells grow and shrink, ebb and flow. And periodically this activity will give rise to a glider, which leaves an area of high activity and ventures out into an area of inactivity.

What happens next is a matter of interest, but unpredictable. Eventually the glider will encounter some other living cells in its path. They may be static patterns or oscillators, or even another area of high activity. However, even if the glider encounters only static patterns or oscillators, a burst of fresh activity will usually result. This new activity may last for only a few generations, or may last for several generations, but usually it will die out again before very long. But very occasionally, the glider will give rise to a whole new area of high activity that persists for quite a long time.

And this does serve to emphasise Archer's point, that neither the macro nor the micro taken alone will allow us to predict on which occasions the activity will fizzle out, and on which it will establish a long term change.

3 The Game of Life as Metaphor

I have to say that I like the Game of Life as a metaphor for many aspects of education at many levels. At the classroom level, having active and inquisitive peers can be stimulating, while having non-responsive peers can dampen enthusiasm. As a consequence, learning activity tends to be concentrated in local areas and over relatively short timescales. Before I became a teacher, I thought that taking a random group of thirty individuals would produce pretty much the same results every time, and one classroom would look and feel much like another. I soon found that was not the case, and that a classroom where the activity feeds off itself is very different from one where not much is happening. The concentration of activity in small, but changing, areas of the field in the Game of Life seems to me to speak of this kind of virtuous or vicious cycle in education. In the context of markets, Mandelbrot (Mandelbrot & Hudson, 2008) has described this as the Joseph Effect, where seven lean years follow seven fruitful years.

At an institutional level, the encroachment of a glider into an area of inactivity might be seen as a metaphor for a change agent or reformer entering a traditional organisation. The outcome is unpredictable, but might be anything from a radical reorganisation of the original structure to a short-term activity that fizzles out as soon as the reformer leaves, or for some other reason becomes ineffective. And in the former case, the radical change may or may not be the change that was intended. Again, this is not modelled in the Game of Life, since intention and anticipation are absent, but we can judge, from our own inability to anticipate exactly what the outcome will be, that the changes may include some unanticipated and unwanted outcomes.

At the personal level the metaphor can be taken further, by equating the areas of the screen with cognate areas, we might think of the individual learning by fits and starts, with development in each stage being limited to specific areas. Virtuous cycles of study, learning, achievement and reward may reinforce motivation and lead to heightened activity in one subject area, while other areas remain stagnant or suffer a retrograde cycle of neglect, failure, punishment and demotivation. But every so often an idea (glider) will be fired off by understanding in one area, and on reaching another lead to a burst of inter-disciplinary speculation, which may amount to nothing, or may develop into a new focus of study.

At the national level, one might speculate about how the patterns are influenced, and what happens when a moral panic is produced in one area or another. But as one would expect the patterns are more stable at the larger level, while it is harder to make predications at the smaller scale. So also, the larger the institution we consider, the more difficult it is to bring about a cultural change. The patterns are remarkably stable overall in the Game of Life, with the results being very similar whether the random pattern used as a starting point is 30 per cent alive or 70 per cent alive. This is not necessarily the case, as one can show by changing the rules slightly. Modifications to the numbers of neighbours needed to sustain or create life can produce very different patterns. And this opens up the possibility of thinking about sensitivity to initial conditions, and how stable, resistant to change, or traditional certain institutions might be.

By no means do I think that I have exhausted the possibilities of the Game of Life as metaphor in education. We might think of using it as a framework for studying children's activity in the school playground during recess, examining which areas of the territory appear to be bustling with activity, and which occupied by children sitting quietly in solitary contemplation. In fact there may well be as many possible uses of such a metaphor as there are imaginations that reflect on educational processes. Systems that have non-linear feedback will tend to exhibit the Joseph Effect, and its opposite, the Noah Effect, when areas of inactivity suddenly switch to activity, and vice versa (Mandelbrot & Hudson, 2008).

Throughout all this discussion I have been at pains to point out that whenever I restart a demonstration of the Game of Life with a fresh random pattern of cells, and set it running, the same pattern occurs. Areas of activity are concentrated between spaces where not much is happening. And when introducing students to the patterns I make sure that I emphasise repeatedly that the pattern is the same. But that raises an important point for comparativists. The initial grid is 1,000 cells by 1,000 cells, or a total of one million cells, and each cell can be either alive or dead. Which means that any one configuration of cells has a one in $2^{1,000,000}$ chance of occurring. If we sat and watched the Game of Life for a thousand years, at one generation a second, we would be unlikely to see exactly the same pattern twice.

Yet no student has ever stopped me and said, 'We have not seen the same pattern twice yet.' Most people are quite happy to accept that 'the same' does not mean 'identical.' But this raises important questions about what it means to make a comparison.

Once I have focused attention on the key features that I am recognising, and given a language that allows them to be recognised repeatedly (static patterns, oscillators and gliders) it makes sense to say that two patterns are the same if they exhibit those features. But before those features of interest have been identified, it is not clear that 'the same' has any identifiable meaning, or at least not an unambiguous meaning. This opens up possibilities for the discussion of the inductive assumptions of positivism, that observation of the facts comes before any attempts to theorise, or grounded theory, where theory is supposed to be derived from observations of similarity and difference.

4   An Area of Special Interest

After I had been using this computer simulation of the Game of Life for some years, which is to say that I had been looking at patterns developing over a considerable period of time, it occurred to me that one particular pattern was of considerable interest. It is of interest precisely because it is problematic. This is a pattern of 12 cells that form, alternately an open cross or an open box, as shown in Figure 2.4. For simplicity and brevity, I will call this pattern the cross/box (also described as a 'traffic light' by Gardner (1970) in the article that originally introduced the Game of Life).

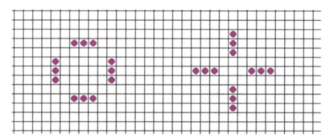

FIGURE 2.4   The cross/box through two generations

An alternative description of the cross/box is that it is an arrangement of four oscillators, as shown in Figure 2.2, that oscillate in synchrony. There is no great mystery about the synchrony; since each oscillator changes between its two positions each generation, once two oscillators are established they will remain in time with each other. The question is whether this should be thought of as a pattern at all.

We know, because we established the rules by which cells interact at the outset, that these four oscillators cannot be interacting with each other. As there is always a dead square between them, and the squares in between them never have more than two living neighbours, no cell can be brought to life as a result of an interaction between two adjacent oscillators. Each of the four oscillators in a cross/box behaves exactly as it would if the other three did not exist. So what should we make of the fact that the three have sprung up in an apparent pattern?

Should we say, following David Hume (1739/1969), that we learn nothing from constant conjunction of two events, and that mere correlation of the movements of the parts of this cross/box pattern tells us nothing about the mechanisms involved, nor should it lead us to suppose a link? And should we follow him further and say that the human mind is predisposed to see patterns, and we have a psychological disposition to see the cross/box as a pattern, even though it exists only in our imagination?

We might think of this as analogous to the Kanizsa triangle illusion, where the observer creates an image which is not present from components that are.

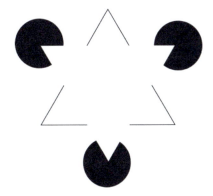

FIGURE 2.5
The Kanizsa triangle

There is plenty of scope here for introducing problems of observing without introducing cognitive illusions that are analogous to optical illusions, as when the context of a figure changes the way in which it is perceived, and therefore affects the outcomes of supposed direct comparisons.

The metaphor might be stretched here to raise questions about whether an external observer can legitimately hope to identify patterns without consulting those who are being observed as to the meaning they impute to the patterns. Of course, in the case of the Game of Life it makes no sense to ask whether the cells are aware of the interactions between themselves and another area of the pattern, because we know the rules under which cells propagate. We can be certain which cells interact. When observing human agents, we might draw a parallel distinction between patterns of behaviour of which participants are aware, and patterns of behaviour that participants are unaware of, but which an outside observer imputes. And it remains a vexed question exactly how much importance we should attach to the latter.

After some time reflecting on the cross/box in those terms, it occurred to me that the cross/box was still more interesting. If it really was a freak accident that occurred when four unconnected oscillators were formed independently and in close proximity, then it seemed to me that it was happening much too frequently. To put this in context, for the glider to come into existence by chance, it needed five living cells to be created within a square space that is three cells by three cells. If we allocated each of a block of nine cells as either alive or dead at random, there are 512 possible combinations of living and dead cells, of which 16 are gliders (four different generations, as shown in Figure 2.3, in each of the four possible orientations). That is a one in 32 chance, which seems compatible with the frequency with which gliders appear.

Of course, the probabilities are slightly smaller than that, because if we are to observe the glider, it must survive at least a few generations, which means that it must be surrounded by and moving into, blank space. But this is just to give a rapid illustration of how we might calculate the odds of a glider occurring, and to indicate how very much less likely the accidental occurrence of a cross/box is, which requires the arrangement of twelve living cells in an area seven cells by seven cells (for the box) and nine cells by nine cells (for the cross). Without doing any calculations, we can see that the cross/box should occur much less frequently than gliders. And yet, when we watch the successive generations of the Game of Life, gliders can be seen from time to time, but cross/boxes are ubiquitous in any pattern that has settled down from its initial random pattern. In any established pattern there will be many cross/boxes, and still more partial cross/boxes where two or three oscillators form part of a cross/box.

That does not exactly close all discussion of chance, however, because a cross/box, once created, will exist for ever unless some other part of the pattern encroaches and interferes. Cross/boxes are very long-lived. In contrast, the glider, in its nature, moves until it eventually collides with another pattern, at which point it is destroyed creating a new area of activity, which subsequently takes on a life of its own or fizzles out. A glider cannot remain static for long periods of time, and typically disappears after ten or twenty generations.

So if we look at an established pattern of the Game of Life and observe a large number of cross/boxes, a substantial number of partial cross/boxes, and very few gliders, if any, we are not at liberty to assert that cross/boxes are occurring more frequently than gliders, because we are not comparing like with like. What we should do is to scale the observations by the life expectancy of each figure, so that we are comparing the number of gliders and cross/boxes that are created in a fixed period of time.

It was while I was turning these things over in my mind that it occurred to me that explicit modelling provided me with a tool that is not regularly available to the comparativist; I could turn the clock back. I could find an area of pattern that included a cross/box and then run it backwards to see what had happened in previous generations. This would eventually tell me whether, although the parts of the cross/box have no present connection, they had had some interconnection at some point in their history.

In the process of delving into the history of the development of patterns in the Game of Life, I came across two patterns of interest, as shown in Figures 2.6a and 2.6b, together with their development through successive generations.

MODELS AND MULTI-CENTRED STUDIES OF EDUCATION   31

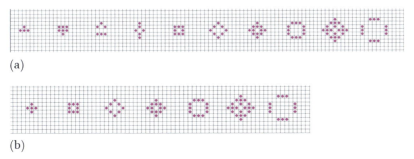

FIGURE 2.6   Precursors of cross/boxes

(This is not an original observation, and like many researchers, I might have saved myself time and effort by knowing the previous literature better (Gardner, 1970).)

It seems unlikely that Figure 2.6 exhausts the possible patterns that could give rise to the cross/box. The two seed patterns I have chosen develop into the patterns, so between the various generations there are at least ten precursors of cross/boxes in Figure 2.6. The initial patterns in the figure involve only four (Figure 2.6a) or five (Figure 2.6b) living cells in specific arrangement, and therefore would seem, other things being equal, to be more likely than, or as likely as, a glider, to occur by chance. Figures 2.6a and 2.6b have a lot in common, following the same evolution after the eight living cells that make up a three by three square with no living cell in the centre. But that prompts the further speculation that nine living cells making up a three by three square might also give rise to a cross/box, which, indeed, it does.

But the central point here is that the puzzle of cross/boxes has been resolved, if it has been resolved, by the identification of a plausible mechanism that could produce the phenomenon, not by any complicated study of the pattern elements that correlate one with another.

Once one knows the answer, or at least has one possible answer, other ways of arriving at the answer immediately present themselves. For example, knowing that one seed shape for the cross/box contains only four living cells suggests an investigation of all possible patterns that start with four living cells in contact with each other. This is relatively simple, as there are very few. The same could also be done for five or six cells, although beyond that, the number of patterns starts to grow too rapidly to make this a fruitful path for further study. But it is unlikely that I would have thought of starting from all possible seed shapes containing n or fewer living cells, had I not known to expect at least one answer with n = 4. So experimental methods are possible, but it helps to have a good idea of how much variety needs to be manipulated in the experimental situation before one starts. Or, which amounts to much the same thing, there is an important role for theory, before one can properly conduct experiments, or interpret correlations sensibly.

But what we can see from this is that the rules of the Game of Life mean that similar patterns tend to reproduce in different parts of a large field. We do not need to look for historical developments that explain why similar cross/box shapes happen in different places. They arise spontaneously, as a result of the rules and random patterns that we can imagine happening relatively often. In contrast with that, the separate parts of a single cross/box do have a common historical origin, which helps us to understand why such symmetrical shapes arise, when at first glance it appears they should not.

And this raises questions about how we are to understand educational phenomena when we come across similar institutions in different places. One examination system looks very much like another examination system. But if we wish to explain that similarity, should we look for historical influences from one to the other, or should we look for ways in which the logic of examination systems produces similarities, even if there has been no historical contact? And one might ask the same for classroom arrangements, text books and so on.

So when Sir Ken Robinson (2010) says that a concentration on academic knowledge is 'deep in the gene pool of public education,' does he mean that one system inherits this characteristic from another, or does he mean that the rules by which education systems are constructed result in this similarity? Both are possible interpretations of what it means to be 'deep in the gene pool,' but the implications for our understanding are rather different.

5   The Next Step

Having used the Game of Life as a metaphor for aspects of educational systems, it is possible to see larger patterns, as I am moving towards here, and to start to ask questions about the methodology of comparison. One can, for example, see that in some cases, and some types of developments, examining historical precedents will reveal the source of similarities across systems and across nations. We can in that sense appreciate the efforts of the early twentieth century comparative educationists who thought that a historical approach was most appropriate in examining similarities and differences across cultures.

But we have also seen that historical contact between systems is not necessary to produce isomorphism, and the idea of trying all possible arrangements of four or five living cells in an experimental approach, we can see the origins of the scientific method, that by manipulating the initial conditions over a wide range of possibilities we can see what the influence of those initial conditions is. In that sense we can understand the impulse of the social scientific trend in comparative education in the 1960s, as scholars like Brian Holmes, Max Eckstein and Harold Noah tried to understand how the rules of development of educational systems led to similarities in the way systems are organised. So we might follow Eckstein (1970) as he attempts to deal with the development of educational systems in terms of urbanisation, rather than in terms of historical influences between different nations.

And we might try out different rule systems in the Game of Life to see how changes in the rules affect the outcomes. One example that I always use when teaching using the Game of Life is to show students the contrast between the Game as defined by John Conway, and a rule set called 'day and night.' Very crudely, the rules of day-and-night mean that a cell lives or dies according to whether most of its neighbours are living or dead. If we set this running on an initial random arrangement of living cells, we very soon see that living cells start clumping together into colonies, with dead areas between them. I see this as analogous to what happens in cities if people have a slight preference for living with people who are culturally similar to themselves; before very long the city is divided into culturally distinct areas, or possibly even ghettoes. So, I live in an area of London where a significant minority of my neighbours are Greek Cypriots. A few miles down the road is a similar area, but with a large minority of Turkish Cypriots.

But more importantly, Conway's Game of Life produces similar patterns across a wide range of initial conditions. Whether one starts from a random pattern that is 30 per cent living cells or 70 per cent living cells, the outcome is recognisably similar, or 'the same' with the caveats about sameness that I have mentioned above. In contrast with that, day-and-night rules bring about patterns that are remarkably sensitive to the initial conditions. Starting with 50 per cent living cells, one can watch the patterns of living colonies ebb and flow over tens of thousands of generations, before finally dying out. Starting the system with 40 per cent living cells, the patterns degenerate and die out in a few thousand generations.

Brian Holmes, on the basis of his understanding of scientific method, stated that what happens in a system is subject to the rules, or laws, that govern the development of that system, and the initial conditions, and he emphasised that the system would be very sensitive to those initial conditions. And we can see that this is partly true. Many systems, perhaps most systems, are sensitive to small disturbances in their initial conditions, and this has been described as the butterfly effect. Weather systems are certainly of that kind, where the flap of a butterfly wing in the Amazon can create a tornado in Texas. But not all systems are sensitive to their initial conditions. The Game of Life, and, indeed, many living systems, produce and reproduce similar patterns, and can maintain themselves in dynamic equilibrium despite quite substantial disturbances.

And for the person who wishes to introduce change into a system, understanding whether the system is or is not susceptible to disturbances, and whether or not, whatever the change agent's efforts, the system will return to its original state, must be important.

This account of how the Game of Life can be used as a metaphor for comparative analysis indicates the way, or one of the ways, in which the issues that have faced comparative educationists over decades can be brought together systematically. I also hope that there is an indication here for my reader, as there is for me, as to why we can never hope to reduce comparative education to a single method. Sometimes historical antecedents are relevant to the understanding of a system, while at other times social science will provide a satisfactory explanation.

But from such simple, not to say simplistic, beginnings, the metaphor of the Game of Life brings in practical reflections on many methodological issues, ranging from David Hume's pronouncements on induction, and the fact that correlations do not imply causation, through to the debates on method in comparative education that characterised and dominated the field in the 1960s and 1970s.

But like any metaphor, the metaphor of the Game of Life has its limits, and we should not lose sight of those.

6   Life Is Not the Game of Life

It has been my intention to illustrate how the explicit development of a model can help us to understand and examine features of systems that occur spontaneously in our social environment. But the features that make explicit modelling useful are exactly the features that make the model limited, and may lead to nonsense if the metaphor is pressed too far. Indeed, this is one of the points that Eckstein (1993) makes about the dangers of using metaphors in an uncritical way. They can restrict thought just as easily as facilitate it.

In the Game of Life, we know the rules of the Game, because that was the basis of the initial model; we chose the rules by which cells would live or die through successive generations. When studying social phenomena, the rules by which the system develops are precisely the point in question. They are not given at the outset by arbitrary decision. So the question of whether, if one were provided with a very large number of patterns from the Game of Life through successive generations, one could deduce, induce, or abduce the rules under which cells operated, is the question that modelling does not help us to address.

We can think of many academic disciplines where explicit models have been set up, and the intricate inner workings of those models explored, only for the models to be mistaken for the real world phenomena for which they are supposed to be an analogue. We might think, for example, of the model *homo economicus*, the calculating human who always seeks to maximise his or her utility, and who has the ability, time, and inclination to calculate how that utility is best maximised. *Homo economicus* can be extremely illuminating, when we compare his or her behaviour with the behaviour of real human beings, as it can give us indications as to where people are acting on economic motives and where they are not. The one mistake that we should never make, although it is sadly a common mistake among economists, is to confuse *homo economicus* with real people.

We might say the same about many other explicitly constructed models, from the free market to the ego, id and super-ego, or such classic distinctions in education as between transformational leadership and transactional leadership, or child-centred and teacher-centred classrooms. These are all valuable examples of what Weber described as polar ideal types, but we should not expect that they exist in the real world.

The limits of the Game of Life as metaphor will probably already have occurred to the reader at some points in my account. Most obviously, the Game of Life allowed me to scroll back through generations, to look for minor indications of where patterns had come from. Turning the clock back is not possible in real life studies, desirable though it may be. But to achieve the same result in real time, we would have to guess where a cross/box was going to appear, and then record all the changes in generations until the pattern appeared. At that point we could go back through the historical record and discover what had brought the cross/box about.

But without some clue as to where to start looking for the origins of a cross/box, the task would appear to be hopeless. We might think of the scientists who, rather than looking for the antecedents or a cross/box are looking for the antecedents of a physical movement in changes in readiness potentials in the brain (Libet et al., 1983). The only clue that they have about where to look is that they should look near the motor neurones in the brain, and shortly before the movement occurs. If there is a tiny antecedent at some other time in some other part of the brain, they will have no chance of finding it, and even if they find it they may not recognise it as what they were looking for.

There are three important lessons that I think should be taken away from this discussion of models. The first, and from my point of view probably the most important, is that even relatively simple models like this, can help in understanding what is happening in education. They can focus attention on aspect of phenomena, suggesting possible links, and highlighting important features. For example, in this case the Game of Life exhibits the Joseph effect, with some areas being active, and activity feeding more activity, while other areas are dormant, and remain dormant over time. These periods of extended trends are then interspersed with periods of sudden reversal. I have taken the term "Joseph effect" from the work of Mandelbrot (Mandelbrot & Hudson, 2008), and he shows that it is connected with a broader family of models taken from complexity theory. But even in this simple example, it focuses attention on the fact that developments in education may not be linear, and may, on the contrary, show sudden reversals and vicious and virtuous cycles. Education is full of such trends and reversals, at both the personal level, as in performance inconsistency, and at the institutional level, when there are fashions and fads in policies, and even at the national level where there are swings in a progressive or conservative direction, or rises and falls of nationalism.

The second important lesson is that not modelling does not mean that one does not have a model. Any research is driven by assumptions and implicit ways of thinking that constitute some kind of model, even if that model is poorly articulated. And if the Game of Life serves no other useful purpose, it highlights some of the assumptions that make up what we normally call common sense, and therefore shapes most of what we call research. For example, most of the time we assume more or less linear relationships will hold; if we spend more time on practising an activity, we will get better at it, more or less in proportion to the time and effort invested. And, although we know from experience that is not necessarily the case, and we have days when nothing seems to get done, even though we think we are putting in the normal effort, those simple assumptions persist, often unexamined. Developing explicit models is a way to challenge and examine some of those assumptions.

And the third lesson is that the model is not "reality." I put "reality" in scare quotes, because I distrust anybody who claims to have access to what reality is. We compare our models with what happens when we observe phenomena, and come to the conclusion that the model more or less fits, and provides an interesting account. But that does not mean that other models may not highlight equally interesting, but different, points. The point and purpose of a model is to focus attention, and to filter out the aspects that are not going to be the focus of attention. One way of expressing this is to say that we are going to study a phenomenon "through the lens" of a particular theory. But it is worth considering what is involved when we literally see through a lens. One does not use a microscope to look at plate tectonics, or through binoculars to appreciate the panoramic beauty of the scene. Looking through a lens picks out some features for special attention, and so does a model.

What people mean when they claim to have seen "reality" is that they have used an implicit model that appears to be common sense to them, and they have been able to confirm their prejudices. Whenever we look at the world we see it in terms of mechanisms and interactions that we expect to see and can understand. Some models are better than others, or produce insights that are interesting, but no model ever captures "reality." For example, if we think that all people act out of self-interest, or that the performance of students in school depends only, or mainly, on the qualifications of teachers, we have an implicit model in mind, and we will probably see only those features that the model suggests, unless we take particular care.

The Game of Life was useful in pointing attention to some aspects of education that we are familiar with, but normally ignore in research, such as the Joseph effect, or the way that action that is linked only to immediate neighbours can nevertheless give rise to system-wide patterns. But it is a very limited model in many ways, not least, in terms of its applicability to education, in the fact that the past can affect the future but the future cannot affect the past. While that is a feature that is common to many models in education, I pick that out as a shortcoming, because it seems to me that the future, future goals and aspirations, play a central role in education. So before I leave this question of explicit modelling, I want to look at one further model, and contrast it with the common sense that so often permeates educational research.

In the preceding argument, I argued that we should start our development of research in comparative education by developing a model of "how things work," rather than relying on observations and common sense. I am going to develop and illustrate that theme further here. And as I do so I will introduce the idea of multi-centred approaches, and contrast that with the single-centred approach that dominates most of our thinking in educational research.

Most of our thinking about education is based on the idea that, if we take a homogeneous group of people, as similar as you like on any measurable characteristic, background, education and so on, and we put them in similar situations, they will behave in the same way. On the other hand, if we find a group of people that divides itself between two courses of action when put in a situation, then there must be some reason, or cause, that we could identify that would allow us to predict which group they would fall into. There must be something in their genetic make-up, their experience or their education that makes them behave differently. People who are the same will react to circumstances in the same way; people who behave differently must be different. I call this way of thinking "single-centred."

As I noted before, this view of education is based on a view of what people are like; they are predictable, and their actions are caused by the circumstances in which they find themselves. People are seen as reactive. We provide a stimulus, and they respond in a predictable way.

In contrast with single-centred thinking, I suggest we should think about the possibility that, if you take that homogeneous group of people, and put them in similar situations, they may nevertheless behave very differently, and not in a way that can be attributed to any characteristic of the persons involved.

Even so, although the behaviour of the individuals who make up the group may be unpredictable, and differ sharply, the behaviour of the group may be quite predictable, in a similar way to the idea that I might be able to estimate how many people will go into a particular supermarket on Monday morning and buy a pint of milk, without having any idea about which particular individuals would be in need of milk on a particular Monday morning. I call this kind of thinking, where groups of similar people can nevertheless do very different things, "multi-centred."

As this example makes clear, many people have multi-centred approaches to their tasks without using what I shall go on in this paper to describe as multi-centred techniques. Supermarket managers, insurance brokers, school time-tablers, railway schedulers and other managers all make estimates of how many people will want to take a particular course of action at different times of the day or week. But they will generally do that by thinking in single-centred terms, about results that cluster around an average. There is a central tendency, it is just we are not exactly sure where it is. If we had more data, we could be more certain about our predictions. Following Michael Bassey, I shall call this "fuzzy" thinking, rather than multi-centred. It puts my original description of single-centredness into a more statistical format, suggesting that a near-homogeneous group would cluster around a central tendency. But it is a single-centred approach because, if we found that the group distributed itself in such a way that the distribution had two or more humps, we would conclude that the group was not really homogeneous at all; there must be some unobserved, or possibly even unobservable, variable that we have not taken into account.

What I am arguing here is that we need to develop models of interactions of groups of people that are more complex than most of those currently used in educational research, and that are multi-centred. And I will argue that pretty well all of current educational research rests on single-centred assumptions, and that what we need is a radical shift. And I shall suggest some ways in which multi-centred policy could be developed.

I have set out many of these ideas out before in my book, *Theory and Practice of Education* (Turner, 2007), but I did not develop how those ideas would be directly relevant in comparative education. So that is what I will attempt in the following discussion. But before I can expect anybody to follow me through an argument that will require a not inconsiderable effort of imagination to picture how educational research could be different, I probably need to explain why such a re-imagination it necessary. And to that end I will start with a little thought experiment.

7   A Thought Experiment

Imagine a homogeneous group of people. Make them all the same class, the same gender, similar life experiences, whatever it takes to satisfy you that they are all the same. Make them clones if you wish. In any event we expect them all the respond similarly to specific circumstances. Divide them into pairs, and give them all the same instructions.

On the count of three, each person will hold out two fingers to represent scissors, their flat hand to represent paper, or a clenched fist to represent a stone. The winner/loser will be decided by the combination of symbols chosen; scissors beats paper, paper beats stone, stone beats scissors, and all other combinations are a draw. One, two, three…

Now we look at our group, and we will see that they have divided themselves into three groups, each having chosen one of the symbols. Each has chosen scissors, paper or stone. Nobody is doing an average kind of hand signal. In fact, the original homogeneous group can now be thought of as nine distinct groups; those who chose scissors and won, those who chose scissors and lost, those who chose scissors and drew, and so on.

Have them do it again. And again. Does an individual do the same thing every time when put in the same situation? It would be foolishness to ask whether all the extroverts chose scissors and all the introverts chose stone, or whether some previous experience pre-disposed some people to choose paper. These people are making decisions in circumstances of uncertainty, where the outcomes do not depend on their choices alone. I will come back to the question of whether this simple game is an appropriate model for educational settings later, but before I leave scissors, paper, stone I want to develop it a little further, and make the analysis a little more formal.

Two players play the game. Let them be A and B. When A wins, B loses and vice versa. Let us suppose that each game is worth a penny. When A wins a penny, B loses a penny, and when A loses a penny, B gains a penny. And when there is a draw no money changes hands. For this reason we call this a zero-sum game, and we can describe the outcomes in the form of a pay-off matrix showing A's gains and losses.

		A		
		Scissors	Paper	Stone
	Scissors	0	−1	+1
B	Paper	+1	0	−1
	Stone	−1	+1	0

FIGURE 2.7   Pay-off matrix for A's winnings in scissors, paper, stone

With nine possible outcomes, all equally likely, and three of them wins, three losses and three draws, we expect A and B to come out of this game on equal terms in the long run. The value of the game, the profit A can expect to make in the long term, is zero (for this particular game).

This is almost as simple as a multi-centred illustration can be, yet it has some very striking features that are common to all multi-centred analyses. The behaviour of the group is fairly predictable, or for large numbers very predictable. They divide sharply between the courses of action in roughly equal proportions. Yet the action of any individual is completely unpredictable. In fact, it is the essence of the game that the action of individuals should be unpredictable; if A could predict with accuracy the choices that B is going to make, she would be able to exploit that knowledge to secure a win on each play.

I think it is important to say that there is some mathematical analysis behind the structure of such zero-sum games, but I do not want to get involved in that here. What I am primarily interested in is the qualitative nature of this analysis, although I shall be drawing upon some of the theorems of game theory. But for the moment, what I am interested in is the zero-sum game as a metaphor, or model, for groups of people making choices in conditions of uncertainty or partial information, conditions that I think we would agree are typical of the conditions where young people make choices relating to their education.

Faced with a range of options, our group of people decide to take one course of action or another. Although no single factor or group of factors in their background can be used to predict what any individual will do, the group divides itself among the options in ways that are predictable and understandable. For me, this addresses one of the important dilemmas of education, namely the extent to which people have freedom to choose, to make themselves over in the image of what they want to be, or whether they are shaped and determined by circumstances and have only the appearance of free will. This is a problem that runs through our understanding of human action. Are the actions of people the result of structure or agency? Are we really free to choose, or are our actions constrained by the opportunities and circumstances we find ourselves in?

While this question has been important throughout the study of society and the development of social science, it is perhaps most strongly felt in education. If we did not believe that people had unexplored potential, that they could choose to change themselves and become better people, in some way more skilful, more knowledgeable and wiser, there would be no point in being involved with education at all. But if we did not believe that people can be shaped and influenced by their circumstances, and persuaded to learn specific things by being placed in a controlled and managed setting, there would be no point in trying to plan education. The rationale for educational policy as such would disappear. In order to engage with education at all, it seems that we need to be able bring together these two diverse, even contradictory, ways of seeing the human condition; people are free to change and to act as knowing agents, but at the same time people are determined and shaped by their setting, their background and their experience. The game of scissors, paper, stone, offers a suggestion of how the two might be combined in a meaningful way to produce an insight into what is happening in education.

In the setting of the game, individuals are free to choose, although the choices they have to make are limited and set by the rules of the game. Within that setting they are free to exercise choice, and their actions are completely unpredictable. However, the situation does determine the outcome, in the sense that the sum of the individual actions, the actions of the group, are completely predictable; the proportion of the group making any choice is predictable. And that is an interesting paradox.

In one way this is not a radical new thought. The ecological fallacy is well-known in the literature and relates to the common, but erroneous, assumption that the behaviour of an individual can be predicted from the behaviour of the group they belong to. But in single-centred analysis, this is a fallacy that is easy to fall into, because we have a very strong tendency to think that the average performance of the group is the performance of the average individual. Multi-centred thinking, as exemplified in the zero-sum game, draws attention to the difference between being able to predict group behaviour and being able to predict individual behaviour; it problematises the link between individual actions and collective behaviour. This is an important lesson when considering policy.

But before leaving scissors, paper, stone behind altogether, I want to look at a variation.

7.1 *Changing Individual Incentives and Group Outcomes*

I want to suppose that for some reason a policy maker wishes to encourage a particular form of behaviour. Let us suppose that this policy maker wishes to

		A		
		Scissors	Paper	Stone
	Scissors	0	−1	+1
B	Paper	+1	0	−1
	Stone	−1	+10	0

FIGURE 2.8 Modified pay-off matrix for A's winnings in scissors, paper, stone

encourage Player A to play Paper more often. And to achieve this result, they change the pay-off matrix to give A a bigger reward if they play Paper when B plays stone, as shown in Figure 2.8.

If A and B continued playing as before, then in nine plays we would expect each of the outcomes to be equally likely, and A would gain a total of nine pence. That would make the value of the game to A one penny per play, on average. But it seems obvious, as it seemed obvious to our policy maker, that with that large reward if A plays Paper and B plays Stone, A will start playing Paper more frequently than average.

But before we congratulate ourselves on having produced a good policy to bring about the desired outcome, perhaps we should have a careful look at this from the point of view of B. When A wins ten pence, B loses it, so B has a strong disincentive to play Stone. In fact, it would probably be smart if B stopped playing Stone altogether, in order to ensure that those losses are not incurred. But if B stops playing Stone, there is no point at all for A to lay Paper. If we assume that B is only going to play Scissors or Paper, then for A playing Scissors always produces a better result than Paper. (In the terminology of game theory, playing Paper is a dominated strategy.) So if B is not going to play Stone, and A is not going to play Paper, we can remove those options from the pay-off matrix and produce the new, simplified game shown in Figure 2.9.

It is still to the advantage of both players to ensure that their choices are unpredictable, but now they should not play their options with equal frequency if they wish to produce the best result for themselves. B should play Scissors twice as often as Paper, while A should play Scissors twice as often as Stone. If both players adopt such an optimal strategy, on average A will gain

		A	
		Scissors	Stone
	Scissors	0	+1
B	Paper	+1	−1

FIGURE 2.9 Reduced pay-off matrix for A's winnings in scissors, paper, stone

one third of a penny each play. That is certainly a loss for B, but it is the smallest loss she can secure given the pay-off matrix, which was designed to encourage A by giving an additional incentive. (For the details of the maths behind these conclusions, see Turner, 2004, pp. 77–97.)

There are several points that arise from this attempt to use incentives to shape collective behaviour, which, after all, is the idea behind most educational policy. The first is that incentives can behave in ways that appear quite perverse. Indeed, there is a growing body of evidence in the social sciences that incentives of this kind often do operate in a seemingly perverse way. The work of Dan Pink (2010) and Dan Ariely (2009) are examples of examination of such effects, which appear to defy common sense. However, in the game theory setting, although such behaviour may seem paradoxical, it is by no means illogical or irrational, as it can be seen to be a consequence of the logic of the situation in which A and B find themselves.

The second point is that, to secure the best outcome, each player must adopt a mixed strategy; they must not make the same choice every time. The idea of a mixed strategy is, in fact, the starting point for multi-centred thinking. Faced with the same choice repeatedly, a player must randomise their choices, selecting between their options in a particular proportion, in order to maximise their benefits. Or, by analogy, if we have a large group of people who are indistinguishable on any background variable, we would expect them to distribute themselves across the options in proportions that were set by the logic of that choice. This is the central insight of the multi-centred approach, namely that similar people in similar situations might respond very differently, but that this does not necessarily make it impossible to develop policy in a planned and effective way.

For example, if I am trying to master a new skill, and my teacher tells me that I am really doing it very badly, I might be discouraged and give up. On the other hand, I might be defiant and redouble my efforts in order to show him that he is wrong. Any attempt to control my behaviour might meet with compliance or resistance. The good teacher will try to shape the circumstances to increase the chances of a positive outcome, even while she knows that complete control is impossible. But in order to do that, she will need to know how to adapt the circumstances to make a positive outcome occur, say, 60 per cent of the time, rather than 40 per cent. I will come back to this point of managing circumstances to increase or decrease the likelihood of a particular outcome, but for the moment, let me go to the next general point arising from the analysis of the modified game of scissors, paper, stone.

The third lesson from our policy maker's effort to incentivise A to play Paper more often is that, although notionally the players each have three options, they end up distributing their choices between only two of them. That also is a robust result of game theory, that the optimal strategy will be a mixed strategy with only two components. That will probably be important if we can develop the multi-centred analysis of policy to the point where benefits can be quantified, as in this example. But for the present I simply want to argue that this result is suggestive of a number of ideas that might be pursued further in research. For example, why is it that in political systems dominated by two political parties, it is so difficult for third parties to become established? Or why, in the "tripartite" system of secondary education established after 1944 in the UK, was there a dominance of two kinds of schools, while the technical schools remained under-developed?

Actually, the optimum mixed strategy of either player has a rather curious characteristic. If A is playing her optimum strategy, she will, on average, win one third of a penny per play, whatever strategy B adopts. If B plays Scissors all the time, A will gain one third of a penny per play. If B plays Stone all of the time, A will gain one third of a penny per play. Or if B plays any combination of Scissors and Stone. Of course, if A knows that B is going to play Stone all the time, she can improve her winnings by using that knowledge. But A's optimum strategy can be thought of as a kind of insurance policy; it secures a stable and predictable outcome whatever B chooses to do. That may be an important idea when we come to think about using game theory in the analysis of policy.

In general, in a zero-sum game, faced with an opponent who is trying to minimise what I can gain, my task is to maximise that minimum, and make sure that I gain at least that maximum minimum. In game theory terminology, this is referred to as "mini-maxing." But we might also think of it as satisficing, a notion that economists have introduced to cover the idea that people, rational people driven by economic motives, do not always optimise their returns, but sometimes settle for just enough. Again, looking at the game through a multi-centred analysis gives a particular insight into what satsificing might involve.

And lastly it should be noted that, although that large incentive was put in the play-off matrix to attract A to it, neither player ends up playing the option that includes it. But that is not to say that the outcome of the game is not influenced by it. The presence of that large incentive makes the game of more value to A, even though she can never actually win that bonus. And that is curious, because it suggests that it is the whole pattern of rewards that is important, and not just some major highlights. And that again is suggestive, or at least worrying. When I, as I suspect many teachers do, tried to encourage pupils or students to adopt a course of action because it would bring them great rewards, either in terms of money or satisfaction, was I actually producing the opposite effect to the one I intended? I do not know the answer to that, but I think that a multi-centred approach might provide ways of collecting evidence to illuminate this question. In the meantime, we might be wise to take care over any motivation that might look too good to be true.

8   Games against Nature

I have used some of the ideas from game theory in order to explain what I mean by a single-centred or a multi-centred policy and contrast them. The core idea here is that a homogeneous group may not all behave in the same way when facing a similar choice. That makes the interpretation of empirical evidence very difficult. We are used to an approach to education where we look for antecedent causes of particular types of behaviour, and to divide the groups of people we are observing into two groups. The group that has our critical factor will behave one way, while the group without our critical factor will behave another. Or, more properly, in statistical terms, the group with our factor is more likely to behave in that way, those without it to behave in another.

I will come back to the question of how widespread this single-centred approach is, and whether I am caricaturing it, later, but those who doubt that this is a mainstream approach to understanding school processes might care to have a look a the extensive literature on the risk factors associated with school dropout. We know that not all children who come from poor neighbourhoods or who have poor diet drop out of school, but the central way of thinking about such problems is to look for ways of classifying children into two groups; those who are more likely to drop out of school and those who are less likely. The thought behind this is that there is some kind of stochastic threshold, and once that is reached the child will drop out of school.

A multi-centred approach looks at the issue very differently. Faced with a choice (the benefits of which and the circumstances of the choice being outside the control of the young person, certainly) on an issue like whether to drop out of school, we will expect some to drop out and some not to, but for there to be no identifying characteristic or risk factor that the dropouts share and the non-dropouts do not. In much the same way, our group playing scissors, paper, stone could be seen to be making different choices, but we would not expect to find a Scissors-factor.

But if members of a homogeneous group can be expected to behave differently (and by implication, members of different groups might behave in the same way), this makes it difficult to believe that we can understand educational processes by applying inductive approaches. Looking at which people do similar things will not necessarily tell us anything of value about the processes involved. So how should we proceed?

What I am advocating is an explicitly hypothetico-deductive approach. The first step is to develop, as I have been developing here, a model of how educational processes work. I am developing the game of scissors, paper, stone in order to illustrate some key processes in education. When I have developed the model, I draw attention to certain key features, such as the paradoxical effect of incentives, or the existence of a mixed strategy. And I can then compare the predictions of my model with actual events in schools and colleges and see whether those features can be seen in naturalistic surroundings (assuming schools to be a naturalistic setting).

The model is certainly abstract, and likely to be only an imperfect description of what we actually observe, but it may nevertheless offer some insights into what is happening. And the question therefore arises as to how much detail we should develop in the model. I have to say, at the moment I think that the model is unsatisfactory. Although it has become fairly commonplace to describe education as a competition, it is rarely a direct confrontation between two competitors, one of whom wins and the other loses. We might think, for example, of the competition for university places, with the members of an age cohort each trying to secure a place at a desired institution. That is a more or less direct competition with winners and losers, but it is not necessarily best viewed as being a direct fight between two candidates, with each trying to damage the chances of the other.

This is a matter of judgement, but I think that before I look at empirical evidence, I want to develop the model a little further to make it intuitively more similar to everyday educational situations. Two person zero-sum games, like scissors, paper, stone, are the simplest kind of game that are described in game theory, which is why I have started from there. But there are many different ways in which the model might be developed. We might, for example, theorise university entrance as a multi-person zero-sum game, where the competition is not between two people, but many people make decisions in the hope of achieving their goal, and the outcomes depend on the collective of all those decisions. Or we might look at non-zero-sum games, where there is an element of cooperation between players, and they cooperate to generate a bigger pool of benefits, and then compete over how those benefits are to be shared out. And those different models might call to mind different processes in education, and it might be sensible to select the multi-centred model according to the phenomenon of interest that is being studied.

But for the purposes of my illustration, I am going to develop the two person zero-sum game by considering it as the foundation of a game against Nature. In this case we consider the player A playing against, not an identifiable player B, but Nature, an impersonal and unidentifiable opponent. Player A must make a choice in conditions of uncertainty, where the outcome depends not on her choices alone, but on a combination of events and decisions of others, all of which lay outside the player's control. All of those impersonal and dispersed happenings are notionally gathered together into one imaginary opponent, Nature. In fact, this is a not unreasonable model for decisions that are made in educational settings. I can choose to study a subject, but whether I can be successful or not does not only depend upon my decision. I can decide to seek a particular qualification, but whether there will be demand for people with that qualification in the labour market by the time I complete my study will depend on the decisions of many other people. And so on. So, in framing these choices as a game against Nature, the decision maker is supposed to be pitting her wits against an impersonal opponent who will be doing their best to frustrate her actions.

And that is the point where the model might seem most unrealistic. It may sometimes feel as though the universe is against us, determined to frustrate our efforts and our ambitions, but Darwin has taught us that Nature is indifferent to our efforts and our ambitions, and has no particular purpose in mind in dealing with evolutionary competition. And this is perhaps where the modelling comes into play with greatest force. Because I have set up the model carefully, in order to be able to draw some conclusions from the analysis, I can build upon a conclusion that I mentioned earlier; the optimum strategy can be seen as a kind of insurance policy, that secures a given level of benefit, whatever the opponent chooses to do.

In that sense, although this form of analysis is called a game against Nature in the literature, the actual embodiment of Nature is completely irrelevant. The person who makes a decision in conditions of uncertainty might choose their strategies in a way to secure a satisfactory minimum outcome, to satisfice, whatever subsequently turned out to be the case. Of course, whether their actual decisions conform with the predictions of the game theory model is a matter for empirical testing, but the model provides some insights into how such empirical testing might be performed.

Games against Nature have been applied to a range of decisions made in circumstances of uncertainty. A classic study of its kind is the study by Davenport (1960) of fishermen in the Caribbean. And I have attempted to model some educational choices made under uncertainty in this way, with interesting, but inconclusive, results (Turner, 2004, pp. 87–97). And further testing is undoubtedly an important future step. But for the moment I am content to argue that the model provides an important challenge to the way that policy is generally viewed.

At this point, one possible objection to the multi-centred policy analysis is the question of whether people, when they face an uncertain decision, actually go through the processes implied by reasoning out the structure of the game they are playing. Do human agents have to be conscious of game theory in order for their actions to be informed by a model from game theory? (This is a specific version of the question that I mentioned before; Do we have to use the ideas of the people we are watching to explain their actions, of can we impose our own classification of events?) Faced with the decision of whether to leave school or stay on to further education, does anybody really sit down and ask themselves, what will happen if I stay on in education, but fail all my examinations at the end? What will happen if I leave education and find myself unable to develop my career in the future? And so on, to construct a pay-off matrix to inform their choice of strategy.

I do not know the answer to that question. There can be no ultimate rules about how to apply rules, and so we have to exercise judgement about how to interpret the models that we develop. On the one hand, we might argue that, even if the people that we are watching making choices do not reason consciously, or explicitly, about their situation, the model might nevertheless be a useful description to explain what they are doing. Elsewhere I have argued that in making decisions about which route to take through busy city traffic, game theory might be able to explain the proportion of the traffic staying on the main roads and the proportion ducking down backstreets, even though each driver has not thought carefully about the optimum distribution of traffic. In the same way, we see children playing scissors, paper, stone thinking carefully about randomising their choices so as to outwit their opponent, but we are not obliged to conclude that they have a well-developed concept of game theory and probabilities to play the game.

As a consequence of the theorem in game theory about the "insurance policy" function of the optimum choices, it also happens that the various different routes through the city traffic should all take the same time. If the drivers are distributed optimally across the routes, all routes should be equal. Were that not the case, some drivers would be able to improve their situation by switching routes, until the extra traffic slowed down progress on the faster route. From which it follows that a distribution where one route has a distinct advantage cannot be an optimal distribution.

The analogous educational situation might occur if the vast majority of young people choose to stay on in education until they are twenty one or twenty two, creating very handsome opportunities for young people who leave academic education early to gain technical expertise. If that pushes up wages for craftspeople we might expect to see a shift away from the competition to get into university, until both routes produce similar benefits. If we see a group of people distributing themselves across options, we should ask how that distribution serves their interests best. We should not, as we are sometimes prone to do, assume that some of them are making dysfunctional or wrong decisions just because they are not doing what we would do, or what we would wish them to do.

On this reasoning, the conscious reasoning of the people involved in making decisions in circumstances of uncertainty is irrelevant. The group might have arrived at the optimal distribution through a process of trial and error, having readjusted towards the optimum whenever there was any advantage in switching. That would suggest that the empirical test of any model need not take into account the perceptions of those involved.

But that might not be the best way of interpreting the model. We have the intuition that how a person perceives the choice that they are making may shape the outcome. Indeed, leadership might be seen as the ability to frame a decision in such a way as to influence the decision made by somebody else. On this interpretation, the perceptions of the person making the choice would be crucial. We would need to ask the person who was making the decision what they thought they were doing, and in that case we would quite specifically mean how they saw the game that they were involved in.

This investigation would be different from a single-centred investigation of the perceptions of those same people. While the sociologist relying on single-centred analysis would ask, "Why did you choose Scissors this time?" the one using multi-centred analysis would be interested in the whole range of outcomes, and how the person was thinking about randomising their choices in the context of the broader game. This would leave a very considerable difficulty over how to aggregate those perceptions to gain an overview of the game they thought they were playing collectively. But that would be one of the areas of interest in any empirical study.

I hope that this short discussion gives sufficient explanation as to how a research programme of empirical study could be built on the concepts of multi-centred analysis.

What I am proposing here is that we should think about the educational situation that we wish to research, develop an abstract or idealised model of how we think it is going to work, and then compare the overall outcomes of our model with the turn of events in the empirical situation we are concerned with. For example, we might look at a critical choice that young people make as they go through education, such as the decision to continue into tertiary education. We could try to quantify the various benefits that they might derive from making one choice or the other, and set up an abstract form of the game against Nature that represents their decision in conditions of uncertainty. Using the model we would try to anticipate how the group would divide itself between the options, and then compare that with the actual demand for university places.

If the predictions of the model are very similar to the observed outcomes, we might congratulate ourselves. But if that is not the case, there might be various ways of interpreting the outcome. For example, if we have set up the model purely in terms of anticipated economic benefits, and people behave in a way we had not anticipated, we might simply reject the model of the game against Nature for this choice, or we might try to improve the model by including other, non-monetary benefits to try to understand what else might carry weight in young people's decisions. The latter course of action should be followed with caution, as we would not wish to make our theoretical position impregnable, or irrefutable, in the face of empirical evidence.

To conclude, the lesson from this quick tour through a number of educational issues is that the relationship between the actions of individuals and the actions of groups is problematic, and not at all obvious or open to simple observation. Knowing what individuals are thinking about when they make choices may not help us to understand why the group of people that they belong to exhibit particular behaviour on aggregate. And very definitely, knowing what the average behaviour of a group is tells us very little about what individuals may do. And this creates very difficult problems for the study of comparative education, where we might like to compare the differences in approaches to education of large groups of people, whether those groups of people are males and females, or members of individualistic and collectivist cultures. It is to some of the implications of those problems that I now turn.

Note

1   Downloaded from www.winlife32.com

CHAPTER 3

Understanding Comparison

1   Introduction

In the previous chapter I have been looking at comparison at the most abstract level, looking at how we might use explicit, conceptual models, to try to understand the circumstances that we find in education. My purpose has been to try to provide a platform that will allow us to question common sense, and try to get beyond the prison of the conceptions that seem to us to be natural. Archimedes is supposed to have said that if he had a long enough lever he would be able to move the world, but it has been pointed out that a long lever would not have been enough; he would have needed somewhere firm to stand, apart from the surface of the earth.

In comparative studies, we like to imagine that we could find the equivalent of Archimedes' firm ground, to see the world as it really is and not through the prism of our own conceptions and prejudices. And, of course, we find, as Archimedes did, that there is no such firm place on which to base our understanding. The best that we can do is to try to imagine ourselves into somebody else's conceptual framework, to try for a moment to see how things could look differently. And I have argued that our best chance of achieving that it through a process of explicit modelling. Those models have included discussion of the relationships of individuals to society, and of society and culture to individuals.

Most of the time we take those links for granted. It is obvious that children acquire their parents' culture through the process of education, and that, consequently, life chances depend upon how well one progresses in education. We see strong correlations between how well children do in school and the previous educational achievement of their parents. And we see a strong correlation between children's performance in school and their future income and quality of life. And we use that as evidence to support our view that children's performance in school is determined by the social capital of their parents, and that their schooling determines future occupational choices. We have read in textbooks on quantitative methods that correlations cannot be assumed to be evidence of causation, but we have no real hesitation in moving from correlations to determinations in this case.

What I am suggesting is that a process of explicit modelling can help us to imagine how things might be seen otherwise. What if both schooling and future life chances depend on the social capital of parents? What if schooling is irrelevant to future prospects, and career opportunities could be explained entirely in terms of family ties and links that could be made socially? Would that change what we do in schools?

In looking at the processes of formal modelling, I have emphasised, at different points, a number of important lessons. What counts as "the same" depends very much on the aspects of what we see that we choose to focus on. Patterns may arise, and look like patterns and cross connections to us, when there is no underlying mechanism that could explain such patterns; patterns of organisation may, like beauty, be in the eye of the beholder. And in seeking explanations for common phenomena, we may look for common historical antecedents, a family tree of innovations, or we may look for functional isomorphism, similar organisations to serve similar purposes.

So, while I hope that all of those lessons can be kept at the back of our minds, in this chapter I want to go in a rather different direction, to look at a more concrete problem of comparative education. In fact, I want to say, perhaps in a moment of hyperbole, that this chapter looks at the one concrete lesson that comparative education has to offer, the one definite conclusion that I have come to after fifty years of studying different educational systems. And I hope that will stimulate your interest: what is the one concrete lesson to be drawn from comparative education, and why is it worth devoting a whole chapter to?

And the answer to that question is this: intergroup variation is always much less than intragroup variation. In previous discussion of modelling, I tried to show how problematic it is to work out the relationship between the individual and the group to which they belong. The present chapter looks at a very specific aspect of that problem.

Consider something as simple as physical size, or height. Take a population of men and women where the average height of men is 176 cm, and that of women is 163 cm. That means the intergroup difference, the difference between the average value for men and the average value for women is 13 cm. But that most certainly does not mean that the height of all men is 176 cm and the height of all women is 163 cm, or even that if we took a man and a woman at random from the population we would know that the man must be taller than the woman. We would expect that the heights of men would fall on a normal distribution, with most men in the middle, although there would be some very tall and some very short men. Similarly, the heights of women would fall on a different normal distribution.

To describe those normal distributions, how widely they are spread out, we use the standard deviation of the distribution. Typically, we might expect the standard deviation of the distribution of height for men to be 8 cm, while that for women might be 7 cm. Not to go too much into the mathematics of normal distributions, this means that 95 per cent of men are between 160 cm and 192 cm tall. There are men who are taller than 192 cm and shorter than 160 cm, but they form a fairly small part of the population. On the other hand, one in twenty is not a very small proportion. Similarly, 95 per cent of women are between 149 cm tall and 177 cm tall. At least one woman in 40 is taller than the average man.

That means that, if we took a man and woman from the population, it is likely that the man will be taller than the woman, but you might be wise not to bet too much money on it. The odds would be better, if we took ten men and ten women at random from the population, that average height of the men would be greater than the average height of the women. But again, it would not be a certainty. The simple lesson from this is that we should be very cautious about drawing conclusions about individuals from information that we have about the group that they belong to. The difference between the average heights of men and women is only 13 cm, but we find each population spread across a range of at least double that. In short, the intergroup variation, the difference between groups, is much less than the intragroup variation, the differences within each group.

And what is true for height is also true for many or most characteristics that we might choose to measure. At about the age of 16, all adolescents in the UK take an examination in mathematics, and we know that, on average, the girls do slightly better on the test than the boys. But the intergroup variation is tiny, while the variation within groups is huge. You would be unwise to assume that a random girl would perform better in mathematics than a random boy. In fact, you might be unwise to assume that the better performance of females would show up in a class of 30, or even in a school of 1,000.

The fact that intragroup variation is larger than intergroup variation is partly an observation about the world, but it is largely an observation about statistics. Looking at large numbers of individuals is different from looking at individuals, and the way that we aggregate statistics means that extraordinary individuals have relatively little impact on average values. We can imagine indicators on which there is no overlap between men and women, but actually it is not so very easy to find them in practice.

So, what lesson do we take away from this, as comparative educationists? There is, of course, a simple lesson about the use of stereotypes and stereotyping. You may have excellent data that indicates that men are better at parking a car in a small space than women. But you would be very unwise to assume that I was better at parking a car in a small space than my wife. The stereotype that men are better at some activities and women better at others cannot be transferred to any conclusion about specific individuals.

Well that seems simple enough. I am not going to laugh any more when I see a description of European heaven or European hell in terms of national stereotypes of cuisine, romanticism, organisation and punctuality. I am not going to take seriously any suggestion that men are from Mars and women from Venus.

When I was first introduced to comparative education, I was introduced to the idea that Germans are romantic and French people are rational. The basis of that national character analysis was that the representative of French modes of thought was the eminently logical Descartes, while the archetypical German thinker was Goethe. Although the main virtue of that analysis is that it is the direct polar opposite of the commonly held stereotype that Germans are rational and the French romantic, it still only replaces one stereotype with another. As serious comparative educationists we need to leave all that behind us. No doubt there are German and French romantics, and German and French rationalists. But whether we can work out any average level of romanticism, and whether that average could inform any specific observation of a French person or a German, are very doubtful. No more stereotypes.

The question we then have to address is whether comparative education, or anything else, can be done, if we really mean to live without stereotypes.

2 An Educational Computer Programme

I am currently piloting a simple educational computer programme. I had best say at the outset that, although I have written the code myself and got it running, the concept is not mine. It dates back to a discussion I had with a fellow student when we were both PhD students, and he described to me an interesting concept in educational computing. Put as simply as I can, you have to imagine a conversation between a person and a computer, roughly as follows.

Computer:	I know all about animals. Think of an animal. Tell me when you are ready.
Person:	Ready.
C:	Is it an elephant?
P:	No.
C:	I give up. What is it?
P:	A cat.
C:	And if I want to know the difference between an elephant and a cat, what question (with a yes/no answer) should I ask?
P:	Has it got a trunk?
C:	And for an elephant, is the answer yes or no?
P:	Yes.

C:	I know all about animals. Think of an animal. Tell me when you are ready.
P:	Ready.
C:	Has it got a trunk?
P:	No.
C:	Is it a cat?
P:	No.
C:	I give up. What is it?...

I doubt I have to go any further for you to understand that the full extent of the knowledge about animals that the computer started with was the word "elephant," and that the person who was supposed to be learning about animals from the computer was actually teaching the computer a taxonomy of sorts. And this process should stimulate reflection on the nature of classification, and which example animals one should choose, and which questions you should suggest, to produce a sensible taxonomy.

Well, I am now also piloting a new version of the programme that begins:

Computer:	I know all about comparative and international education. Think of a country. Tell me when you are ready.
Person:	Ready.
C:	Is it France?...

Of course, there is a great deal of interest to be examined here. Does a person's classification of countries depend upon his or her past experience and country of origin? It is not difficult to imagine that a native of Central America might have a sharper vision of the distinction between Guatemala and Honduras than somebody who lives in West Africa, while the latter might have a more definite question to distinguish between Ghana and Sierra Leone. And does the taxonomy develop differently if it starts from a different place? If the computer starts knowing the name of France, does that produce a different kind of taxonomy than if it starts with Uruguay?

Those questions are very interesting, and I am developing a new version of the programme that will save the decision tree that the person constructs as they teach the computer about differences in national character. But that is not at the forefront of my mind at this moment. The point that I am making here is that nobody has ever said, "I do not understand the question; I do not think that it is possible to generalise about countries in that way. Variation within countries is always greater than variation between countries, and there is no simple yes/no generalisation that can be made to distinguish between them."

And yet it seems logical that some people could respond in that way, and perhaps should respond in that way. In looking at international comparisons, we gloss over those intragroup differences to produce generalisations that are almost certainly false. And, of course, this is not just a comment that applies to national difference. It applies equally to descriptions of the characteristics of the genders, as I have said, between social classes, native speakers of a language and non-native speakers, the global north and the global south, urban dwellers and rural dwellers, and any other dichotomous classification of people. If we had appropriate metrics, we would probably find that the differences between tables and chair, or between apples and oranges, were dwarfed by the variance within any classification of furniture or fruit.

It looks as though the whole project of comparative education, in fact of comparative anything, is dissolving in front of our eyes. And yet people have no difficulty talking about groups of objects or groups of people as though they had some kind of independent, homogeneous existence. The Japanese are polite, the English rude, the Thais smiling, and so on. East Asians are collectivist, while Europeans are individualistic. This is how language works, by creating a label to handle a group. It would be impossible to speak at all, if such classifications and simplistic generalisations were prohibited. So we are caught in an impossible dilemma, between using language in a way that seems to make real, or reify, groups that actually house great variation, and between paying attention to the obvious logical and empirical fact that such a use of language hides, or makes invisible, huge intragroup variation. And probably the best we can do is to use language, which is, after all, the only tool that we have, while trying to guard against the worst excesses of reification.

There are many ways of being collectivist, as well as many ways of being individualistic, and while we may recognise some kind of truth behind the classifications of Hofstede (Mason, 2007), we should also keep in mind that they are complete nonsense. How do we manage those two things together?

For the moment I can only commend you to Tyrrell Burgess's (2002) definition of intelligence in the *Devil's Dictionary of Education*: the ability to keep two contradictory ideas in mind without being paralysed. But not for the first time we find ourselves trying to square a circle. And it is worth noting that this particular conflict of ideas maps directly on to the issue that I raised already in Chapter 1, between people as masters of their own destiny, and free to make their own choices, or people as shaped and constrained by their background, circumstances and social group.

While I was thinking about the previous paragraph, by accident I came across the fact that Stephen Jay Gould, the biologist and historian of science, apparently concluded that there was no such thing as a fish. He did not, of course, mean that there are no creatures that live in the oceans. He meant that the category "fish" is so various and varied that it hardly makes sense to group all the instances of sea creatures into one category with a single label "fish." This may be the conclusion of any expert, that common understandings of categories start to blur at the edges when you study them too closely. So it is worth emphasising that the difficulties that arise from the fact that intragroup variation is always greater than intergroup variation are not unique or special to comparative education. However, they arise with more force in the area of comparative education.

I am English, but I am also a Londoner, and Londoners are a bit different from the average run of English people. You might be unwise to generalise to the views of all English people after talking with even a large number of Londoners. So the difficulties of dealing with national differences are serious, even before we come to questions such as what makes a school a school, or what counts as literacy.

It is tempting to think that we might be able to overcome such difficulties by refusing to generalise. We will recognise the importance of context, and talk only about specific cases. This is what I found in this school, but other contexts are different, and nothing can be transferred from this case to other cases, however similar they may look. But, for good or ill, that is not the way language works. Language groups together classes of things and gives them a common name, despite any variation within the group. Nouns bring together classes of objects, verbs bring together classes of actions, and adjectives bring together classes of characteristics. If we take a vow to refrain from generalising, it will amount to a vow of silence. So we must generalise, even though we recognise the flaws that such a process must entail.

3   An Historical Approach

Since this difficulty of dealing with classifications that are problematic is always with us, and has always been with us, it is worth considering how comparative educationists have dealt with it in the past, in the process of developing our field of study. And the earliest exponents of comparative education drew on a heritage of historical studies based in nineteenth century scholarship, at a time when the nation state was coming to prominence in the management of the world order. Perhaps unsurprisingly, scholars such as Schneider and Hans sought to identify that which defined the nation: the essence or spirit of the nation. And in doing so, they emphasised the intragroup homogeneity, that which the members of the nation held in common and separated them off from the rest of the world.

Hans, for example, identified the nation as a group that shared a common language, a common religion, common ethnicity, common mores and common historical experiences, while sharing a piece of territory in common. With hindsight, this looks like a wilful attempt to ignore what I have described as the only certain lesson that comparative education has to offer. It is a determined attempt to argue that intragroup variation is negligible, and certainly less important than intergroup variation. Such an approach is much less acceptable today, and I think that there are three reasons why that is the case.

In the first place, geographical mobility means that it is much harder to find countries where such a sense of uniformity is even plausible. Secondly, views of history, and what counts as history, have changed dramatically over the last century. And thirdly, there is a dynamic in twenty first century states that tends to exaggerate and emphasise division and difference. I will come back to that third issue later, but first let me explore the first two aspects of these changes since the time when Hans wrote and described the uniform nature of nation states; changes in those states themselves and changes in the way that history is viewed.

In the 1950s when Hans was writing, the focus of comparative education was firmly on Europe and North America. Even in the case of Russia or the USSR, the emphasis was on its European heritage rather than its Asian roots or presence. And in Europe, the creation of the nation state had been based on creating a sense of common institutions. Either formally, as in France, or informally, as in England, there had been efforts to produce a uniformity of national institutions. Whether language was policed by a formal institution like the Académie Française, or simply promoted through institutions with other purposes, as was the case for "BBC English," the emphasis was on creating a homogeneous entity as the nation. And in the cases of Germany or Italy where the unity as a nation was more recent, or more open to doubt, the mechanisms of management were perhaps even stronger. This made a view that intragroup diversity was negligible not merely a description of a historical fact, but also a norm and value that was to be promoted.

These days, when the focus in comparative education has moved away from Europe, at least to some extent, it is very much easier to point to countries where the idea that the population shares a common linguistic heritage or historical experience cannot be sustained for a moment. Nigeria, India and Malaysia spring to mind immediately, but in fact it is hard to identify a country today that would meet Hans' criteria of nationhood. Even in the Europe that he described in terms of separate and identifiable national character, the geographical mobility of people has ensured that any categorisation of the population of a country in terms of common characteristics is highly questionable.

A second element in this move away from viewing nations as having a common purpose and common heritage has been a change in the way that history is viewed. The nineteenth century saw the rise of the great man theory of history; history was the account of the deeds of kings and queens, heroes and villains, who bent countries to their will and purposes. Although this theory was challenged in the nineteenth century, it seems only to have been challenged to the extent that history was seen as the activities of an elite. And it was rather easier to argue that an elite was homogeneous than to argue that a whole population had common values and purposes.

In the second half of the twentieth century we witnessed a fairly dramatic transformation in what counted as history. Mass Observation sought to introduce the everyday experience of ordinary people into recorded history. And this move toward egalitarianism was reflected in various calls for the histories of those who had previously been ignored by the historians to be given more recognition. The inclusion of women and ethnic minorities in history, or the development of their different histories, or different perspectives on history, have made it more difficult to argue that nation states follow an uncontested historical trajectory, or that the population speaks with one voice.

For all these reasons, from the demographic changes in the populations of states, to the different views of what counts as history, a historical approach to comparative education, as propounded by Hans, has become less attractive. Most obviously, we are more aware than before that there is no biological justification for describing race in the terms that he did. Like any other categorisation of people, when you get up close to classifications of race, the categories dissolve and serve no scientific purpose, although clearly they may continue to serve political purposes. We need to assert with absolute clarity that there is only one race, and that is the human race. But even there we need to recognise that the entirely fictional classifications of race may, nevertheless, have very real practical consequences in the world.

It should be noted, however, that Hans' approach to history is not the only possible use of history in comparative education. Vygotsky contrasts the fields of science and history, arguing that it is science that seeks generalisations, while history seeks to recognise and record the individuality and unique qualities of one-off events. In that sense, Hans may be seen as seeking a science of history, rather than history itself. By seeking to isolate the factors and traditions in history, he was attempting to go beyond history and develop a science of historical development.

In Edmund King we have an example that comes closer, I think, to a purely historical approach. King emphasises the unique and context bound nature of his encounters with individuals in educational settings, and, beyond the sole generalisation that predictions and generalisations are impossible, does not attempt a science of history of the type proposed by Hans.

For all of these reasons, historical approaches to comparative education have become less attractive. Not only that, but the very idea of using nation states as the best or appropriate units of comparison has been called into question. Ironically, this latter case has more often been made in terms of the growing homogeneity of the world, rather than in terms of the categories of nations falling apart, as it were, from the inside. But for whatever reason, and on the whole one would have to say for very good reasons, nationhood has come to be seen as problematic in comparative education.

On the other hand, that seems not to be, from my perspective, a reason for rejecting comparisons on the basis of nation states. It is, after all, nation states that legislate for education, that make financial provision for education (or fail to make financial provision), and that manage and collect data on educational systems. Again there seems to be an unavoidable paradox here, that we cannot construct a comparative education without taking into account nation states, even though we know such a categorisation is deeply flawed. I come back to the conclusion that to be involved in comparative education is to use categories of explanation at the same time as calling those categories into question, and to live with any resulting discomfort that sitting on the fence may produce.

And I hope that it will not have escaped notice that this discussion of methods in comparative education echoes and reflects the dichotomies that I mentioned in earlier chapters between individuals as shaping societies or societies as shaping individuals. These difficulties run through our chosen subject area like a vein of coal running through a mineral deposit, stimulating efforts to dig it out.

4   A Dynamic of Diversity

I promised earlier to come back to a third aspect of diversity in societies in the twenty first century, namely a dynamic that drives and exacerbates diversity. I do that now.

I am writing these thoughts during the COVID-19 pandemic in June 2020, but the thoughts themselves have their roots further back, at least in 2019, when a student asked why it was that, now that we had entered the age of mass education, even mass higher education, when we would expect a majority of people to be able to think critically for themselves, things actually seemed to be going from bad to worse. As evidence of that deterioration he cited the rise in popularism, the rise in far right politics, the spread of fake news and palpably false conspiracy theories, and the rise of "post-truth society" in general. And those are certainly interesting, and challenging, questions for those of us who have put our faith in education as the motor for social advancement, reduction of inequality, and greater understanding and tolerance.

But if the current pandemic has done nothing else positive, it may possibly have provided a metaphor that is helpful in understanding this paradox: herd immunity. Those of us who have had a naive view of democracy, that a simple majority is enough to secure a decision, may have hoped, and may still hope, that when more than 50 per cent of the population had experienced higher education, a more enlightened approach to politics, policy and life in general might have prevailed. Those of us who had actually worked in universities, and had experienced whether those institutions were a model for enlightened society might have been less sanguine, but if we devoted our working lives to higher education we must have had some thought that higher education would make the world a better place. An educated electorate would not tolerate a bigoted politician who lied without shame and then denied that he had done so.

Thinking about this from a different perspective, however, it is clear that, although the 50 per cent threshold is important, it is by no means the only important threshold. Measles is a highly contagious infections disease that may prove fatal. If more than 93 to 95 per cent of the population is immune to the disease, either because they have been vaccinated, or because of previous exposure to the virus, then a pandemic is unlikely as one infected person would not come into contact with enough susceptible people to produce the spread of the disease. Above that threshold, society has herd immunity, while below it society is vulnerable to a pandemic.

If we now turn our attention to the spread on nonsensical conspiracy theories, bogus remedies for diseases and specious politics, we might have hoped that once more than 50 per cent of the population could think critically about their political and scientific opinions such things would disappear. (Indulge me for the moment in the conceit that having experienced higher education can be equated with being able to think critically; I know that is a question that may need further examination.)

Faced with stories that are interesting, unexpected, unusual and palpably false, and comparing those with stories that are dull, run-of-the-mill, predictable and probably true, we know that the former spread on social media faster and farther than the latter. And the reason for that may be a consequence of the characteristics of the stories, as described here, or it may be because those who transmit them are more interested in the responses of their followers than in the content of the story. But for whatever the reason, it is clear that many more than 50 per cent of the population have to exercise critical judgement, evaluate the content, and then fail to forward false messages. The threshold for herd immunity to fake news may be 93 to 95 per cent, like measles, or it may be higher or lower. But it is clear that those of us who hoped that, once a majority of the population were educated to a sufficient level, it would no longer be possible to mislead the general populace were far too optimistic.

Before I leave the metaphor of herd immunity altogether, one last comment is in order. It might still be possible to create a local epidemic of measles, even where the average level of immunity is above 95 per cent. All that would be necessary would be to gather those who were not immune into a concentrated location and expose them to the virus. The result might not spread to the whole population, but it might nevertheless have a large impact locally. We might be witnessing something similar on social media, where, by design, accident, or algorithm, people of like attitudes are gathered together to share their views.

But even though the simple majority rule of 50 per cent plus one may not be the be all and end all of democratic decision making, that does not necessarily mean that the 50 per cent threshold is without any significance. The theory of cooperative games suggests that in order to control decisions in a committee, it is necessary to convene a winning coalition, and under normal committee rules that would mean a majority of 50 per cent plus one. Moreover, since holding a coalition together consumes resources, and holding a large coalition together consumes more resources than holding a small coalition together, the general goal is to secure the minimum winning coalition. That necessarily means that a large minority will be excluded, or feel excluded, from effective decision making.

In the past it may have been possible to hold together an implicit majority by asserting the divine right of kings to rule, by presenting leaders as those who know best, or by depending on the gullibility of the general public to believe campaign promises would actually be implemented. We have to hope that, as the percentage of the population who think critically about such matters increases, those who have thought that it was their right to rule, and had used such measures to maintain their rule, will be made increasingly insecure in their position. But we can hardly expect them simply to resign themselves to the new situation and let the new society develop. We would expect them to lie, to cheat, to hoodwink anybody they could, and to become increasingly belligerent toward those they expected never to be able to win over. Between the time when 50 per cent of the population thinks critically about policy, and the time when 95 per cent of the population does so, we might expect to see increasing desperation on the part of politicians who fear they will be losing their positions of privilege, and increasing polarisation in political contests.

If one is of an optimistic disposition, one might see the rise of populism and the increasing polarisation of debate as positive signs, as indications of the spread of critical thinking and the success of mass education. In much the same way one might expect an increase in activity in a violent confrontation as it nears political solution, as there is so much to gain in those last moments before the final settlement as parties to the dispute jockey for position. But I may be reading too much into what I discern as recent trends in politics, and these may not be indications of a more tectonic shift.

Whatever one's conclusions from this discussion, my general point is that there may well be internal processes in modern society that lead to increasing divisions in the perspectives that people have on social issues, and increasing polarity in discussions. At its most general, my argument is that there may be an internal dynamic in modern societies that actually makes it more difficult to generalise about the attitudes and norms that prevail in a particular country or community. All of my previous discussion of intergroup and intragroup variation was based on the implicit notion that populations are distributed on a normal distribution for many variables. That is to say, if there really are dynamic pressures in society to move people toward extremes, the population may move away from a normal distribution where the majority are in the middle and very few at the extremes, to one where fewer are in the middle and more are at the extremes. In more radical cases, the population may actually divide more completely so that there are two peaks rather than one.

Such deviations from normal distributions in populations add force to my previous assertion that intragroup variation is always greater than intergroup variation. But equally important is the fact, as described by Mandelbrot, that such non-normal distributions increase the likelihood of chaotic behaviour of the system, and in particular vicious and virtuous cycles, as described by the Joseph effect.

5   More Models

Ever since Socrates was condemned to death for corrupting the youth of Athens, and probably longer, dictators and autocrats have tried to prevent the education of people that might lead to making them ungovernable. And although democracies have paid lip service to the idea of needing an educated electorate, their actions have not always matched their ideals. In this chapter I have illustrated the argument mainly in terms of democratic institutions. However, I am very far from believing that only democracies have moved in the direction of populism and post-truth in response to the spread of education.

Totalitarian and oligarchic systems have also moved toward closer supervision of official media, careful management of the circulation of opinions via unofficial media, and outright lies and nonsense when it was useful in clouding critical judgements on government policies. It is, however, my assumption that all governments govern, to some extent, on the basis of the consent of their people. The threshold of 50 per cent of the people may not have any particular significance in an undemocratic system, but somewhere between 50 per cent and 99 per cent, depending on the level of physical violence the government is prepared to use, there is a point at which the effective consent of the people to be governed has been withdrawn. Although the numbers may differ, we might therefore expect to see qualitatively similar phenomena in different systems of governance.

I want to make quite explicit what I have been doing here. I have been setting out a model of how a society might be expected to respond to different aspects of increasing diversity. I have tried to articulate that model, so that changes, and mechanisms of change, can be posited and examined, in a variety of actions that might be described as "thought experiments." The insights provided by such thought experiments can then be applied, or held up against, actual events, and even compared with events that do not fully conform to the specifications of the model. An example of this last point is the application of a model developed to illustrate the dynamics of a democratic system to a system that is not democratic.

In this particular case, I have suggested that such a model of society could indicate that, as higher education and/or critical political awareness is disseminated in society, political division and policy difference may be expected to increase. We might then look at various societies with a view to evaluating the model, and seeing whether it does describe some important features of the societies that we are interested in.

If the model fails that simple test, it can be discarded and we can go back to developing a new theory or set of theories. But if the model passes that initial test, nothing has been "proved" about the efficacy of the model. In much the same way as one cannot describe events without language, one cannot examine events without some form of model of interactions. Any model focuses attention on specific evidence, results in other issues being ignored, and there is the very serious danger that it will select only that evidence that supports the model. However, I remain convinced that explicit use of models is superior to the implicit use of models, which may be made worse by the assumption that no models are being employed and that the researcher has direct access to "reality."

The central point of this chapter has been the observation that, for a number of reasons, it has become increasingly difficult to regard nation states, cultures, social classes or institutions as homogeneous entities. But that is not really the end of the matter. I have to this point only addressed the question of describing national character in terms of Hans' analysis of factors and traditions. Coping with the difficulty created by the use of categories, that the use of a category or classification implies a grouping that has something in common, while recognising that intragroup variation always exceeds intergroup variation, does not involve moving from one method to another. The dilemma arises in connection with any method, because it is integral to the way that we think. Above all, it applies to the classification of observations that is essential for a scientific, or social scientific, study of education. In the 1960s and 1970s considerable practical work was done on reducing the ambiguities of educational terms, through meetings of experts that looked at the "relevant data" to be used in comparative education. The development of the International Standard Classification of Education (ISCED) was a major step forward in facilitating the practical comparison of educational systems, so that everybody knows what they are talking about when they compare "secondary" or "tertiary" education. But while this solves some of the difficulties of cultural translation, it does nothing to solve the problem that what counts as a school, a teacher, or a parent may involve massive intragroup variation.

So it is worth pausing for a moment to think sympathetically of the plight of a masters student approaching comparative education for the first time, with, say, a simple comparative study of pedagogic practices in elementary schools in India and China. What evidence can one call upon for such a comparison? Knowing that there is huge intragroup variety, for example between schools in Delhi and schools in a rural area of Andhra Pradesh, does it make sense to talk about pedagogical practice in Indian schools? Or in China? Is there any generalisation that we might be able to make about the attitudes of parents in China and India that might not be contradicted in specific cases? It is no wonder that the question of what counts as comparative education looms large when one starts to think about such a project. And the problem is exacerbated by the fact that at least some of the policy makers in India and China will be using the stereotypes that we know are not logically defensible in order to create a sense of national unity and solidarity.

And, if you thought things were complicated enough already, this is where it gets really complicated. If identifying what it means for other people to be identified as "Chinese," "Indian," "French" or "Samoan," we also have to face the fact that national and cultural identity will be at the heart of how each researcher thinks about himself or herself. The fact that categories become porous and diffuse when you start to examine them closely is not something that can remain confined to student essays and erudite books: it is something that is bound to affect the way that we think of ourselves, as researchers, as scholars, as people. That is to say, we continually reconstruct ourselves as we learn more about the subject that we are learning.

I have already noted that we should not think of ourselves as collecting a subject that is ready-made. The key question for any student of any subject is what they hope to make of that subject. It has become fashionable to speak of the curriculum in terms of skills, or knowledge and skills, that can be collected and attached to a person who is fundamentally unchanged in the process. That seems to me to be a very poor way of thinking about curricula. A person who has really understood that other people see the world in a very different way should be changed by that process, and should have a better understanding, perhaps more humble, view of their own perceptions of the world.

In the sections that follow, I want to look at this process of self reconstruction through two key concepts of complexity, and relate them to the processes of education. These two new metaphors are the non-random walk and Stafford Beer's viable systems model. I will illustrate these two metaphors primarily in relation to institutions, and how institutions follow a path of continual self reconstruction and renewal.

I have chosen to focus on the institutional level for two main reasons. First, the history and inner workings of institutions are more readily available and identifiable than the history and inner workings of individual people or national organisations. At the same time, it is easy enough to see how the metaphors might be extended to cover both personal and national self reconstruction, which are processes I shall examine more fully later in the book. The second reason is that, standing, as they do, between the personal and the national, institutions are perhaps less emotive topics for discussion than either the macro or the micro scale.

Finally, precisely because institutions are of a particular scale, it is almost impossible to consider a school or a university without at the same time recognising that it is made up of individuals and that it fits within a national system. Thinking about institutions almost inevitably sets up the discussion that I want to elaborate later, on the nesting of one system within another within another, each of which is in a continual process of self-reconstruction.

I want to go into this issue of self-reconstruction in some detail because it forms a central theme in the whole story I want to tell about how education systems work and about how we ought to understand their operation. In addition, I want to present an argument that this reconstruction takes place at several different levels. Individuals are reconstructing themselves in terms of who they are and how they address their activities. Institutions reconstruct themselves in a pattern that is rather similar. And fields of study, such as comparative education, are continuously reconstructed over time. And even whole nations, national systems and national character are transformed through a process of reconstruction.

Moreover, this perspective on human activity as a process of identity construction on many levels offers an important way of understanding certain methodological questions that necessarily arise in the context of comparative education.

As noted above, I am going to look at the process of reconstruction in relation to two theoretical models or metaphors. Although the process happens on the various different levels that I have mentioned, it is, as I have said, easiest to illustrate the process in relation to the development of institutions. I will illustrate my points by taking a quick review of a single institution over the sweep of its history, and to analyse this history I will use two theoretical models. First, I will introduce the concept of a non-random walk, and later I will use Stafford Beer's viable system model.

The theoretical understanding of random walks was introduced at the beginning of the twentieth century by Einstein, who developed a mathematical treatment for the phenomenon of Brownian motion. Brownian motion is the slight jiggling motion of pollen particles in water, or smoke particles in air, as the particles that are visible under an optical microscope are jostled by the multitude of smaller, invisible molecules that make up the substance where the larger particles are suspended. One important feature of Brownian motion is that the future behaviour of particles and their migration has no relationship with what has happened in the past; each particular period in time is independent of what has gone on before.

Einstein developed a mathematical representation of the random walk and demonstrated that the distance a particle moves from its point of origin is proportional to the square root of the time taken, or $x = kt^{1/2}$.

Non-random walks can be defined in negative terms in the sense that they are not random walks. That is to say, the most important feature of a non-random walk is that it has to have a memory, as the future behaviour of the walk depends on what has happened in the past. Random walks need no memory, as the future does not depend on the past. Non-random walks have a memory and the particle moves away from its point of origin either more rapidly or more slowly than would be the case for a random movement. Non-random walks are either attracted back to, or repelled from, their starting point.

It is perhaps worth emphasising this point that random events have no memory, because the gambler's fallacious reasoning is generally based on the idea that they do. If I toss an unbiased coin, there is a 50:50 chance that it will come down heads. In a sequence of tosses, however, if the coin comes down heads five times in a row, I imagine that there as an increased probability that it will come down tails next time; the chances of six heads in a row are only 1 in 64. But coins have no memory, and each hazard is completely unconnected to those that went before.

On the other hand, people and institutions do have memory. They do have a tendency either to repeat similar patterns or to avoid repetition and seek novelty. There is an old joke about two friends watching a film who have a bet about how the film ends. The film ends, the matter is decided, and the loser pays up. Then the winner confesses that he had seen the film before, and consequently it was not a fair bet. "I had seen it too," said the loser, "But I never expected them to make the same mistakes a second time." This is a reflection on the nature of memory, and how it can be misunderstood. Films and other recordings have memory in the sense that they are designed so that they repeat themselves exactly. Treating them as though the outcome is a random event is the height of foolishness. On the other hand, people have memory in that they learn from mistakes, at least sometimes, although it may be unwise to bet that they will always learn after only one instance. Treating a film of a people as though one were observing actual people is, of course, a mistake.

A non-random walk exhibits memory in the sense that it can "remember" where it came from, and either be attracted back to its starting point, or repelled away from it. The tendency may only be slight, so that not every move is back towards the starting point. Nor is every move away from the starting point. But on average, and over time, the non-random walk moves from its starting point at a slightly larger or smaller speed than a random walk. Put in mathematical terms, analogous to the formula produced by Einstein, $x = kt^H$, where H is not equal to one half. One might think of the random walk as a special case of a more general family of non-random walks.

In very crude terms, one might think of a person's movement over a lifetime as a possible non-random walk, where the point of origin, the national culture, language, and sense of place draw the person back, so that even if they migrate long distances, the connection with the origin is never completely severed. For most people this may seem a very natural way in which memory affects them, although there will undoubtedly be others who have the opposite instinct and want to get as far away as possible from their origins.

One of the concepts of complexity that I find most difficult is the concept of the strange attractor. Conceptually, however, it is linked with the idea of a non-random walk, and the fact that a non-random walk moves away from its origin at a speed that is different from that of a random walk. The concept of a strange attractor in complexity theory is the idea that particles that are moving on a non-random walk are not merely attracted back to, or repelled from, their starting point but are attracted to or repelled from every point along their pathway.

Consider again the gambler tossing the coin; since the sequence has no memory, it might as well start in one place as in any other. The next throw of the dice or toss of the coin will not be affected by what has gone before. So one can choose any point in a sequence and treat it as though it were the beginning. However, if we introduce memory, there is the possibility that one point will be remembered as special, a starting point, our "roots," which have a particularly strong pull on us. That might be an ordinary attractor. But the non-random walk shares with the random walk the idea that any point on its progress can be taken arbitrarily as the starting point for what follows. This means that the actual starting point must not be special, not stand out as different from other points along the pathway. And the result is that the motion is attracted back to, or repelled away from, every point along its path.

The outcome is that motion that follows a non-random walk demonstrates chaotic behaviour. A strange attractor represents the whole motion of the non-random walk, and the idea that the motion is attracted back to all of the places where it has previously been. I shall return to the metaphor of the strange attractor at intervals through the course of this book, because this idea, that there are points in our history which we continually revisit and reinterpret, without ever getting back to exactly the same spot, seems to me to be a particularly rich way of looking at human and social behaviour.

Benoit Mandelbrot used the concept of a non-random walk to examine the behaviour of stock markets (Mandelbrot and Hudson, 2004). Typically, when stock markets rise this creates a sentiment in the market that is optimistic and the market continues to rise, sometimes producing bubble of high prices driven by unrealistically high expectations. At some point the market suffers a dramatic reversal and the opposite effect is produced, where a generally pessimistic estimation produces a collapse, or the bubble bursts. Mandelbrot described this feature of sequences or groups of similar movements of the market as the "Joseph Effect," after the Biblical character who predicted seven years of good harvests followed by seven years of famine.

In between these periods of self similarity, where bull or bear markets reinforce themselves, there must be a sudden switch in direction when the bubble bursts or when the depression turns around. Mandelbrot describes this as the "Noah Effect," again named after a Biblical character, in this case one whose history was marked with sudden reversals. The overall image that is produced of a non-random walk is one of periods of sustained growth or collapse, interspersed with sudden and cataclysmic changes.

In order to illustrate this model of the non-random walk more fully in an educational context, I will present a brief overview of the history of an institution in relation to the model.

I work for the University of South Wales, or rather I have recently retired from the University of South Wales. The University of South Wales is, in fact, a new creation, established in 2013. The institution originated as the Mid-Glamorgan College of Mining more than 100 years ago, at the beginning of the 20th century. Over the years the institution has gone through a number of changes as it has grown, and as its mission has shifted.

Like many institutions, its development follows a periodic cycle that is analogous to the non-random walk, with periods of gradual evolution and development, interspersed with incidents when the institutional mission is re-examined, and there is a deliberate attempt to rebrand or rename the institution. In those occasional episodes of self examination and conscious self-creation, the institution is attracted back to, or repelled from, earlier key transformations. And one of the key points of reference in any organisation is the foundation story, or foundation myth, which embodies the key characteristics and purposes of the institution.

However far the institution has moved on from its beginnings, the foundation story is part of its characteristic self-image and the institution continually revisits, or is attracted back to, that initial starting point. For example, it is part of the culture of the University of South Wales that, when things get difficult, colleagues will say something along the lines, "It could be much worse; we could be under ground and hewing coal." Part of this sentiment is a reference to the idea that the institution started as a mining college. But the expression also encapsulates an indication that colleagues feel themselves to be tied into the local industry and needs of the local community, even though mining no longer happens in South Wales.

Another element of this foundation myth might also be the strength of the sentiment among colleagues that the University of South Wales is most definitely not Cardiff University. Originally funded from a levy on the tonnage of coal produced by local collieries, the owners of those coal mines played an important part in the establishment of the college of mines, and, in return for the generous financial support they provided, wanted the new institution to be responsive to their needs by providing the skilled manpower that was needed for the coal mining industry. As a result, they resisted the foundation of the school of mines as part of Cardiff University, then as now an institution focused on academic rather than industrial values. Practical knowledge, links to local industry and not being Cardiff University therefore form key reference points in the identity of the institution which recur forcefully from time to time (McIntyre, 2013), although in the meantime the institution has developed its academic pedigree and fruitful collaborations with Cardiff University.

The institution did not remain a monotechnic college devoted only to mining, and over the intervening period other professional interests, such as teacher training and nursing education were added. These new activities were different from mining, but similar enough in that they were driven by the needs of the local community to have an appropriate supply of public service professionals. These different efforts to add training for public service professions were not all equally successful. The University South Wales maintains strong and thriving school of nursing, although its engagement with initial teacher education has been rather more patchy over the years.

The history of the institution reaches, as it were, another crisis point in the mid-1970s, when the government established polytechnics by bringing together various public sector higher education institutions. The institution became the Polytechnic of Wales, the only non-university institution of higher education in the principality of Wales, and in the process it brought together a range of higher education activities funded by the local government sector, typically based on para-professionals like teachers and nurses, but also creative arts and a range of activities that had previously not been catered for in the university sector. This recasting of the institution was a stimulus to revisit the purpose and mission of the institution. The Polytechnic of Wales was located in the heart of the coal mining area, an area which was, by the 1970s, in decline and suffering from some depression and underdevelopment. The Polytechnic of Wales added a business school, though its central focus remained on public sector business and policy. In this way the institution was re-invented, but within boundaries that were derived in part from the earlier history of the institution.

As the Polytechnic of Wales, the institution adopted a new mission, however, of taking on responsibility for the kind of professional training in which it was engaged across the whole of Wales. In this sense the names of institutions can be important, and the "Polytechnic of Wales" signals a change in direction from the "Mid-Glamorgan College of Mines." This is more than symbolic, with the name being one of the mechanisms that reinforces the self-similarity, and promotes the Joseph Effect, while a change of name can indicate a shift in orientation, or the Noah Effect. The national orientation of the institution to the whole of Wales persists in some of its outreach activities and its connection with higher education in further education institutions across the country.

The institution therefore continued with a mission that involved a revisiting of the connection with the local community first established by the mining college with its connection to the main industry of the local community and a re-analysis of where the institution stands in relation to public services.

In 1992 all the polytechnics in the UK and were granted the right to change their name to University. The re-classification of public institutions that were in the control of local government as autonomous universities occurred at the same time across the UK. All similar institutions were taken away from local government funding in 1992 and placed in the framework of national funding from central government.

It is worth reflecting that the addition of the word "university" to the names of the institutions that had formerly been called polytechnics brings together two non-random walks. The non-random walk of the institution comes into contact with the non-random walk of the idea of a university. It was perhaps a mistake, or perhaps at least an anomaly, for the word university to be applied to all higher education in the UK. Applying the word university to this wider range of institutions carries with it certain traditions, certain ideas of autonomy and institutional organisation, which date back to the mediaeval universities of Oxford and Bologna. But, in fact, although the UK has a number of institutions that might readily be regarded as traditional ancient universities, the vast majority of institutions that are now called universities, and indeed the institutions where the majority of students who are currently enrolled in universities are studying, are institutions that would previously have been outside the university sector of higher education and they provide courses that would not have been included within the traditional functions of universities.

Calling all higher education "university education" carries with it certain overtones about traditions which draw upon a specific history, and therefore a specific non-random walk. The word "university" is stretched and developed, changed while remaining the same, by its application to institutions that have quite different activities and traditions. Even the traditional ancient universities are no longer rigidly constrained within the pattern of the mediaeval university. But the focus of my interest is that the institution is also changed by its adoption of the label "university."

People are involved in education and those people may well have seen this transition as an opportunity to reconstruct themselves differently in terms of their scholarship and status at the same time as they reconstructed their institution. University status was accorded to both individuals and institutions at a stroke. People like me went from being polytechnic lecturers to being university professors, with a consequent impact on both my status (upwards by contagion) and on the status of professors (downward as its rarity value was reduced). Polytechnics dealt with this new status by moving out of education that did not lead to degrees and increasing their involvement with research, a process that has been described as "academic drift." Academic drift is itself an interesting term, which carries many of the same overtones as Brownian motion and non-random walks. It describes a process that implies change, but which also retains a memory of its history and development.

So, like all other polytechnics in the UK, the Polytechnic of Wales became a university, which was simultaneously a step in the development of the institution, but also a step in the development of many individuals involved, who saw the change as beneficial to them personally. In this way the non-random walk of the institution is linked with the non-random walks of the individual career paths, without the two levels ever being causally interconnected. Individuals can leave the institution, and the institution carries on in its own way and with its own culture, while the individuals may move to other institutions, not necessarily in education at all. The paths of individuals and institutions cross, run parallel and separate in ways that are complex.

The Polytechnic of Wales became the University of Glamorgan in 1992. The title "University of Wales" was already being used by another institution, so the new institution could not adopt that name. But it is worth reflecting whether the new name was not chosen to reflect the importance of the creation myth of the new institution, and its origins as an institution of Mid-Glamorgan. The University of Glamorgan existed from 1992 to 2013, and at which point it merged with University of Wales College Newport, to create a new institution. The change of name, rather than the imposition of the name of one or other of the pre-existing institutions on the new entity, suggests that there is to be a radical rethink of where the institution needs to go and where it is going. The change of name thus symbolises that this is a merger and not a takeover, and that in some way the non-random walks of the two institutions must be combined in a way that respects both of their histories.

All of these changes are signalled in an interesting way by the selection of the new name of the institution. Incidentally, the choice of the new name was one of the few aspects of the new institutional arrangements that was opened for discussion among all the staff of the institution, so the new name does arise in a real sense from the distributed wisdom of the institution. However, despite the name, the University of South Wales is not really the University of South Wales. It is certainly one university of south Wales, but other institutions may also lay claim to that position, most notably Cardiff University. Exactly what the name means and represents, what special identity the institution lays claim to through its name, will be worked out in the future through a process of self-recreation.

Once again, what I am pointing to here is the phenomenon whereby the institution recreates itself in the light of certain key points in its history. The origin stories of the two institutions will be particularly important, but there are also other key points where the mission of the university has been revisited. In this way the institution develops a characteristic identity which persists despite changing personnel. Students come and go. Members of staff come and go. But the institution develops a character of its own and picks out those people and appoints those people who are in some way or other in accord with that underlying current, that underlying process of the institution recreating itself. The institution recreates itself within a broader tradition of higher education, and is itself the context where people recreate themselves. The institution certainly is driven by heads of department, by deans and by vice chancellors who want to build their empires, create their own personal reputations and develop their own CVs. And what those individuals can do, and what they can achieve, is not entirely independent of what the institution does. We see a process of reconstruction that is going on at different levels, but the levels are not directly or causally connected, although there are strong linkages between levels.

An important feature of complex organisations is that they have this characteristic of fractal behaviour, or holographic behaviour, where the whole can be seen in the part. Patterns of reconstruction at the institutional level are reflected in every piece of the institution in self-similar ways. Furthermore, the patterns that are seen at the institutional level are repeated at the system level and so on up to the level of the national system of education and perhaps beyond. Different levels of performance, and different levels of analysis, exhibit similar, but not identical, patterns, and there are reciprocal connections between levels in a way that is both illuminating but also allows for the freedom of development in a non-deterministic way.

One of the interesting aspects of Mandelbrot's analysis of stock markets, which relates to this concept of fractal patterns, is that the sudden fluctuations in the of behaviour of stock markets can never be removed by looking at events in greater detail. If one looks at a chart, for example of the performance of the stock market over the years, there are sudden ups and downs in the level of the market. If one then zooms in, so that the scale on the chart is in days rather than years, the same patterns can be seen. Zoom in again so that the timescale is in minutes rather than days, and once again the same pattern is repeated. The same patterns can be seen at different levels of magnification, so that, apart from the labelling on the axes, one cannot easily tell the difference between a chart of market movements over the last century, and a chart of market movement over the last ten minutes.

I should perhaps comment, parenthetically, on the use of the word "same" here, as it is obviously a matter of comparative interest. The patterns are the same, in the sense that they exhibit the Joseph Effect and the Noah Effect, criteria that I have described earlier, and that I am directing attention to when I describe the patterns as "the same." In fact, each pattern is unique and unpredictable, so the patterns are only "the same" in this restricted sense. But that is the nature of comparison.

These patterns of trends over time are also present in the development of an institution, and one can see that over more than a century, between the foundation of the institution and the present day, the institution develops its plans, absorbs smaller colleges and then gradually re-focuses on a few large campuses and then expands again. It passes through expansionist phases when it merges with some other institutions and takes on new activities. It follows these phases with periods of consolidation, when it divests itself of small campuses and concentrates its activities again, with the institution gradually repositioning itself and reflecting upon its mission, and how it is to serve the local community.

And this process also happens at rather different levels of magnification. One sees the internal organisation of the institution changing, as faculties change shape through merger or splitting, through closure or expansion. A law school is established that is later integrated into the business school. A course on educational management in the human resource management section of the business school gives rise to a grouping of staff who concentrate on education, and this is eventually merged with some other activities in other departments to create a subject area that stands on its own. But in a later stage of consolidation it is recombined with other departments. At a different level of magnification, there are also periods of expansion in courses, when new courses are established to recruit new students with new interests. But at a later point there is an effort to rationalise academic programmes and to ensure that all courses have at least a minimum number of students enrolled on them.

These periodic processes of expansion, consolidation and reorganisation are typical of institutions of higher education, at least in the UK, and possibly further afield. The patterns will be different in systems where ministerial approval is required to add courses or faculties to the university, but where institutions have the autonomy to organise themselves as they see fit, patterns of expansion and consolidation can be used to reflect the importance being attached to certain areas of intellectual activity.

These patterns of expansion and consolidation need not necessarily be happening in a synchronised way; pruning back one area may be the basis for overall expansion of the institution, so that some areas may have periods of consolidation while others are experiencing a flourishing of new and expansionist developments. But at course and department level, the institution will adopt certain patterns of behaviour to reflect a particular focus, and departments and courses will be tailored and adjusted to the needs or intentions of the institution. These patterns will be reflected throughout the different levels of the organisation, right down to the department level, so that, whether in casual conversation or in discussion of the development new programmes, individuals will refer to the history and the location of the institution and to both its ancient and more recent history of development. This is part of the process of self reference which moves the institution gradually towards its new destiny in the process of a non-random walk. The institution is brought progressively both back to where it started and also to reinterpret its starting position in such a way that it can move on to do new things, and different things. This interplay of activity and inactivity, of expansion and contraction, is reminiscent of the patterns that I have already described in Conway's game of Life.

The non-random walk combines both novelty and inertia in a way that is illustrative of the development of the characteristics of a group of people who are at the same time more than the sum of its parts, or the individuals who constitute the group. The group is created from and develops from those individual level activities, but is not exactly determined once one has described those individual level activities. There is a pattern of progression, often characterised as two steps forward and one step back, that seems to recur in many areas of human endeavour, from learning to play a musical instrument to developing a multi-national consensus.

One of the most celebrated features of complex system is the butterfly effect, the idea that very small inputs or perturbations of the system can produce very large differences in outcomes. The butterfly effect gets its name from the idea that a tornado in Texas can have its origins in the flap of a butterfly wing in the Amazon rainforest. Obviously, not all tiny inputs can have huge and catastrophic outcomes, and the butterfly effect includes the idea that on occasion huge inputs can have little effect, or no effect at all. Complex systems seem to be able to pick out the influences that they will respond to, as schools appoint the staff that they think will further their mission, or universities post profiles of successful students on their websites in the hope of attracting a clientèle that matches what they offer in the way of courses. At an individual level it often seems that people will only learn when they are ready, and while teaching can support learning, it can never create learning.

I should, perhaps, at this point highlight a methodological issue of importance that arises from this discussion. In discussing any kind of social endeavour, a scholar needs to make some decisions about what entities exist in society, and what needs to be described and explained. Strict methodological individualists will argue that only individual people count. Only individuals can have opinions, make decisions or take action. For those theorists, it makes no sense to talk of an institution having a purpose, or of a country deciding to do something. At the other end of this methodological spectrum are those who think that only groups of people are important, and that the opinions, decisions and actions of an individual must be understood as reflections of that individual's group membership, as a man/woman, member of the working/upper class, or racial, or national, identity.

Archer (1995) has discussed the spectrum in terms of another key methodological debate in the social sciences, that of agency and structure; are individuals free agents who can make decisions about their intended actions? or are they constrained and determined by the social structures in which they find themselves? Archer argues that both extreme ends of this spectrum are mistaken. The radical individualists ignore anything beyond the individual ("There is no such thing as society") and in so doing look to explain all social phenomena in terms of the properties and characteristics of individuals. Archer calls this stance "downward conflation," where events that can only be described at the collective level, such as culture, are treated as a property of individuals. At the other end of the spectrum there are theorists who are radical collectivists, who deny the importance of individual decisions, and seek explanations for historical trends in class relationships or national movements. Archer calls this stance "upward conflation," which she regards as the mistake of ignoring the effect that individual decisions can make. One group of radical collectivists, for example, might speak of "false consciousness," the inability of the individual to recognise what is the consciousness that is appropriate to his or her class position.

What this discussion should make clear is that my own position leans toward the individualist end of the spectrum, but that groups of people, whether a university or a nation, have emergent properties, properties at a group level that are linked to but not reducible to properties at the individual level. In this way, it does make sense to speak of a university having a mission, even though it could not have a mission if individuals had not written it, argued for it, ratified it and adopted it.

I hope that this discussion of the institution in terms of the metaphor of the non-random walk captures in simple terms what I am trying demonstrate in an understanding of organisations through a process of self-reconstruction. At the same time, I hope that the reader will fill in the gaps of my account, to extend the metaphor to an understanding of how the processes of self-reconstruction at different levels interact in such a way as ultimately to produce something that can be described as "national character," where people in national systems as a whole have key points that they return to in their discussion of what it means to be American or French or British or whatever, or indeed what it means to be part of this nation as opposed to being part of a splinter group. I will be returning to the question of national character and national identity at a later point, and I will there want to pick up on this question of how national identity develops, and whether cultural differences can be recognised without creating stereotypes.

The second metaphor that I wish to employ to examine this process of self-reconstruction is Stafford Beer's viable system model. This model emphasises a different aspect of the process of self-recreation, namely its purposefulness. To a considerable extent, the non-random walk is the outcome of a process that is merely accidental, in the sense that the movement of smoke particles in a smoke cell or of pollen grains suspended in water are at the mercy of the random collisions of invisible molecules that move the particles that we can see. Smoke particles cannot have a sense of purpose, and cannot pick out those directions that match their purpose.

Stafford Beer's viable system model invites us to think of an institution which is responding to changes in its environment and which, in order to remain viable, must adjust to the changes in its environment. That is, the viable system model describes an organisation with a purpose, and that purpose is to remain viable in an uncertain environment.

Now, an institution will have certain responses that it can produce in reacting to changes in its environment, and in order to maintain its viability. In particular, most institutions are fairly conservative in wishing to maintain viability in something close to the condition in which they find themselves. A system will try to return to something like its present condition, and in order to do that it must have an array of responses which are as varied as the changes in its environment. If the environment can change in ten different ways, then the institution needs at least ten different responses, so that it can react appropriately to the variety of changes in its environment. If the environment can change in a million different ways, then the organisation must have a million different ways to respond in order be able to maintain itself in roughly the condition. So the responsiveness of an institution needs to be matched to its circumstances.

In addition, the responsiveness of the organisation needs to be handled in a range of different ways. Beer first points to an immediate, almost unthinking, reaction which is designed to bring the organisation back into equilibrium with its environs, so that it can continue to perform its primary task. The system needs an immediate monitoring system that monitors its operation and responds to changes in its operations so that it can bring them back to the proper condition. For example, the University provides courses, and it must monitor student recruitment in such a way that if recruitment drops to such an extent that the existence of some courses is threatened, it can respond immediately to increase recruitment. In this example, we can see what Beer describes as System One and System Two of his viable system model. System

One is devoted to performing the basic function of the system, in this case the teaching of students. System Two monitors and corrects deviations from expectations which arise from variations in the environment of the system. When some change occurs in the environment which threatens the viability of the whole system, System Two must be able to react immediately to bring itself back to something like the homeostasis that existed before the change in the environment. System Two can typically handle much of the variety in the environment, but not all the variety in the environment will be handled in that way.

In order to cope with variety in the environment, System Two must incorporate a, necessarily simplistic, model of the environment. Beer illustrates this in terms of the thermostat. The thermostat monitors and controls the performance of a central heating system. The thermostat, which is System Two to the central heating system boiler's System One, incorporates a picture of the environment which has only two states; the environment is hot enough, or the environment is not hot enough. And if the environment is hot enough, the thermostat turns the boiler off, while if the environment is not hot enough, the thermostat turns the boiler on.

In much the same way, the admissions process of the university will be monitoring recruitment to those courses that the institution, as a university, has to run in order to maintain itself as viable. So, if interest in a programme goes down, the university might lower its entry requirements for that course, while if a course becomes more popular, it might raise entry requirements.

But just as a boiler and a thermostat cannot respond to all possible changes in the environment, so System Two, with its simplified model of the environment, cannot cope with all possible changes. For example, it the temperature is too hot, the heating system does not have an appropriate response, as the model it incorporates only specifies the two states, "hot enough" and "not hot enough." Similarly, the university that can only respond to changes in recruitment by raising or lowering its entry requirements will not be able to respond to all possible changes in its environment.

The university will also need to be thinking about closing courses that have stopped recruiting and establishing new courses that it is not currently running in order to attract new students. This involves an element of forward planning about the necessary requirements to maintain viability in the future, and planning courses that might replace losses in student numbers. So the viable system needs a System Three that can be handling variety by planning responses, not in the immediate day-to-day activity of the institution, but it must be planning the logistics of securing the necessary wherewithal for the performance of the institution. In this way, variety in the environment that cannot be handled by System Two of the university can be passed on to System Three, which handles much of the longer term activity. For example, in a university this will involve the accreditation of new programmes, the rationalisation of programmes and so on. These are not responses that can be produced on the spur of the moment, and hence a different system, with a specific time scale on its horizon, System Three, is necessary.

For the university to remain as a viable system, it must also be thinking ahead about what the future environment is likely to do and so there must be, in the institution, somebody who can anticipate future developments in the environment so that plans can be made, and responses prepared, so that when the time comes System Three will have available appropriate responses to environmental changes. This might be handled through processes such as quinquennial review of activities and forward planning, so that variety in the environment that cannot be handled by System Three will be handed on to parts of the system which look at planning for the longer term future. And this process of anticipating what the environment is likely to do in the future is the responsibility of System Four.

Finally, and here we link back again to the metaphor of the non-random walk again, and the process of self-recreation, the institution also needs to be thinking about its identity, what sort of organisation the institution is, and what sort of activities are compatible with this overall mission, and which kinds of activities are not compatible with the total vision of how the institution sees itself. So in his viable system model, Beer posits the existence of System Five which manages and looks after those long-term questions of identity. System Five has to deal with continuity in extremely variable environments, so that the university decides what its core activities are, and what is involved in being a university *per se*, as opposed to being, for example, a long term student hostel and restaurant.

The overall structure which results from the combination of these five systems is shown in Figure 3.1.

In addition to having the characteristic functions associated with each of the five systems, an institution that is faced with a changing environment that it needs to handle must also be able to pass information appropriately between systems, and in a timely manner. System Two will handle such variety in its environment as it can, and it must then pass the unhandled variety on to System Three. Similarly, System Three will handle such variety originating in the environment as it can, and pass the remainder on to System Four. The channels of communication between the various systems must be capable of handling sufficient variety, because otherwise the responses of those systems will either be inappropriate, or they will be too late.

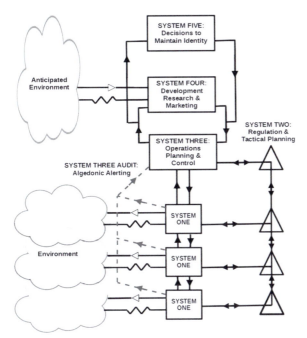

FIGURE 3.1   Stafford Beer's viable system model (adapted from https://en.wikipedia.org/wiki/Stafford_Beer)

Finally, Figure 3.1 shows a network of algedonic alerting, analogous to the pain systems within the body, which can alert the higher order systems when something is going drastically wrong.

The function of self-reconstruction is most closely identified with System Five, but that activity is based on the messages received from other systems, and is therefore described in the complete viable system model.

I have suggested that the non-random walk captures the unpredictability of human behaviour and of human institutions in its "accidental" movements to and fro. In that sense it may be identified with the fuzziness or woolliness of human activity. The viable system model, by way of contrast may look mechanical, rigid, and above all predictable. It should be noted however, that the two models are closer than they may initially appear.

I have noted the fractal quality of non-random walks and that features do not disappear as one focuses in more closely on a specific aspect of the complex system. The viable system model also incorporates the notion of fractal construction, namely that each part of the system is a microcosm of the organisation as a whole. Beer observes that each System One must itself be a complete viable system. These are not identical copies of the whole system, but self-similar models of the larger pattern.

For the university as a whole to be a viable system, it must be a made up of systems that are viable at a lower level, and its departments and faculties must also be viable systems. And the sub-parts must be viable systems, with departments, courses and even the individuals who engage with the institution as teachers or students being viable systems. The idea of fractal organisation is like a Russian doll model, with each level of the organisation including inside it a stacking system of viable systems.

Moreover, to operate as a viable system the organisation needs an environment which is a viable system. A viable university needs a national system of higher education, and a national system needs a world system, all of which are viable.

It is at this point, when one sees the overall structure of viable systems nested one inside the other, this model converges with that of the non-random walk. The connections in the viable system model are not mechanical and deterministic. A change in the environment elicits a response in the viable system, but that response is not a perfect adjustment to the environment. It is mediated by the view that the system holds of the nature of the environment, and it is managed by means of messages, necessarily imperfect, that pass between the different levels of organisation.

The immediate response of the viable system comes from System Two, but the strength and direction of the response made by System Two may be subject to later correction or modification in the light of messages passing between System Two and System Three. And so the viable system does not run on the iron rails of certainty, but follows something like its own non-random walk as it accommodates and adjusts to the viable systems that make up its environment and its constituent parts.

Moreover, the environment that the system is responding to is itself a system that has its own responses that are going on continuously. A system therefore responds to changes that are uncertain and poorly understood. Looking outward, the viable system sees an environment that is not merely changing, but is changing according to a pattern that appears to be able to pick out its own influences. Similarly, looking inwards, the viable system is made up of viable systems that it must try to coordinate, while they, at the same time, are following purposes of their own in their efforts to remain viable.

In conclusion, we can see that the two models, that of the non-random and that of the viable system model, have in common this idea that patterns of behaviour are repeated. The patterns at each level are not directly controlled by, nor completely determined by, patterns of behaviour at higher and lower levels within the system. Nevertheless, the patterns that repeat at each level within the system are "the same." I will return to this question of what it means to be "the same" at a later point, because this is one of the necessary underpinnings of any kind of comparison. But for the time being, I hope that this introduction will be sufficient as an outline of what I think is important to understand about how people reconstruct themselves within systems and how those personal reconstructions interface with the reconstruction of institutions.

This introduction forms the basis for what I consider to be an important understanding of comparative education at a minimum of two, and possibly more, different levels. In the first place, it provides a framework for understanding the work of individual comparative educationists. Those individual comparative educationists were/are reconstructing themselves, positioning themselves, and adopting certain theoretical and methodological positions, and in the process of doing that they have shaped the field of comparative education. We need, as scholars who are fitting ourselves into the field, an understanding of the field which we aspire to develop, move on, shape or contribute to.

At the same time, much of the substance of comparative education is precisely about understanding different cultures, different national settings, and different understandings of education. In order to come to terms with the variety of ways in which the world is conceptualised, we need to see how other people's national systems are reconstructed and what it is that individuals are doing. We need a framework within which it is possible to talk about national character without stereotyping or insisting that all individuals are completely determined by their national or cultural setting. We need a framework that allows us to recognise that there is a sense in which Japanese scholars and British scholars approach educational issues from a completely different perspective, without losing sight of the fact that there is more within group variation than between group variation, and that knowing that a scholar is Japanese or British in no way allows us to stereotype them and prescribe how they think.

This brings me once more to emphasise the key lesson of comparative education; the difference between the mean performance of any two groups is always small compared to the difference between individuals within the groups. It is easy to lose sight of this as we characteristically talk of male characteristics or female characteristics, about German philosophy or Japanese art. Nevertheless, we need constantly to remind ourselves that such generalisations carry significant risks. On the other hand, simply because it is usual and useful to talk about American literature or Latin American music, I wish in the course of this book to develop, promote or one might almost say rehabilitate a notion of national character. When I started to study comparative education, a notion that there was, or is, a living spirit that characterises a nation was a common idea. It has since fallen into some desuetude in the face of studies that seek universal explanations of human behaviour. I regard the latter as a mistake, and the idea of national character, not in any simplistic sense but as a non-random walk/viable system, will feature prominently in the course of this book.

The overall framework of personal and social reconstruction also provides a framework for addressing a range of important methodological questions that we have to confront in comparative education. I have already hinted in that direction when I have suggested in the analysis that certain ideas, such as the idea of a university or the idea of a teacher, are plastic concepts which can be applied to different settings. In general, we have a deep attachment to words, and think that words represent natural categories. So we think that an institution has changed fundamentally when we change the way that we refer to it from "polytechnic" to "university." Calling institutions "universities" and "polytechnics" carries with it the idea that those institutions will be evaluated, changed and orientated in accordance with different criteria. Changing the name of something certainly changes how it behaves, and what our expectations are. In that very broad sense, we need to be able to accommodate the idea that the world is socially constructed, and depends upon the way that we describe it.

Words are important. However, without adopting an entirely realist position, I believe that there are certain incontrovertible facts that form the basis of our thinking. There is some substratum of experience, which we shape and reshape with the use of language. Although we can recast the world by describing it with different language, the world cannot be recast into just any shape, and the essential inelasticity of things eventually rules out some possibilities.

This question of whether the world is socially constructed, and, if it is socially constructed, whether there are limits to the freedom with which scholars can apply language, is, of course, a crucial one in terms of understanding our education systems. Whether we are able to describe other people's activities in our terms, or must take into account the way in which they interpret their actions, whether we are seeking objectivity or are happy with a subjective understanding, what are appropriate categories for comparison, and what are relevant differences between similar situations, these are all crucial methodological questions that every comparative educationist must come to terms with. Our decisions about these basic questions have an impact on how we collect information, on how we analyse it and how we interpret it.

These are issues that, like many other issues raised in this chapter, I will need to come back to again and again in the course of this book. But in this first instance I have offered a sketch of a framework for analysing how individuals and groups are related, and how the individuals, who form part of a group, can exert on influence that group, and, conversely, how the possibilities that the individual can choose are shaped by the group he or she belongs to. And this will be the model which, again repeated at different levels, will form the structure of this exploration of comparative education.

CHAPTER 4

Mapping the Field

1   The Field as Context

This chapter provides an overview of the field of comparative education. Many people have attempted such a mapping. The usual starting point is to offer a definition of what makes the field, and there are two common ways of approaching this. The first is to define the field in terms of content, and the second is to define it in terms of method. I will argue that both such approaches are mistaken, as is any combination of them.

What I will offer instead is an image, as I see it, of a self-identifying group of scholars (comparative educationists) who choose to construct themselves as members of this field, as I do. We therefore see the field through a double refraction, where I try to present my understanding of how they understood themselves. Any scholar will change over the course of his or her scholarship, and so the scholars whom I describe are themselves on a non-random walk through the field and through their experience. But as with any non-random walk there are points where they are attracted back to, points of anchorage, as it were.

I am going to pick one of those points of anchorage as the leitmotif of this chapter: the idea of scholarship as the pursuit of science. "Science" is a good word, by which I mean that it conjures up positive feelings. No scholar is going to present himself or herself as unscientific. Anti-scientific possibly, and anti-positivist science, certainly, but never unscientific. I have chosen as the metaphors for structuring this book ideas that spring from complexity "science" – non-random walks have their scientific credentials even more firmly established by having attracted the attention of Einstein.

As teachers, as professionals and as scholars we are presented with experience that is essentially fragmented and anecdotal. It comes in isolated events, like individual grains of sand. We recognise it as being subjective. And our task is to find ways of bringing those grains of sand together into some sort of organised scheme, to build a heap of sand, or better still a sandcastle. We think that then we will have some objective understanding. That question of how we bring subjective experiences, even a very large number of subjective experiences, together to produce something more certain, something objective, which we might call knowledge, has been one of the major recurrent themes of philosophy through the ages, and I do not expect to solve it in this volume. It is, however, a question that every scholar must examine and must take a position on.

My reading of Kant (1781/2007) (in the *Critique of Pure Reason*) is that he faced the problem of how Newton had put all those observations of individual stars and planets together to produce a theory of how the universe operated; how had he got it right, in spite of the difficulties? In contrast with Kant, my reading of Popper (1959) (in the *Logic of Scientific Discovery*) is that he had a different question, after Einstein had published his theory of relativity; how had Newton got it so wrong? And perhaps more importantly, how had people taken the wrong answer to be correct for nearly two hundred and fifty years? So what it means to be a science has itself been on a random walk over the centuries, and there will be many interpretations of what it means to be a scientist. I will argue that each of the scholars whom I look to as anchor points in my experience of comparative education was presenting himself or herself as a scientist, although they differed sharply in what they thought that the term "scientist" implied.

It is at moments like this that I am rendered almost speechless by the daunting nature of what I am trying to describe here. "Each of the scholars... was presenting himself or herself as a scientist." Is that what I intended to say? Might I not better have expressed that thought by saying that I find it helpful to understand the stance of each as a claim to be a scientist? Or perhaps I should have said that I think it will add to my reader's understanding if I suggest that each scholar can be understood as making a claim to be a scientist. Some explicitly claimed to be applying a scientific method (or the scientific method), but not all did. To what extent am I allowed to impose my interpretation on them retrospectively? The whole question of what it is to make a claim about other people can open up at any time with the simplest of sentences, and is in danger of making the whole project, not only of comparative education itself, but of scholarship in general, completely impossible.

The matters that we deal with in comparative education, as in many other fields of study, are infinitely complex, and it is right that we should examine the foundations on which we stand critically. Archimedes is supposed to have said, "Give me somewhere to stand and a lever and I will move the Earth." And like him, most scholars crave some firm ground to stand on, although on close inspection all firm foundations seem to crumble. So we have to content ourselves with recognising that all foundations are only provisional and will need critical examination at some point – perhaps a little later. The matter is complicated, and as I like to observe to my students, that is all to the good; were it otherwise, we would not need to be studying it in a university, or running postgraduate courses on it, and this book might have been written decades ago. So let me simply say that I am going to try to bring some order to my understanding of the field by thinking of the competing voices in comparative education as presenting claims about what a science of comparative education might be like.

But before I get into that more complex and fluid account of what the field of comparative education might look like, let me examine what I have identified as the two common approaches to defining the field of comparative education, and offer my critique of those. Taking first the idea, of defining the field or the discipline by the first approach, by the content of the subject, the clearest example is that of Harold Noah (1974), who in his presidential address to the Comparative and International Education Society (CIES) talked about "fast fish and loose fish." The metaphor here is that there exists an ocean of knowledge in which whales, or topics, swim. Some have been harpooned, but there are other whales that are still swimming free. Building a discipline involves harpooning those whales that do not yet belong to another discipline, so making fast a fish that had previously been loose.

Even leaving aside the fact that whales are not fish, I cannot imagine why anyone would think this was an appropriate way of defining a discipline. It would mean defining comparative education by looking around for topics that had not been addressed, and claiming them for the discipline. Differences in body language between five year old pupils learning arithmetic in Japan and the UK: nobody has studied that, so we could make that part of a comparative field of education. But, apart from the fact that you know this could be a comparative education study, because it already incorporates a prior notion of comparison, most of the things that we want to look at are already "fast fish" tied to some other discipline. Assessment and testing is already part of psychometrics, or statistical analysis, or education more generally, but that does nothing to diminish the interest in the comparative aspects of PISA (however misguided the actual design of the PISA comparisons may be).

If we look at the example of the established sciences, the content that is appropriate for the study of physics is the entire visible universe. Similarly, the subject matter of chemistry is the entire visible universe. Moreover, the subject matter of the field of biology, or the discipline of biology, is living matter wherever it occurs in the visible universe. So the contents of these disciplines overlap almost completely. In the same way, history covers all those events that relate to human culture, as do sociology and psychology. All events or social interactions are equally approached by any discipline.

Sara Delamont (2005) offers an interesting insight when discussing a related topic in connection with the study of education in general. Starting from the idea of education scholarship as a branch of the social sciences, and recognising that one of the purposes of the social sciences is to "render the familiar strange," she argues that education researchers should, not infrequently, turn their attention to education in unexpected settings. Although most of our time and attention is necessarily spent looking at schools and universities, and national systems of governance and funding mechanisms, we should necessarily look, from time to time, at other, perhaps more marginal activities that are educational. What happens in zumba classes? How do novice anglers learn from other people on the river bank? What makes a street in Beijing into a "classroom" for tai chi?

This is not a random collection of "loose fish" but a purposeful attempt to bring insights to possibly ossified educational theory. What makes a topic part of comparative education is not the study itself, but the intention of the scholar to link it in some way with the literature, the theorising and the prior activity in the field.

A similar objection can be made in the case of defining a discipline in terms of method. Again, this approach seems to me to be mistaken, since a scientist will use whatever method is needed to arrive at a solution to the problem they are struggling with. That does not mean that discussion of method is not important; I think that the often heated debates about method that took place in the 1960s constituted one of the most fruitful periods in terms of developing the field of comparative education. Indeed, I would go further and say that the current lack of discussion of method, as though these questions had all been settled once and for all, is a major source of weakness in comparative education as it is currently represented in conference publications and journal articles.

I want to argue that the definition of a field of study is much too important to be regarded as something static that can be settled once and for all. The definition of a discipline is something that is crucially important to any scholar, and also very personal to him or her. Some years ago I worked in the North East London Polytechnic's School for Independent Study. For most people, the definition of independent study would have involved a phrase like "working on your own," "private study," or something along those lines. I had a colleague, however, who took a very different view of the matter (Robbins, 1988).

He argued that whenever a scholar creates their own body of work, they hold it up against a backdrop of previous work. That previous body of work defines the context for the scholar's work and the approaches taken. If we properly understand that backdrop, we have a route into the entire area of interest of the scholar and the kinds of theories which he or she will apply in the body of his or her work.

For Robbins, independent study meant that the scholar in question was free to choose which backdrop of previous work they held their own work against. The historian holds their work up against history texts and the work of previous history scholars. The geographer holds their work up against the previous work by other geographers. The difference between the human geographer and the historian is not the content of what they look at, nor the methods they use. The difference between them is the way they frame their work against a pre-existing body of work.

In that sense, a comparative educationist is somebody who chooses to hold their work up against a backdrop of other scholars' work, where those scholars are deemed to have created the field of comparative education. There may be certain minimum requirements in content matter. For example, it might be suggested that the content must be in some way related to education and the development of young people. But almost anything can be argued to be in that category if one chooses. For example, I will argue in some detail later that there are major debates in comparative education about the content of history textbooks, partly because this can be politically contentious but also because history constitutes part of the way in which a society views itself. As such, history is an important cultural element which enters into discussions about education.

So, if it is legitimate to argue that how a society engages with its own history is an important topic for study in comparative education, then almost any aspect of culture can be relevant to comparative education. In a way, it is the presentation of an argument that a topic is part of comparative education (or any other discipline) that is more important than what the topic actually is.

If one follows this analysis, that one holds one's work up against a backdrop of previous work, then it follows that new work extends and develops, and possibly even rewrites the field against which the work is considered. So, when I say that I am going to provide an overview of the field of comparative education, I mean of course an overview, and I mean more specifically my overview.

There is a story written by Borges about the work of an author, Pierre Menard, who sets out to rewrite Cervantes' Quixote (Borges, 1970). Borges describes his task, and states that Menard had seen two ways of completing the task. The first was to put himself into the mindset of a sixteenth century prisoner, and hope that the same impulses would lead him to produce the same words. The alternative, the path Menard actually chose according to Borges, was to set out to rewrite the Quixote word for word, but with the same words carrying an entirely different meaning, because they are imbued with the sensitivity of an author from the twentieth century.

In much the same way, any scholar rewrites the field with a study that is presented in the context of that field. Each scholar offers a personal stance, describing their own study in the context of what has previously been published. And at the same time he or she offers a reinterpretation of how the field or discipline has developed, and what the contributions of specific authors mean. To capture this in a nutshell, Harold Noah and Max Eckstein describe the work of early pioneers in the field as "travellers' tales." In doing so, they invite us to see their own work as a move toward a more scientific approach to the analysis of comparative data, but they also invite us to see the work of Matthew Arnold or Michael Sadler as the mythical stage of a pre-science, or a precursor to their own scientific work. In this way they give their work a context, but they also give a new interpretation to that context.

In offering an overview of comparative education, I offer my own particular interpretation of what those previous authors have meant to me. But more importantly from my point of view, I set out the grounds on which I hope to add to them. I think Brian Holmes offered me the following advice on many occasions. Of course, I may be mistaken, and he may have offered me the advice only once, but, in my criss-crossing my own development in the non-random walks that I have made through the field, I am continually being attracted back to it as a motif. Consequently, in my mind it seems to me that he gave me the advice many times. This is how a person can pick up the stimuli that motivate him or her, and those stimuli can have a huge impact even though they may have seemed insignificant at the time. This is the butterfly effect at work in the life of a scholar.

Anyway, to the advice that Holmes gave me: he said, "It is not enough to be thought of as a Holmesian. You have to be a Holmesian but… or a Holmesian and…" This captures the plight of the scholar quite concisely. Nobody can make a reputation for making a contribution to the field if he or she simply parrots the thoughts, however eminent, of Bereday or Hans, while adding nothing of their own. But on the other hand, no scholar springs fresh from nowhere without context, and each must locate his or her work in the context of what has gone before. The interpretation of what has gone before provides the argument that what is being offered actually is new.

It is worth noting that Holmes took it for granted that I would be a Holmesian of some sort. These revisited moments of personal history often have this double feature that makes them both influential but at the same time chimerical. I have never been able to decide whether this assumption that I was destined to be some kind of Holmesian was the product of his certitude that his own position was correct, or that it was simply a recognition of the fact that I could not build on anything other than what I was experiencing. Sometimes I think that he was a truly inspired teacher, who could pick the moment to say exactly the right thing to motivate me, and other times I think he simply said what he said, and it is only with hindsight that I have attached significance to those sayings. Probably both things are true; I have attached unwarranted significance to the things that I remember from the past, but I have selected the things that I attach significance to for a reason, and part of that reason is that they were important events in the first place.

As one constructs one's journey through the field, one builds upon the questions and answers that have been left by previous scholars, and then a new contribution requires a very personal interpretation of what was there already, of what is to be built upon. Each scholar will have his or her own mental map of the field of comparative education and what I offer here is no more than sketch of my own imagination of the field.

In line with my overall methodological position that I would not wish to apply an approach to somebody else that I would not be happy to see applied to me, I allow myself the liberty to reconstruct the field and to locate myself against it. I must also bear in mind that all the scholars that I describe are also, in their own way, each re-interpreting and re-constructing the field in the light of their own insights, and their own ambitions to contribute to the field. In particular, because my own concern has been throughout with seeing how one might develop what might be broadly be called a scientific approach to comparative education, I interpret each of those scholars on whom I have drawn as having tried to locate themselves as a scientist of comparative education.

I do not say this in a narrow sense of trying to claim a special priority for one form of method. If we think of "science" as being the embodiment of the best forms of thought, wherever they come from, and scholars as trying to advance the best, however they are motivated, then I think that we can see all scholars as advocating what they see as the best approach, which can perhaps be described as "science."

When we describe disciplines and fields as more or less fixed areas of study, we not only make a mistake, but above all we do a disservice to younger scholars, who come to see the development of the discipline and their place in the discipline as being a question of fitting pegs into holes – sometimes square pegs into round holes, but always pegs into holes. We give young scholars, especially undergraduate scholars, the idea that there is, out there, an approach and a discipline which would be suitable for their temperament. We underestimate, or underplay, the role that active construction plays in the development of the young scholar. History, geography, sociology or comparative education does not exist as a body of knowledge that the young scholar can collect or receive. The important questions are, What is your personal connection to the field? What are you going to make of what you find in the field?

We need to be very careful about the culture that we promote. If we promote a passive culture, in which the student simply receives the work of established scholars, then plagiarism is seen as sensible. If comparative education is seen as a discipline that builds up through a process of accretion, then why would a scholar struggle to put something in their own words, when others with more facility have already struggled to explain it so clearly? Why would one make an effort to encapsulate the idea of cultural relativism of educational processes, when Michael Sadler has already captured it so expressively in the oft quoted snippet (Sadler, 1900, p. 50, cited in Hans, 1967, p. 3):

> We cannot wander at will through systems of education like children in a garden picking a leaf from one plant and a petal from another and expect them to grow if we put them in the ground.

If an idea has been so beautifully captured in a metaphorical expression, why should anyone struggle to put it differently? But if each scholar has to re-create and re-interpret the field as a whole, and not simply tinker at the edges, it is that personal relationship between the scholar and the content of the field that is of interest. This cannot be plagiarised because this is a question of the route that has formed part of each and every scholar individually. What we want to read about, even in our undergraduate essays, but especially what we wish to read about from our colleagues, is not what happens in a school or what happens in other countries, but how those scholars engage with the evidence they find. It is these very personal connections that make comparative education live.

It is noticeable that many of the pioneers in the field of comparative education had very personal reasons for being engaged with the international aspects of education. Nicholas Hans had left Odessa in order to become a scholar in Western Europe. We can think of him as naturally having had an engagement with the international development of education and comparison. Lauwerys fled from the German occupation of Belgium with his father during the First World War, and one thinks of him also as having had very personal and compelling reasons for engaging with international aspects.

In my own case, or in the case of Brian Holmes or Edmund King, the personal drivers are less obvious. But I think that they are also in some way apparent in the interaction between the personal and professional aspects of comparative education. The personal and the professional are very much tied together. When we read the works of King, we might very well conclude that his style is anecdotal, but it is actually the anecdotal which is engaging and drives our interest in reading about the cultural experience of everyday exchanges and the confrontation with other cultures which King captures in his narrative and descriptions.

It is much more difficult to see the person, and the anecdotal connection, in the work of Holmes, but this can sometimes be seen in a positive way. I think that his personal commitment to a way of thinking about science drives much of what one reads on the page.

What I intend to offer here, then, is my own interpretation, but also my interpretation of how other earlier scholars were interpreting the field. These interpretations involve wheels within wheels and do not provide a very stable or comfortable place. And that, I think, reflects the nature of the way in which we work within the discipline.

Although my goal in this chapter is to provide an overview of the field of comparative education, I want to avoid asking the question of what comparative education is and providing some kind of definitive overview of what makes of the field. All I can offer is a picture of how I have reconstructed the field of comparative education in my head and how I see the key debates and positions that have been adopted in the field. Each scholar reconstructs the field for himself or herself as an observer. To try and provide an essentialist or definitive overview of the field would be both frivolous and overambitious.

When one thinks of mapping the field in this way, one almost inevitably thinks of Roland Paulston and his efforts to locate scholars on an intellectual map (Paulston, 1999). I hope that what I am doing here will be seen as something rather different. Paulston, I thought, was using maps as a way of identifying the "other"; we are over here, positivists are over there, structuralists are over there. Although explicitly he admitted the idea that the positioning on maps was contested, it did not actually feel very much like it.

In contrast with that, I am using mapping as a metaphor for making sense out of our surroundings, in this case the field of comparative education. The overall map that I offer is my map, so where I see another scholar on my map says as much, and possibly more, about me than it says about the scholar in question. Moreover, I gladly acknowledge that other scholars have different maps. I want to consider their process of mapping, not as a way of locating them on my map so much as, I hope, an empathetic way of trying to understand what they were trying to do in the field, and how they saw it. This is something more like those cartoon maps of a New Yorker's view of the world, or a Bostonian's view of the world, in which landmarks that are near and important are drawn much larger than those that are less significant of far away. In that sense, it is the differences between the maps that are interesting, creating a kind of comparative cartography of the field.

What I think is possible is to look at the way that an individual constructs the field and to give some sense of those key points to which they continually return and use in the recasting and redefinition of the field for themselves. Of course, many of those key points about which any contemporary scholar reconstructs the field will be those key authors and previous thinkers who they take as having marked out the field beforehand.

What I also want to do is to try and give a sense of my understanding of those key authors and key figures and their role in constructing the field and positioning themselves in certain intellectual locations, or of locating themselves in certain intellectual positions. Many of the pioneers of comparative education themselves, as I have already noted, had a personal commitment to international connections in education. Nicholas Hans fled from Odessa. The family Lauwerys fled from the invasion of the Germans in Belgium.

There is none of that in my background. I was born and brought up in suburban London and had had relatively little contact with education abroad. My schooling and my university had all been conducted in England, so I first came across comparative education quite by accident. I was a teacher in a secondary school in east London, studying part-time for my postgraduate certificate in education at what was then the North East London Polytechnic. This was a two year, part-time course and at the end of the course I took the six, three hour written examinations.

Sometime later I received a letter from Brian Holmes who was the external examiner on the programme. He told me that I was not going to pass. But he also told me that he wanted me to go back and retake the necessary examinations, and that once having successfully completed the certificate I should go and study for a master's degree in comparative education in his department.

I think that even this brief anecdote addresses some very important aspects of Brian Holmes' character. Firstly, it was not atypical for him to collect waifs and strays into his department because he had taken an interest in them. And secondly, it was my interest in the philosophy of science that had been evident in my answers on my failing examination papers that made him offer me a place in his programme.

Later, I was to learn most of what I know about the role of an academic from him, including the strongly expressed view that it was the function of the external examiner to protect students from the prejudices and biases of internal examiners. It has only just occurred to me that there may not have been anything personal about his invitation to join his course; he may simply have been putting his principles into practice and compensating for what he thought would otherwise have been an unjust outcome, the failing of a student who had something interesting to say, however incoherently they said it. And that, actually, was his first principle of examining, that it is the examiner's job to find what is of value in what a student has to say, however well it is hidden.

Let me pause for a minute there to revisit this question with hindsight. Over the course of several years working with Holmes, and of listening to the people that he invited to give guest lectures, I came to know some of the people who he knew and obviously respected, and I came to know and respect them in turn. The list included eminent scholars, among them Basil Bernstein, Tyrrell Burgess and Maurice Kogan. But on this question, of the responsibilities of examiners, I am reminded of a comment that Tyrrell Burgess made to me much later: "I refuse to fail a student merely because they have not answered the question."

Eventually, as will be clear, I enrolled in the masters in comparative education, which included among the many teachers on the programme, Edmund King, Brian Holmes and Robert Cowen. Of course, the first question I had, although I am not even sure if it was fully or explicitly expressed, when Holmes invited me to join the masters course in comparative education was, What is comparative education?

The answer Holmes offered me was to tell me to go and read *Comparative Education* by Nicolas Hans (1967). Like so many things that Holmes did over the years, I am not absolutely sure whether his choice was inspired by some great insight or whether it was simply that accidentally he hit upon exactly the right thing to do for me, to lead me to comparative education. I went away and read the book, and this was my first introduction to comparative education.

I was overtaken by the vision that Hans offered, the broad sweep of understanding of international education and comparative education. As a child and throughout my formal schooling I had had no interest in history, and what little interest I had developed in history had come through my interest in the philosophy of science and therefore the history of the development of science. But I was absolutely captivated by Nicolas Hans' book. This was history, but it was not a history of a concatenation of events, or of specific lives and specific life happenings. It was a history of themes and ideas which brought together a synoptic view of the causes and reasons for events. It was, if you like, a science of history rather than history as commonly conceived.

I eventually grew dissatisfied with Hans' approach to comparative education. But as an introduction it opened up a vista of what it would be like to have a comprehensive understanding of the forces and factors that helped to shape and form educational systems. It was my starting point in comparative education.

I later became aware of other precursors of comparative education, such as Marc Antoine Jullien de Paris and Michael Sadler. And I think that for me, as for so many other comparative educationalists, these are precursors that one looks to, and uses as a foil to contrast one's position against, as much as real influences on the development of comparative education. But for me Hans was the starting point. His text was the most accessible book on comparative education in England at the time. It had sold well, which meant that it was on the shelves of the library at the North East London Polytechnic, and the sweep of the vision and the easy flow of the language make the book extremely readable.

Actually, as anybody who knows Hans' writing well will understand, that is quite ironic. The library at the University of London Institute of Education has a typescript prepared by Hans which is a history of technical education through the seventeenth to twentieth centuries. It involves some of those key factors to which Hans returned in the course of his historical explanations, the strange attractors in his intellectual life, most notably the prominent role of the Freemasons in establishing state systems of technical education. But the text is almost unreadable.

In the early 1980s both Brian Holmes and George Bereday (independently) suggested that I should edit that text and prepare it for publication. I did quite a lot of work on the text, but in the event the prospective publisher would only consider publishing it if I could add updated material for the post-war period. To complete the book in a way that lived up to the breadth of Hans' vision proved to be beyond me at that time. As a result, the text remains as a typescript in the archive of the University of London Institute of Education. But in the process, I learned to appreciate the work of the editor of *Comparative Education* by Nicholas Hans, whoever he or she was.

Throughout 1975 to 1977 I studied for the masters in comparative education at the University of London Institute of Education, and that, of course, brought me into contact with the works of other theorists of comparative education, most notably Holmes himself and Edmund King, but also George Bereday and Harold Noah and Max Eckstein.

The heady days of the methodological disputes in comparative education in the 1960s were already past, although some of the personal animosities remained. But if I have to form some sense of what was going on in that debate, I think it would be true to say that most of the content of that debate was about those scholars positioning themselves as scientists of comparative education. I have already suggested that Hans was offering one view of what it means to be a science by developing an abstraction from historical developments, to identify those key factors which shape history. To me, with a background in physical sciences background that I shared with Brian Holmes, this was a very 19th-century view of what constitutes a science.

But this was a broadly attractive approach, which is to say that it is an approach that is relatively easily grasped by non-scientists, to study the circumstances of education, and to extract those factors which were the key elements. This was an approach that Holmes himself described as being based on the philosophy of John Stuart Mill and his method of similarities and differences (Mill, 1843/2012). As Mill described it, one could hope to identify the cause of an outcome by looking at natural experiments, such as those to be found in the field of comparative education. By looking at those causes which are always present when a particular outcome is produced, and at those causes that are always absent when that outcome is not produced, one could eventually identify which causes are linked with which outcomes.

The word positivist has become a common description applied to those people who hope to develop in social sciences an approach that is analogous to the physical sciences. For that reason it is not unusual to see Brian Holmes described as a positivist, or a neo-positivist, in the literature on comparative education. From my perspective, the word positivist has taken on so many meanings that it is in fact quite rare that all of them apply to any one scholar. Moreover, it is normally applied with a derogatory sense which I am trying to avoid in my description of other scholars. For the moment, however, let me distinguish at least three meanings of the word positivist, because I think by using those different meanings one can understand a number of different ways in which people tried to position themselves as scientists.

The first meaning of the word positivist, which is derived from the philosophy of Auguste Comte, suggests that science is a development from its mystical origins, its prehistoric origins, towards some kind of modern science. I think that one can see the influence of this idea, that science is a progression from myth into modernity, when Noah and Eckstein, like many comparative educationalists, pick precursors of comparative education. Picking primitive precedents makes it possible to contrast ourselves with that mystical prehistory, and show what progress has been made. What we do now is contrasted with that pre-scientific phase of comparative education, described as travellers' tales, to suggest that in the science of comparative education there is progress towards a higher objective of more scientific understanding.

The second meaning of the word positivist also invokes the idea of progress. But this time it describes science as a collection of observations, with theories being derived from those observations through a process of induction. By building up a solid foundation of case studies, one is eventually able to induce overarching laws, or an understanding of regularities. I think that, in this sense, Hans can be seen as a positivist, although he would certainly not have been positivist in the other ways.

And a third meaning of the word positivist asserts that those things that are real are the things that can be measured. In its strict sense, this idea of positivism derives from the philosophy of Ernst Mach, who, in order to make sense out of quantum physics argued that quantities that could not be measured should be deemed not to exist. So, for example, it makes sense to talk about the momentum of a particle only if it is, in principle, possible to measure it.

This is a serious problem for quantum physicists, where Heisenberg's uncertainty principle states that it is impossible to measure certain pairs of physical states simultaneously, but outside the world of sub-atomic particles it appears to have only metaphorical application.

Notwithstanding that, the metaphorical transfer of the principle that only those things that can be measured are important to the field of education in general, and comparative education in particular, has done terrible damage. Measurement focuses attention on standardised tests such as IQ rather than on less easily measured phenomena such as emotional well-being. Some of the force of that metaphor can be seen in the way that PISA has captured the imagination of policy makers around the world, or the influence of league tables and rankings on various aspects of education. Once a concept is quantified, it appears to acquire hypnotic effect.

This type of positivism has flourished dramatically in recent years, building upon a basis of reasoning from strict rules and efforts to develop studies based on truly statistical approaches, such as Peaker's work to base explanations in the IEA studies on rigid rules (Peaker, 1975). In terms of the philosophical foundation for such approaches in comparative education, we can look to Noah and Eckstein's aspiration that eventually the names of countries should be replaced by the names of variables.

This question of using quantifiable entities rather than more fuzzy concepts is an important one, since it speaks directly to the question of national character. The positivist assumption is that it will eventually be possible to replace such fuzzy concepts with strict measures. For example, it may be possible to speak of countries with such-and-such a range of per capita income, so many television sets per household and a specific range of values on the GINI Index, rather than talking about the differences between Francophone and Anglophone cultures. That is certainly a positivist ambition, in the sense that it implies that only elements that can be strictly quantified should remain in ideal explanations, and that the use of such vague concepts as culture, religion and language should eventually be banished from our lexicon.

For reasons that I hope will become clear, I most certainly want to retain some of those fuzzy notions, such as national character, but I recognise that the move toward quantification is well under way. I have already noted the hypnotic effect of international comparison that is based on numbers in the thinking of policy makers. But one rarely, if ever, hears nowadays about national character in presentations at conferences of comparative education, although religious heritage and culture have not yet been completely abandoned.

So I do not want to be simplistic and simply label everybody who is trying to become a scientist as positivist. I think that it is important to try and draw out some of those different meanings about what it means to be a scientist. Perhaps I should make a slight diversion into my understanding of the history of science and the philosophy of science to develop this theme further.

I take it that an important starting point in the philosophy of science is the work of Isaac Newton. Newton managed, from some necessarily limited observations of the behaviour of planets and their orbits, to produce some surprisingly successful and purportedly universal laws about gravitation. And the crucial question for philosophy was how he had managed to produce laws that could be universally applied from an evidential base which could not possibly be sufficient to support such generalisations. This was the crucial question for philosophy; how can we be in possession of theories which apply to an infinite number of cases when we have only actually observed a relatively small and finite number of cases. That is the core of western philosophy for centuries, and we can see the attempt to address this question as a central theme of the work of philosophers from Hume to Hegel. But for me the most important, as well as the most stimulating approach is represented by Immanuel Kant's *Critique of Pure Reason* (1781/2007), in which he argued that knowledge of the kind that Newton offered was synthetic a priori knowledge, and consequently justifiable.

To summarise three hundred years of philosophy of science rather crudely, from the 17th to the 20th centuries the central question of epistemology was, How did Newton manage to get it so right on the basis of insufficient evidence?

At the beginning of the twentieth century, Einstein produced the theory of relativity, which was in some ways a development of, but in other ways a refutation of, Newton's work. As a result of Einstein's new insight, the philosophy of science shifted from being concerned to demonstrate that Newton was justifiably correct, and instead moved to the question, How did Newton get it so wrong? And that was coupled with another question which in some ways has more psychological or emotional force: How can it be that we were fooled for 300 years?

The key philosopher of science for this second phase of philosophical reasoning was Karl Popper (1957, 1959), who suggested that there was an asymmetry in the relationship between theory and evidence, in the sense that no amount of evidence could demonstrate a theory to be true but it takes only one instance to demonstrate a theory to be false. I will come back to some of the ramifications of that philosophical position, because it seems to me to be crucial for a number of methodological issues. Most importantly, we increasingly see the randomised clinical trial, or the randomised controlled trial, being held up as the "gold standard" in scientific method. A direct transfer from the methods of medicine, as the name implies, this suggests that the only way to arrive at new understandings depends upon the weight of numbers. In so doing it devalues the anecdotal accounts of cultural exchange, as offered by Edmund King, and the use of unique case studies, as advocated as a starting point by George Bereday. And more importantly from my point of view, it leads to the undervaluing of professional experience, gained by researchers and practitioners in the classroom, through a series of unrepeatable encounters. These are questions about what counts as a sound basis for drawing conclusions, and they must be central to everything that we consider in terms of comparative method. But before coming on to those questions in detail, I want to conclude this brief and personal mapping of the field of comparative education by describing my initial encounters with two of the classical comparative educationists whom I have already mentioned.

2 Weaving the Personal and the Professional

I twice met George Bereday in the spring of 1982. I had just started working in the Department of Comparative Education at the University of London Institute of Education, and Brian Holmes had arranged for me to go to the annual meeting of the CIES in New York. I took advantage of that opportunity, my first visit to the USA, to visit some schools, and to go and visit a few scholars to whom Holmes had provided introductions.

Among those who I met were Henry J. Perkinson, author of *The Imperfect Panacea* and Neil Postman, the author best known, at that time, for co-authoring *Teaching as a Subversive Activity*. Holmes regarded Perkinson as the personal demonstration of the effectiveness the GI Acts in the United States, which promoted the education of ex-servicemen after the Second World War. Perkinson used the provisions of the Act to fund a period of study in the UK. More importantly, this introduced me to the core concepts of *The Imperfect Panacea*, namely that Americans suffer periodic bouts of moral panic, when they complain that their education is failing as compared with the Prussians, the Russians or the Chinese, but nevertheless have enough faith in the panacea of education to conclude that a reform of education is the answer.

Neil Postman asked me what I had seen in New York, and I told him the names of the schools that I had visited. He asked me to make him a promise, that I would never say or write anything positive about schools in America on the basis of what I had seen. That introduced me to a very important perspective on comparative education, which is the observation that any sample which arises from personal experience is biased and partial and will provide a rather biased view of what is going on in that country. This is particularly true if the sample of school visits and observations has been selected by a native of the country, since people have a natural tendency to wish to demonstrate the best, the brightest or the most interesting aspects of their educational system. It creates methodological difficulties for any comparativist who wishes to draw any conclusions on the basis of personal experience, however.

But for me, the most important introduction was the opportunity to go and visit George Bereday in his office at Teachers' College Columbia. This was a really exciting time for me. It was the first time I had been to America, in fact the first time that I had been anywhere as exciting and stimulating as New York, and at that time the area around Teachers' College was both exotic and threatening. And, of course, I was to meet one of the charismatic founders of the field of comparative education.

The larger than life George Bereday was bound to make a major impression on a young comparative educationist. I remember that he introduced himself and gave me a brief introduction to his personal biography:

"Have you seen," he said, "The film A Bridge Too Far?"

This is a movie about the Second World War, where paratroopers were dropped into Arnhem to seize a bridge over the River Rhine, preparing the way for the Allied advance into Europe.

"It is quite a good film," Bereday added. "There are only two criticisms I would make about it. The first is that they used an English actor to portray me. And the second is that they killed me off much too early."

In this way he introduced me to some of his colourful background as a Polish paratrooper in the Second World War, as well as to some of the dangerous excitement about what it meant to be a comparative educationist.

Later in the week I saw Bereday again, when he gave his presentation at the CIES conference, and expounded two great principles of comparative education.

"I am going to keep your attention by the well known comparative method," he said, "Of having bulging eyes and waving my arms about a lot."

And that is exactly what he proceeded to do. In the course of his exposition he pronounced the golden rule of all comparison, that you can say anything bad about your own country, and anything good about other peoples' countries, but not the other way about.

George Bereday was that very rare combination of a charismatic personality coupled with a strong basis in theory. I think that his theoretical position was wrong on a number of counts. In the first place he argued that comparative education is not itself a discipline, and that in order to become a strong comparative educationist one first needs to immerse oneself in a discipline such as sociology, anthropology, psychology or history.

I think that idea, that the study of education is parasitic on a number of contributing disciplines, is profoundly wrong. The excitement of education studies is that it combines the introspective or psychological perspective, of what goes on inside a person's head, with the external or cultural perspective, or what goes on outside a person's head. Sociology, psychology, anthropology or history each deal predominantly with either the inner personal history or the external social history, but only in the study of education are both intimately connected. Psychology and sociology are derived from a study of how people develop in social settings, and therefore derived from education studies, and not the other way around.

The second point on which I think Bereday was mistaken is where I agree with Holmes' analysis of his work. Holmes thought that Bereday expressed in the clearest possible terms Mill's method of similarities and differences, moving from juxtaposing descriptive accounts of two or more different case studies and then proceeding to induce an understanding of the underlying causes and effects in operation in educational systems. The comparative method, on this understanding, serves the function of the experimental method, in circumstances where experiment is impossible or precluded on moral grounds. So, in an experiment, one would manipulate various inputs, and observe the effect of those changing inputs, with the intention of eventually concluding that increasing this input produces that outcome. In education, where it is morally objectionable to deliberately provide an inferior education for a child in order to find out what the impact of a better education is, experiment is unacceptable. So we look to the comparative method as a kind of naturally occurring experiment; it would be morally unacceptable for us to deprive children of access to books in an effort to identify what the impact of books is on educational outcomes, but there is nothing to stop us looking at systems where the children do not have books. This is essentially an inductive way of proceeding, which Hume had long since discredited on logical grounds. This is an approach based on a 19th Century view of science which I regard as philosophically insupportable (Turner, 2017).

However, one has to give credit where it is due, and if the case could be made for Mill's method of induction, then Bereday made it in the clearest possible way. In addition, if one looks at the *de facto* state of the field after a decade or so of the 21st Century, one would have to conclude that Bereday's method has come to dominate. While methodological questions seem to attract little attention, most presentations at comparative education conferences would fit very easily into one or another of the stages of Bereday's method.

Another giant among the founders of comparative education who was just at the edge of my awareness when I joined Holmes' doctoral seminar was Joseph

Lauwerys. I met Lauwerys only once, and could not claim to have known him well. But he was the focus of what I think of as the first piece of academic work that I undertook. Under the guidance of Robert Cowen, the members of the doctoral seminar prepared a *Festschrift* for Lauwerys (McLean, 1981). Because I had a background in science, I was given the task of reviewing and writing short reflections on the various scientific publications that Lauwerys had written. Among the books and articles that I read for that project three stand out.

The first was a glossy text book on biology and ecology, which taught me for the first time that the Sahara and the great deserts of the Middle East were man-made, or at least sheep-made. Apparently sheep, unlike most grazing animals, are able to graze grass so short that it eventually dies, whereupon the top soil is no longer anchored by the roots of the grass, rainwater flows off the surface or soaks away, and a vicious cycle of soil erosion and infertility follows. I found this a remarkable revelation, but apart from a few daydreams about farming the Sahara, there was not much that I could do with it.

In many ways more remarkable to me personally were the personal links that this volume suggested between Lauwerys and Otto Neurath and Lancelot Hogben, authors who had been on the bookshelves when I was growing up and whose works had been part of what inspired me to become a scientist in the first place. Hogben's *Science for the Citizen* and *Mathematics for the Million* served me as reference works when I was stuck with anything that my school textbooks failed to develop, and it was many years before I realised what an eccentric view of the history of science Hogben presented. But those personal links between Lauwerys and what I was most familiar with suddenly made comparative education seem very near, as though it was what I had been travelling towards for a long time. I have come to think that providing personal links is one of the important functions of teachers. My students can read a book by Holmes or Bereday, but they can no longer meet them. That presents a risk that the written words may appear more weighty than they deserve. Personal connections can reinforce the idea that books, all books, were written by fallible human beings, and therefore deserve to be critiqued. That is one of the reasons (among others) I have tried to include a few personal anecdotes in my account of how I came to be a comparative educationist.

The other two articles by Lauwerys that I reviewed for the *Festschrift* were published earlier, and dealt with the use of radio and film in the school respectively. This was at a time when professional storytellers could make radio broadcasts, or eminent scientists could make films about their work, so that all children could have access to the very best presentation, however weak their teachers. I suppose that we have all experienced such things. I had certainly used films to show the addition and subtraction of colours, mixing paints (subtraction) or coloured light (addition) to show the rules that govern the result when two colours are mixed, when I could certainly have done those same experiments myself in the classroom.

Lauwerys' argument was that the new media (radio and film) were wasted if we simply use them to reproduce things that teachers were already doing perfectly well beforehand. In that circumstance, radio and film were doing no more than pushing the teacher to one side and "teacher proofing" the curriculum. And that was of very little value, if any. What was important, he suggested, was finding out what the new media could do that could not be done before. And then it should only be used to do those new things which we wished we could have done, but could not do previously. So, new media made it possible to do new things which would have been desirable but were previously impossible.

Real examples of such innovation are harder to find than one would hope. The introduction of film loops in Nuffield Science courses to show the movements of birds and animals or the use of film to show conditions of weightlessness would be two clear examples, but good instances are actually disappointingly rare. But more importantly, I have been reminded of those papers by Lauwerys on many occasions subsequently, normally when talking to an advocate of the use of computers in the classroom, or when testing a piece of educational software. What do these things really do that we have always wanted to do but could not do before? There probably is an answer to that question, but not many people seem to be asking the right question.

I found this brief encounter with Lauwerys stimulating, but in the end not terribly rewarding. Lauwerys had a reputation as a great lecturer. It was part of the folklore of the Institute at that time that he had been scheduled to give a lecture, and the demand for seats was so high that the lecture theatre was full to overflowing, as was the supplementary lecture theatre where the lecture was to be relayed over loudspeakers. And the topic of the lecture was, "The Importance of Teaching in Small Groups." In contrast with that, the meeting of the London Association of Comparative Educationists where I saw him speak was decidedly low key, but he had a commanding personal presence. So he had charisma, but, in spite of those two or three bright pinpricks of insight that his writing offered, I found his exposition unsatisfying because it did not provide a theoretical basis on which to build.

Nicholas Beattie often told me – by which I mean that he told me once, but that I have had cause to reflect upon it often – that when he was first appointed to lecture in education he had gone off to his lecture notes of Lauwerys' lectures with a view to using the material for his own lectures, only to discover that there was no substance to the lectures at all. Lauwerys was a brilliant raconteur, and used his extensive personal experience to capture an audience, but there was little theory or integration in his thinking. Although it is also true, and this is the main theme of my account, that a lecturer or author can really only reconstruct his or her own experience in teaching; trying to borrow somebody else's experience is bound to end in tears, or at least disappointment.

Anyone who wants a further insight into Lauwerys' lifestyle might try reading Graham Greene's *Our Man in Havana*, which includes a character who is a professor of comparative education, and Robert Cowen once told me that it was based on Lauwerys.

3   Toward a Science of Comparative Education

Thus, Lauwerys had huge charisma and charm and was a great public performer, but from my perspective was ultimately wanting in theoretical terms. Holmes, by way of contrast had a kind of charisma, but you would not describe him as a great performer in public settings. He was much more at home in his seminar, and the intimate discussion which was possible in a seminar, than in a lecture. But he provided a theoretical basis that stands years of exploration, and I think that there are some points that I am only now coming to understand. And that may mean there are further points that I have not yet come to understand, but I have not yet recognised their importance.

Perhaps it was that combination of charisma and theory that Lauwerys and Holmes presented together that made them a good team, and led to the rise of the University of London Institute of Education's eminence in comparative education.

Bereday had both public presence and theoretical depth. And I have to say that, for me, King had neither, at least in person. On the written page he had that ability to pull together an anecdotal narrative based on his personal experiences in other countries and cultures, but I did not find him an inspiring lecturer. He also had aspirations to provide a theoretical basis for comparative education, but again, I found his insights rather limited.

According to my reading of Popper, we should make every effort to construct laws that describe our experience. And as was noted in the context of Newton's Laws, and Einstein's refutation of them, any such law will go beyond our experience, and consequently there is no ultimate justification for believing that it will prove to be true. However, our goal when developing generalisations, and the more general the better, is to stimulate further research. The generalisations can be applied to circumstances with which we are not familiar, and if the generalisation survives that test we may place a little more confidence in its application in the future.

That means that what is crucial for Popper's method is the development of scientific laws, albeit decidedly provisional laws, which are continuously tested against new circumstances. When they are refuted, they are discarded. I think that this would appeal to any physicist's notion of scientific development, and it certainly appealed to Holmes. Holmes argued that we should be looking for such generalisations or sociological laws, in the form, "If this, then that." For example, "If we introduce comprehensive schools, the average level of attainment among pupils will rise."

I have always believed that this was true, and have said so on a number of occasions. In fact, there was a time when, whenever I met Charl Wolhuter, he would ask me, "Have you found any sociological laws yet?" I have since come to the conclusion that laws in this precise form are rather too mechanical, too simplistic. We know that people, as complex systems, are able to pick out the influences that will have an effect on them, as are institutions. Such simple causal laws are, therefore, not in the right form. I will come back to this question in greater detail later, since it will form an important part of my vision of the future of comparative education. For the moment I simply wish to emphasise that Holmes was very much persuaded by this particular aspect of Popper's work.

However, the issue is further complicated by another strand of Popper's philosophy which is more evident in *The Poverty of Historicism* than in *The Logic of Scientific Discovery*. Popper argues that predicting the future is always undesirable or even reprehensible, and that in particular there are no laws of historical development of the kind proposed by Marx. I think that it was this second aspect of Popper's thinking that Edmund King took to heart in his development of a comparative education which was essentially a descriptive account of education in completely unpredictable circumstances. I have some sympathy with that position. After all, if the flap of a butterfly's wing can have catastrophic consequences, what hope is there for predicting where educational systems will be a few years hence.

I add this last point simply to say that both King and Holmes saw themselves as the defenders of a Popperian position in comparative education, and both with some justice. Unfortunately, the fact that they aspired to something that was nominally similar but conceptually very different probably only added to their personal animosity. But it is clear to me that more than one approach can be taken, in good faith, to maintain a Popperian scientific approach to comparative education. And if one adds in non-Popperian approaches, Bereday seems to me to be advocating a scientific method based on John Stuart Mill, and Harold Noah and Max Eckstein an approach that might reasonably be called positivist, in the sense that it seems more closely allied with the philosophy of Ernst Mach.

The 1960s to the 1990s, the years that formed the context of my induction to comparative education, therefore seem to me to be a period of contesting ideas about what it meant to be scientific in approaching comparative education. The clash of ideas about what it means to be scientific was certainly productive, and I very much regret that such debate seems to have gone out of fashion for a much more pragmatic view that we should just get on with comparing.

What I carry away from those discussions, however, is a certain dissatisfaction with the question of what comparative education is, if that question is meant in some essentialist and fixed terms. I think that questions like, What is physics? or What is chemistry? are fundamentally mistaken, whether we define subjects in terms of content or of method, the two most common responses to the question. The content of physics is the whole universe, and the content of chemistry is the whole universe. What distinguishes physics and chemistry is not content. It is not even really method, which are fairly interchangeable between them and grow more similar every day. There is a difference in focus, or a difference of attention. That is to say, the difference between disciplines is not to be found so much in the disciplines themselves as in the attitudes or intentions of those who pursue them. In which case it might make sense to ask about the intention with which comparative education is studied. Or perhaps not, as intentions are intensely personal.

So to avoid unnecessary complications of generalising, I will simply say what I intend when I study comparative education, and while I commend it to others, I am not sure it actually describes what other comparative educationists are doing, or think that they are doing. The metaphor that comes to mind immediately is that old riddle about coming to a fork in the road where two identical twins live, one of who always tells the truth and the other always lies. You need to know which road leads to London, but may only ask one question. Which question should you ask? The answer, and it is obvious when you are told, is to ask one of the twins which road the other would say goes to London (and, of course, go the other way). This riddle captures the idea of seeing the actions of one group through the eyes of another which, to me, seems so central to a study of comparative education. How would an English person describe a French school? How would a French person describe an English school? And can those two answers be reconciled in some way which respects the culture and meanings of both cultures?

Although it is possible to imagine comparisons that are between other things than countries or cultures, I think that it is the effort to grasp what it is like to be a citizen of another country, a speaker of another language or a member of another culture that is the ultimate fascination of comparative education, an effort that is always, ultimately, doomed to be a failure.

So when I look at Noah and Eckstein's proposal that the goal of comparative educational study is to replace the names of countries with the values of variables, I have to say that I find myself in complete opposition. Their suggestion is that we should try to explain the phenomena of education with reference to variables that can be observed and measured. We might think of variables such as urbanisation or industrialisation as general variables that might explain the development of particular aspects of education, as when Noah and Eckstein offer us a comparison of the teaching profession in New York, London, Amsterdam and Paris, on the grounds that the education systems of major cities in industrialised and highly urbanised countries will be inherently comparable, because of their similarity in terms of those variables.

Their suggestion is that, once those variables have been used to explain everything that can be explained, only then should the fact that countries are different be invoked, to explain the residual differences that remain. National culture and national character is only to be used to explain what is left over after everything possible has been explained in terms of some of those other larger facets.

My response is to argue that this is a more general case of the specific principle that is seen at work in multiple regression, and the objections that are relevant in the analysis of regression are applicable here also. In multiple regression, an arbitrary decision has to be made about the order in which variables are entered into the regression. The variables that are entered in first tend to account for most of the variance. That is to say, if we have two variables, each of which accounts for some part of the variance alone, but which also together account for some more of the variance (a very likely occurrence when the variables are themselves inter-correlated to some extent, as is very often the case in studies in the social sciences) then whichever of the variables is entered into the regression first will seem to account for the variation that is explained jointly.

That means one of a number of things. It might mean that the variance attributed to a particular variable depends upon the arbitrary choice of the order in which the variables are entered into the regression. Or it might mean that multiple regression is an inappropriate way of allocating variance, or relative influence, to any of the variables being considered.

In a very similar way, if one starts from urbanisation, GDP per capita, industrialisation or age distribution of the population, or any other general variable, one will be able to explain many things about different countries, and what is left to be explained by language differences, cultural differences or national idiosyncrasies will be relatively little. If one starts from national character, what is left to be explained in terms of those other variables will be correspondingly reduced.

It is, in the end, an arbitrary choice. And I choose to see things first and foremost from the perspective of national and cultural difference. Industrialisation has become part of the national character of those countries where it has been long established, as has relative wealth or relative poverty. That is not to say that these differences can be or should be cloaked in some kind of sanctity; wanting to change the world is perfectly respectable. But it is to say that what makes different nations different is the first order of business for the comparative educationist.

At bottom, comparative education is part of that impossible but endlessly entertaining pursuit of trying to find out what it would be like to be somebody else. What would it be like to see this problem as a German would? How would a Nigerian think about this situation? And this not for reasons of incurable nosiness, although incurable nosiness may be an asset for a comparativist, as it may be in many other occupations. The key question, as I think Michael Sadler suggested, is to inform us if there are ways in which we might live better. That may take the form of borrowing best practice, and there are certainly times when borrowing something that other people do will provide us with a way to live better, or it may simply be to see ourselves as others see us, which oftentimes will be a stimulus to living better on its own.

There are many academic disciplines that concentrate on what is common to all people. Most obviously, biology focuses on what makes us living organisms. But psychology, in its central thrust, seeks an explanation of the human psyche which is common to all people. Evolutionary biology refers us back to a common environmental influence produced by the machinations of natural selection on the savannah of Africa. World culture theory points to a convergence of cultures towards a single, common culture. Globalisation is highlighted as a universal influence that makes us all increasingly similar. Neuroscience seeks to explain our reactions, learning styles and motivations in terms of our common physiology.

I can see no objection in principle to people wanting to feed those elements into the mix ahead of national character, so long as we recognise that in so doing they have chosen to minimise the role played in human society by national culture and subtle variations in culture from place to place and time to time. But what I am arguing is that what makes a discipline is neither content nor method, but a focus or intention. And a discipline that puts the focus on universal principles is not comparative education. Actually I would go further than that and say that a discipline that puts the focus on the universal is not very interesting. For me, the fascination of comparative education has been exploring the way in which different people, on account of their different induction into diverse cultures, conceptualise situations in very different ways, and consequently respond very differently.

For me, then, the content of comparative education is everything that can have a cultural influence, and which can help people to interpret their surroundings. This will include language, history and geography. In short, the content of comparative education is everything. And therein lies the fascination that the universe which we share can be conceptualised in very different ways by people from different perspectives. In his *Devil's Dictionary of Education* Tyrrell Burgess (2002) offers the definition of the word intelligent as being able to hold two contradictory ideas in mind at the same time without being paralysed (see p. 107). Comparative education requires the application of intelligence of this sort.

Similarly, the methods of comparative education are anything and everything; anything that will contribute to developing an understanding of the frames of reference which people bring to bear in order to conceptualise their surroundings. On one occasion this will require economics, on another psychology and on another history. Indeed, on some occasions it will require all of them in some sort of bricolage.

But suppose that we wish to try to understand the obstacles that rest in the way of the development of a country as it moves from a situation, or a period in history, when the economy was centrally planned, to a situation where there is a free market economy. In asking questions about how people think about their environment, economics will probably be a central tool, but not economics of a simple sort. What will be necessary is some kind of comparative economics; what is the difference between the way that an inhabitant of a centrally managed economy and an inhabitant of a free market economy would think about this issue? How will they prioritise actions, and why will they have such difficulty in seeing things from the alternative perspective? This is not just economics; this is intelligent economics.

And this, I think, is the problem with the suggestion that a comparative educationist should first have a solid grounding in one of the "foundation" disciplines, as first posited by Bereday, and as more recently expounded by Martin Carnoy. That training in a foundation discipline will necessarily lead the scholar to prioritise or privilege certain methods. The sociologist will see universal sociological trends, while the psychologist will see the expression of universal dispositions. What is left for comparative education to explain, as I understand it, will be the mere crumbs on the table after the feast.

What I want to say is that sociology is relevant, or psychology is relevant, only to the extent that social trends or psychological responses have become part of national culture, and are reflected in the idiosyncratic responses and behaviours observed in a country. Those are the moments that illuminate the life of the comparative educationist, when we get an insight into how the inhabitants of this place or that place understand themselves, so they do not think that they are being rude, or obsequious, or arrogant, or any of the other things that the untutored observer will imagine them to be.

I am not interested in explaining everything that I can in terms of the material culture, race, social class and gender, and then, as a last resort looking to see what is left that can be explained in terms of national character. What I want to understand is how that very specific mixture of materialism, bigotry, class consciousness and racism feeds into and helps to construct what it is to be English. And, naturally, that will both shape and be shaped by the way in which the English construct and interpret their history. Of course the tools of the sociologist, the economist, the historian and the anthropologist will be important, but unless one is prepared to have a try at all of them, and unless one first starts from a fascination with what it is like to be somebody else, the outcome is unlikely to be comparative education.

The insights that lead to what I describe here as comparative education can come from anywhere, and can hardly be planned for. It is true to say that London and Beijing are both large cities and so have certain characteristics in common. As large cities they have that impersonality that can make city life rather alienating and anonymous, an emotional distance from one's neighbours that is out of proportion with the physical closeness. There will be exceptions to this in some communities in large cities, as I imagine there are in the hutongs of Beijing or in certain culturally homogenous enclaves of London.

But the fascination and excitement of comparison comes when one's expectations are confronted with the expectations of a Chinese person who has concepts that are quite different from one's own, and what that means in terms of everyday behaviour. I know, for example, what it means to be literate in English. I also know, at an intellectual level, that expectations about literacy are somewhat different for somebody who is Chinese and uses the Chinese language. People from different parts of China may be mutually unintelligible when they speak, but should be able to understand each other quite well in writing.

However, the comparative moment came on a taxi journey across Beijing, when a taxi driver, completely unable to understand where I wanted to go, handed me a piece of paper confident that I would write down my destination in Chinese characters and that he would then be able to understand. There is something vital and living here about how writing and speaking tie together, and this comes together in a unique way in specific circumstances. One can learn English without learning to write, and many people do. I am not sure if one can learn Mandarin without learning at least some writing; I have certainly come to the conclusion that my own shortcomings in learning Mandarin arise at least in part from the fact that I was trying to take a short cut and learn to speak without learning to write.

And this so obviously has links with education. How do Chinese children learn to read and speak? What general attitudes do they learn about literacy in the process? And how do the beliefs that adults hold about literacy shape debate about the curriculum, either in general, or specifically related to proposed reform/simplification of the writing system?

So anything from a conversation with a taxi driver to the content of a history text book can be relevant content for comparative education. And to explain that universe of content, we had best not be too rigid in limiting the methods that we bring to bear, or we may not be able to understand anything at all.

The idea of comparative education, as I see it, is not to isolate different elements, whether they are material or conceptual, but to show how they integrate into something that might be called national life. It is relatively easy to see that primary and secondary schools in England are separated, usually physically separated in different buildings, at about the age of twelve, while schools in Scandinavia and in many other countries are not, but are single schools that serve the child's whole school career. However, discussions about the reform of schools in England never examine whether this is a helpful arrangement. It is worth pausing for a moment over that, since many aspects of Scandinavian schooling have featured in debates about educational reform.

There is a deep-seated belief that has informed the development of schools in England, that the age of eleven is important because it marks the division between before and after puberty, and that children before puberty should be separated from children after puberty. The underlying principle is that the young children should not be corrupted by the older and worldly-wise secondary school pupils. It is an assumption that one finds built into various youth organisations as well as schools, and perhaps also reflects the ambivalent attitude that we have to children, thinking of them on the one hand as innocent, and on the other as a dangerous threat in need of control and correction. This is not, I think, a view of children that Scandinavians share.

That divergence of attitudes to children may also inform or be related to other aspects of our approach to education, and the division between a nurturing, supportive environment for the young and a stern and disciplined (in both meanings of the word) environment in the secondary school. This difference in attitude and difference in ambience may also contribute to making the transition from primary school to secondary school more difficult, as the child moves from the homely and friendly atmosphere of the primary school to the threatening adult environment of the secondary school. And that question, the difficulty of the transition from primary to secondary school, is a major centre of debate on school reform in the UK, with many primary schools and secondary schools working together to reduce the perceived gap, introducing pupils across the boundary gradually, introducing secondary school teachers to primary school children and so on.

Interestingly, neither the division, nor the dichotomy of attitudes is evident in Scandinavia. So while Scandinavian experiments with comprehensive education (horizontal integration) have been the focus of more or less continuous debate and interest in England for forty years, unifying primary and secondary education (vertical integration) has attracted almost no attention at all. And that is because childhood, and reflections on childhood, are taken to be natural phenomena, and therefore not in need of discussion. It is this process, whereby certain social constructs come to be thought of as "natural," and therefore to all intents and purposes disappear, that constitutes a major interest of comparative education. Comparison can change the naturalness, and therefore the visibility, of phenomena, thereby achieving what the sociologists promised us, to make the familiar strange.

I am therefore suspicious of those comparative educationists who argue that one needs to have a home discipline before turning to comparative education. In that vision, comparative educationists are sociologists, economists or psychologists first and then bring the tools of their home discipline to comparative education. This seems to me to be a complete misunderstanding of what comparative education is. At its best it uses that variety of insights, but it is the integration of work across diverse and sometimes conflicting frames of reference that bring it to life.

As is the case of education as a whole, comparative education is not a receiver of wisdom from fields like psychology, which concentrates on what happens inside people's heads, or sociology, which concentrates on what happens between people, but contributes to both precisely because it does integrate both elements, and it is the integration that is important. Perhaps we should rethink what it means to be a "donor" discipline. It is certainly wrong to think of education as an area in which psychology is applied and sociology is applied. Comparative education must capture the approaches of various strands of education; it must address the sociological, the economic, the psychological and the anthropological, but I do not think that it needs to be deferential, or carry any idea of a debt to those disciplines. Rather those disciplines exist because they have applications in the real world of education, to the extent that they do, and the real world of education is always, to some extent, comparative.

At the end of this quick ramble through the field of comparative education as I understand it, I should, perhaps, offer some kind of conclusion. Needless to say, I wish to present myself as some kind of scientist, a scholar who has a way of bringing together these idiosyncratic observations and building them into something bigger and more important than just a collection of random facts. In that effort, I have borrowed my metaphors from areas that are acknowledged, more or less, to be "scientific." Non-random walks are taken from complexity science and Stafford Beer was primarily an information scientist.

But, in fact, this is not where I wish to base my claim to being scientific. I want to base that claim on an aspect of the work of Popper, but not one that either Holmes or King chose to emphasise particularly. Popper suggested that the goal of science was to produce hypotheses that are as comprehensive as possible, since the more situations they cover, the more opportunities there will be to refute them.

From a philosophical perspective, there have been three major ways of underpinning theories of truth; authority, coherence and correspondence. I see no immediate reason for thinking that there is an indisputable source of authority that we could rest our claims to truth on; divine inspiration may be possible, and some texts may be divinely inspired, but identifying which they are, and which parts of them are divinely inspired, seems to me to be an eminently human and fallible activity. So I think that I had best leave revealed truth to one side.

The next main support for claims of truth is coherence; the parts of the theory hang together logically and do not contradict each other. Since any conclusion can be derived from a contradiction, this must be an important characteristic of the truth, but for most people it is not enough. It is not enough because there may be many logically coherent schemes that are different, as there are many geometries, each of which is self-consistent, but not all of which can correspond to the nature of the world.

And that neatly raises the question of correspondence to the fact, or correspondence to the world, which is the third foundation for claims to truth. Popper proclaims himself to hold to a correspondence theory of truth; a theory is true if and only if it corresponds to the facts. I have always found that rather unsatisfactory, as it appears to imply that there are certain pre-theoretical facts that the theory can be tested against. However, as Popper himself notes, all alleged facts are in some way dependent on theory. This appears to me to open up the danger of an infinite regress, and an ultimate difficulty in knowing whether a theory does, in fact, correspond with the facts.

What is less obvious in Popper's writing is that he also certainly adheres to a coherence theory of the truth. He argues that logical deduction must be used to derive the implications of a hypothesis, which would be enough to ensure coherence. And he also argues that we should try to generalise our insights. This does make it more likely that they will confront inconvenient or falsifying facts. But it also makes it more difficult for it to be coherent, and therefore raises the game of those seeking truth in that way as well.

So, I think that, in general, I must interpret my claim to be scientific as being an attempt to be coherent, to try to apply the same theoretical frameworks across the whole gamut of educational experience. An institution can be seen (as I hope I have shown) in the light of a non-random walk, or illustrated by the metaphor of the viable system model. But so can a university, a kindergarten, a ministry of education, a policy think tank, a nation or an individual. My goal is precisely to provide a theoretical framework across a wide range of settings. The result is bound to be, I am afraid, rather eclectic.

But I want to go further still than that. I want to say that any theorist who is worth his or her salt should be quite happy to see his or her theories applied to himself or herself. The theories of learning that are applied in developing an understanding of schools should also apply to the ways in which the theorist develops his or her own work. If I look at a school system and believe that it can be understood in terms of national character, I should be equally content if another observer chooses to explain the bias and focus of my interest in terms of my national character.

At one point I was starting to develop a study of comparative plumbing as a hobby. The workings of toilet cisterns are fascinating, and there are characteristically different designs of cisterns in the UK, Scandinavia, the US and Japan. (Actually there are three distinct designs in the US, for the rich, for the poor and for corporations.) I was first seriously attracted to this study by the observation in Kuala Lumpur of the cistern in a decrepit backpackers hostel (UK style) and a modern five-star hotel (US style). That colonial history can be traced through plumbing seemed an opportunity that was too good to miss. Moreover, if different nations can have such different approaches to pouring five litres of water down a toilet, then how much more different are their approaches to something as intangible as education likely to be? But I finally gave up the study when it occurred to me that an obsession with the lavatorial arrangements of foreign countries was just a little bit too stereotypically British.

But I hold to the general principle, which I shall return to periodically, that educational theorists should only advance those theories that they are happy to see applied to themselves. My pursuit of that claim may lead me to introduce more of my own personal history into this book than is usual in a book on comparative education, and more than the reader will care for. I trust that the reader will bear with me, however, as it is important to me.

In conclusion, in this chapter I have tried to offer an overview as to how the field of comparative education has been constructed by a range of participants, and suggested that the field or discipline or whatever it is cannot easily be defined in terms of either content or method. Rather, it is defined by a diverse range of activity which shares a common purpose of trying to see the world through the cultural prism, or prisms, of others.

This does not mean that methodological questions are unimportant, which is, perhaps, why the aspiration to scientific rigour is a common theme among practitioners of comparative education. Items of individual lived experience, elements of personal histories, have to be transcended in some way to produce hunches, hypotheses, generalisations and laws that have more universal application. Some practitioners, such as Holmes and Bereday, achieve that more successfully than others, such as Lauwerys and King, but method cannot be ignored. Exactly what that leads me to in terms of conclusion will have to be left in abeyance for the moment.

CHAPTER 5

National Character

1   Introduction

In this chapter I want to examine the idea of "national character." When I started to study comparative education, this was a common notion. Based on the work of scholars such as Vernon Mallinson, and possibly further back to Hans and beyond, the idea was that each nation had its own history and values, and the members of that nation were likely to behave in broadly similar ways. This was a scholarly attempt to introduce more rigour to a common notion, that one can characterise all the nationals of a particular country by some typical behaviour. It is difficult to pick out examples of such stereotypes, since most of them are derogatory and designed to mark off the "other" as strange and incomprehensible.

And, of course, therein lies the principal danger of such stereotypes. National character was intended to be much more subtle than that, of course. For example, Mallinson suggested that it would take years of living in a country, of learning the language, of immersing oneself in the country, to appreciate and understand the national character. That would make comparative education, beyond case studies of two or three countries, a physical impossibility for any scholar.

Over the time that I have been involved in comparative education, the concept of national character has become less prominent. It has come under pressure from two directions. On the one hand, there has been a rise in the popularity of the thesis that the nation state is no longer the most appropriate unit of analysis; we all come under the influence of the global market, and we have all adopted the consumerist values of Hollywood, and we are all subject to the dictats and agreements of international organisations such as the World Bank and the General Agreement on Tariffs and Trade. On the other hand, national character has suffered from being broken down into its component parts. People, all people of all nations, it is suggested, can be classified as introvert or extrovert, as individualistic or community oriented, as urban or rural, and so on. The argument is that if we incorporate enough of those personal traits in our analysis, then the need for nation specific variables, such as national character, would disappear.

There is some merit in both arguments. We are all subject to trends that are orchestrated by global organisations or fostered across national boundaries by multinational companies. The World Trade Organisation does set the rules for international commerce. And there may be greater differences between rural and urban people in France than between urban people in France and Italy. But even so, I find that the arguments are not completely convincing. It is not merely that the case for globalisation and for personality traits that are universal are not really comparative.

It is true that the rise of such international organisations as the European Union or ASEAN mean that some decisions are taken at a regional level rather than at the national level. But to argue that this means that the nation state is irrelevant to analysis of education because the nation state is no longer fully sovereign is to make a serious mistake. In fact, no single nation is ever fully sovereign and its decisions and legislation are to some extent constrained by international agreements and expectations. International organisations may make those external influences more visible, more tightly specifiable, but they do not create the influences from nothing. It continues to be the case that if you want to know what legislation frames a national system of education, it is the national legislature to which one must turn, and the working out of the legal ramifications takes place, for the most part, in the national courts.

The explanations in terms of personality traits are equally universalising, and suggest that there are no fundamental differences between, for example, the British and the French; there are universal characteristics like extroversion and introversion, and the British and the French are said to differ only in the amount of each characteristic that any individual is likely to have. For me the real problem is that these various approaches beg the most important comparative questions.

If we try to explain international developments using the analysis that we have all become consumers now, we have immediately lost sight of the fact that Japanese people and Australian people may be consumers in completely different ways. To take a concrete example, I have been trying to understand the principles on which Chinese society is organised. In that process I have taken Gu Mingyuan (2013) as my guide. He tells me that Chinese society, deeply influenced by Confucius, is a deeply moral society. One of the guiding criteria of moral behaviour is Confucius' concept that is normally rendered into English as the "superior man" or "gentleman." Now the British also have a concept of "gentleman," so I am already equipped with a concept that should help me to understand the Chinese approach to ethical questions. But the comparative question still remains; is the British concept the same as or different from the Chinese one? I will come back to this question in greater detail, but it seems to me that there is a great deal here that merits close examination. If Chinese society is essentially moral, is that sense of morality one that I can easily apprehend, or is it a moral sense that is essentially Chinese?

So my concern is that when we say that the world is now globalised, we are actually saying much more about our determination to view all the world through the lens of a specific culture, normally some variant of western culture, than we are actually saying about the world. When we say that everybody is now a consumer in the global market, we are actually announcing our intention to analyse all behaviour that we look at in terms of a model of market competition, and in that process we may well overlook other, perhaps subtler, similarities and differences. In particular, we may well lose the things that I regard as fundamentally comparative, namely the effort to try to see things in the way that other people might see them.

So my purpose in this chapter is to argue that there is a way to reinvigorate the concept of national character, so that it can be used in comparative analysis. This is not really a new enterprise. In his book, *Comparative Education: Some considerations of method*, Holmes (1982) presented four models of curriculum selection. Based on the idea that one could answer Herbert Spencer's question, "What knowledge is of most worth?" in national terms, identifying what knowledge would be crucial to being educated in different contexts, Holmes identifies a number of documents that he argues frame the idea of what it means to be educated in the case of England, France, the USA and the USSR. He says that he first put these ideas forward at the second conference of the Comparative Education Society in Europe (CESE), held in Berlin in June, 1965.

At that meeting, Joseph Lauwerys gave the keynote address in which he also introduced the idea that what counted as an educated "gentleman" was different in those four countries, and set out a description of what such a model of the educated person would look like. The ideas in both those presentations can be traced back to an editorial in the Year Book of Education of 1957, jointly written by Lauwerys and Holmes, and it is perhaps not surprising that, working closely together, they should develop the ideas in parallel. However, I think that they were attempting to do different things in their presentations.

In Lauwerys' hands, the four traditional ways of thinking about the content of education become elements of resistance or obstacles to change. They are, so to speak, facts in the educational landscape that explain why reforms that are applied in different settings, such as the expansion of secondary education, follow different trajectories in different countries. That is an interesting use of these paradigms of national character, but in Holmes' hands they become something much more. They become a way of measuring tendencies in different settings. This is, perhaps, the approach of the physicist, to say that these are abstract ideals that can be used to assess the extent to which actual ways of thinking conform to these ideals. In the same way, the abstract gas laws describe the performance of an ideal gas. One should not confuse the idea of an ideal gas with the fact of an actual gas such as nitrogen or carbon dioxide, although one might conclude from empirical evidence that nitrogen behaved more like an ideal gas than carbon dioxide does. In the same way, one might hold the Indian Constitution up against the ideal typical models of the USA, England and USSR and ask which tradition had more influence in its framing. It is this concern with measuring and the tools of measurement that separates the intentions of Holmes and Lauwerys.

However, the distinction is slight, and may disappear altogether when one starts to apply Holmes measuring instruments to specific cases, when it may be argued that conformity with national character tends to put a brake on educational reform. There is always the danger that such models will slip into stereotyping, and that we will be tempted to explain the behaviour of specific individuals in terms of ideal types when we ought to know better.

My argument is that Holmes went some way to ensuring that his use of ideal types was not stereotyping, and that it was not assumed that the ideal types themselves predicted specific actions. But his ideal types are static, and it is all too easy to start seeing them as descriptions of actual mindsets and approaches. In this chapter I hope to go further, by viewing national culture as a non-random walk, as offering anchor points to which people of a nation are attracted, but not mechanically or causally connected. I believe that in this way it is possible to find an intellectually acceptable role for national character in comparative education.

When I was becoming a teacher there was a mood abroad, which I still think is important, that stereotyping people was wrong, and unfortunate from both an intellectual point of view and from the point of view of practical policy. It was thought to be intellectually wrong to label children as being of a particular type, and worse still to treat them on that basis, because there is always wide variation within any group of similar people, and variation within and group is always greater than the variation between groups. And it was thought to be wrong to develop policy on that basis, on the grounds that stereotypes were then likely to become self-fulfilling prophecies.

Incidentally, that mood has shifted somewhat, with some groups of people choosing to self-label, to identify themselves as having an immutable character, as having been born with certain tendencies and dispositions. Sadly, the rise of an understanding of modern genetics in popular culture, though probably not modern genetics itself, has done nothing to diminish the damaging view that we are determined by our roots, and that "bad blood will out." It seems to me, however, that anybody who is involved with education has at least a professional commitment to the idea that people can change, and so I remain strongly attached to the idea that I absorbed in my early training that stereotyping people is wrong, because it fails to respect their personality and their intentions, and it also produces bad policy.

On the other hand, it is also clear that people from different countries do behave in very different ways. People from different cultures or from different countries have very different ways of interpreting events. The Chinese behave very differently from the Japanese and Americans behave very differently from the French. Quite often it is even possible, in such simple matters is clothing, to distinguish the French person from the British person, and that at some considerable distance. It does seem that there are characteristic ways in which people of particular nations tend to behave.

I have already commented on the weaknesses of using national stereotypes, and the general principle that intragroup variation always exceeds intergroup variation, and so I simply reiterate here that it is right to discard the idea of national stereotypes as a simple and straightforward explanation of the behaviour of the inhabitants of a particular country. What Holmes offered in this regard was the concept of an ideal typical model. The notion of the ideal typical model is based upon Weber's analysis and the use of an abstraction which is not necessarily observed in the behaviour of any specific individual.

I should perhaps make a slight aside here, because I think that Holmes' original idea was to banish the idea of national character from his problem solving method, instead replacing it with an ideal typical curriculum model that was drawn from documents, such as constitutions, the writings of philosophers and so on, as I shall describe in this chapter. However, as time went on, the idea of "mental states," which might be seen as deeply held beliefs which can motivate our actions without us being fully aware of them, came to play a larger and larger role in his thinking, and he sometimes compared his use of mental states with Mallinson's use of national character. I will return to this question more fully when I come back to discuss Holmes' problem-solving approach to comparative education in more detail. I restrict myself here to saying that I reject the idea of mental states in accordance with my first principle of only using theoretical frameworks that I am happy to see applied to me, and I do not care for the notion that my motivation is always clearer to some outside observer (whether that is Freud or Pareto) than it is to me.

Yet we are faced with what seems to me to be the overriding fact of comparative education, that people from different countries do have different ways of conceptualising things, and that, despite differences, there is something that can be seen as typifying a national approach. For this reason, Holmes' idea of ideal typical models seems to me to be a valuable tool for giving substance to that insight, and so I devote a good deal of attention to ideal typical models as a tool that is of great potential benefit to comparative educationists.

My understanding of the ideal typical model is again coloured by my experience of the physical sciences, and in particular by the idea of an ideal gas. The behaviour of an ideal gas is exactly described by the gas laws, Charles' Law and

Boyle's Law. An ideal gas can, therefore, be seen as "ideal," not in the sense of being a goal or objective to which other gases aspire, but in the sense of being an abstract measure to which all gases approximate, and against which the behaviour of real gases can be compared. For example, as gases approach their boiling point (as they are cooled and approach liquefaction) and are about to turn into liquids, their behaviour deviates from the behaviour of an ideal gas considerably. Even so, the notion of an ideal gas still serves as a useful generalisation of how gases behave well above their boiling point and also provides a measuring stick against which to assess the degree to which a real gas deviates from the behaviour of an ideal gas in specific circumstances.

I think that Holmes offered the ideal national ideal typical national models in something of the same spirit, in that the ideal typical French person or American person was not supposed to prescribe exactly how the nationals of those countries would behave in all circumstances. The ideal typical model was supposed to be some sort of guide as to how people might be thought of in general, and what kind of assumptions they may take for granted in evaluating a problem. There would certainly be deviations from the ideal type, and there was no assumption that the ideal typical model would necessarily be exemplified in the behaviour of any real individual.

There are two further important aspects of Holmes' view of ideal typical models that need to be borne in mind. The first is that he was extremely insistent that ideal typical models should not merely be dreamt up, but that they should be developed on the basis of some background in the literature. So, for example, the ideal typical model should be drawn either from the national constitution or legal framework, or based on some literary and/or philosophical sources which might form the basis for establishing the national ideal typical model. In that way Holmes hoped that it would be possible to have some kind of objectivity in the drawing up ideal typical models, so that any scholar could propose their own, or critique the basis on which a model had been prepared.

Holmes himself proposed that an American ideal typical model might be based on elements drawn from Constitution of the United States and the philosophy of pragmatism. On that basis other scholars would be able to see how the ideal typical model was constructed, and if necessary contest the basis on which it was prepared, in order to make their own ideal typical model. In this way the ideal typical model could be used as a kind of standard against which the behaviour of particular individuals and organisations could be compared and interpreted. The ideal typical model was not to be seen as applicable to the behaviour of particular individuals.

The other important aspect of Holmes' work on ideal typical models was that he did not assume that everyone in the nation was thinking in the same way. One might easily reach the mistaken conclusion that the use of an ideal typical model means that every American should be seen as conforming to an ideal typical model based on pragmatism. For example, Holmes argued that the philosophy of John Dewey was central to constructing the ideal typical model of American nationals. He was not of the opinion that every American believes in the truth of the work of Dewey or approves of his prescriptions for education. What he argued was that, in coming to an understanding of educational debates in America, an understanding of Dewey was crucial in the sense that most of the contributors to an educational debate would be arguing explicitly or implicitly for or against a position which could most easily be understood in terms of Dewey's philosophy.

On the one hand there are those who follow Dewey, or at least, if they are not consciously aware of Dewey's philosophy, they have been influenced by Bruner or Kolb or Schön or some other author whose work was more or less firmly based on Dewey's precepts. And on the other hand, there are those who oppose the views of Dewey, and appeal to some notion of "traditional" education.

So, we could therefore see that the Progressive Education Association and the very different position of the campaign for the one hundred best books can both be understood in terms of their shared contestation of a perspective that derives from Dewey. Similarly, the call for a strengthening of high school science, advocated by Admiral Rickover in the context of the National Defense and Education Acts, can be understood as a contribution to a debate that makes sense in terms of Dewey's philosophy, although nobody would ever confuse Rickover with a Deweyan.

This sense of the ideal typical model, that it frames and shapes an understanding of national debates without specifying that most citizens are on one side or the other, is an important insight into how Holmes understood what he was proposing, and a useful counterpoint to the idea that an ideal typical model represents some kind of average over the whole of society.

Nevertheless, I think there is a danger in using ideal typical models, because there remains a normative element in the concept, that in some way in ideal typical model represents something that can be applied to all individuals, or perhaps represents some kind of status to which all nationals of that specific nation should want to aspire. What I want to propose is a slight variation on the concept of an ideal typical model. Or perhaps I should express that slightly differently. The main danger, I think, rests in thinking of the elements that make up an ideal typical model as being static. Instead I want to propose that those elements should be seen as the strange attractors in the national psyche, to which people return again and again in their debates.

This sense of a strange attractor goes beyond what Holmes suggested, although I think that his account of how ideal typical models should be interpreted as pointing towards a concept of non-random walks and strange attractors, a language which was not available to him when he described the important idea of ideal typical models. In a personal sense, I have read some of the work of Kant, and some of the work of Popper, and though there are points on which I differ from each or both, nevertheless, as will be evident to the reader, I find both useful in framing a discussion of what it means to be a scientist. In a similar way, as described in the previous chapter, institutions engage in the process of self-development with reference to key events which form, depending on the attitudes of the reformers of the time, either the valuable traditional values which need to be reinvigorated for the present time, or the dead hand of history that needs to be brushed aside. Nor do all the members of an organisation need to be of the same mind for an understanding of those key points in the organisational history to be useful in interpreting the positions of contemporary protagonists.

The national ideal typical model as strange attractor takes this process one step further, one level up in the hierarchy, to suggest that national debates about what is or is not appropriate to our country can be understood in terms of some kind of ideal typical model.

This can be very clearly seen, for example, in the case of the United States Constitution, and especially the first ten amendments that make up the Bill of Rights. Any external observer of discussion of gun laws in the United States is doubtless bemused to see such strong attachment to the carrying of weapons or to the proliferation of weapons. This debate has its roots in the Constitution and the Second Amendment in particular, which enshrines the right to bear arms. The right to bear arms was important because the authors of the Constitution intended it as a defence against their own government, and a way of preventing the kind of governmental tyranny that was their main reason for breaking with European political institutions. An armed citizenry was therefore seen as a constraint on the unbridled power of the Federal Government. In times of danger the armed citizenry would be called upon to come to the defence of their State. This trade-off was specified to ensure a balance of power between the citizenry and the government that would prevent oppression.

If one looks at this rationally in the modern context, one can see that the United States has long since given up the idea that it should rely on its armed citizenry to defend it in time of trouble. In order to secure the balance of power envisaged by the authors of the Constitution, every citizen of the United States would need their own battleship and aircraft. Even though the irrationality of the position set out by the Constitution can be seen, there remains a strong attachment to the original concept, which is enshrined not only in the right to bear arms, but also in a strong distrust of any action on the part of the Federal

Government, and a marked preference for small government and private provision of social welfare.

Of course, nobody would be tempted to argue that all citizens of the United States are in favour of the unabridged right to bear arms. The nation is divided on the issue, and apparently very nearly equally divided, which is one of the reasons that a heated debate continues. And, indeed, the point can hardly be made too often in any discussion of comparison that within group variation is almost invariably greater than between group variation. The difference between the most individualistic American and the most collectivist American will be much greater than the difference between the average American and the average English person. The purpose of the ideal typical model is not to suggest the one way in which all citizens of a nation should think, or do think, but to explain for the outsider what the key points of reference are in the debate, and to explain why it is important. The Second Amendment is unique, in that precise form, to the United States, and captures a specific point in the history of the nation, which is very influential in many debates and not only debates about gun control.

This is a debate that recurs from time to time, and people come back to the same key points around which national debates are framed and set. The right to bear arms is rooted in a distrust of government. And this distrust of all government is evident beyond the realm of gun legislation. I remember going into a fast food joint in Chicago, and selecting from the board a meal that was on display for $4.95. When I came to pay the shopkeeper said, "That will be $5.17." I am always taken aback by this conversation, because whenever I arrive in the US I am likely to forget the taxes.

"Where I come from," I said, "The price that is displayed is the price that is charged."

"What a dishonest government you must have," he replied, "To hide the taxes away like that." In contrast with that attitude, my natural reaction is always, "What dishonest shopkeepers you have, not to display the full price."

That wariness that the government is always trying to take away "our" money, or "our" rights, runs through many different strands of thought in the US, and perhaps helps to explain, not only the widespread acceptance of neoliberalism in the US, but also much of the missionary zeal with which some American institutions have sought to spread it around the world. This attitude toward government and money is in stark contrast with a different tradition. When asked by his disciples whether it was right to pay tribute to Rome, Jesus is reported to have answered that the money has the picture of Caesar on it: "Render unto Caesar, that which is Caesar's." In other words, it is governments that generate money, and citizens only have money in their pockets at the behest of government. These fundamental differences in approach cannot easily be captured in personality traits, even quite large arrays of character traits. There probably is a difference between collectivism and individualism enshrined in this difference over the meaning of money, but it is not clear that the collectivism/individualism distinction exhausts differences in attitudes to money and taxes.

This conversation with the burger flipper is one that I routinely have, in my mind at least, every time I return to the US. The conversation makes sense, to the extent that it makes any sense at all, only in the context of a general distrust of government, an attitude that is fairly firmly enshrined in the US Constitution. It is that kind of use of the national ideal typical model as a strange attractor which explains the hidden background of daily conversation that is envisaged here. The man serving me distrusts government, so thinks it rational to display the price without tax so that I am aware of the impact government has on his business. I distrust shopkeepers, so I expect them to display the price they are going to charge. Of course, this individual shopkeeper may not distrust his government any more than I distrust mine, but the fact remains that there are very different practices for displaying prices in the UK and the US. In this way the Constitution provides the setting to untangle this mutual incomprehension.

In the case of United States, it is also clear in an institutional sense, because the Constitution is explicitly used by the Supreme Court as a way of examining social norms and of developing consensus about what should or should not be regarded as legitimate things to be done and legislated for in the United States.

Let me interject an observation here about the nature of theorising in comparative education. Even when we appear to be dealing with very specific instances of behaviour, we cannot, and should not, avoid the large philosophical and methodological issues that lie behind that discussion. So, for example, the American shopkeeper might think in terms of the government taking "his" money, a turn of phrase which, sadly, is becoming more and more common in political debates in the UK. But this specific discussion of whether money has its origins in my work or in my government's policies mirrors the methodological question of whether social movements are driven by individual choices or by the cultural influences of classes and nations. It is almost impossible to describe a particular comparative, cross-cultural scenario without using terms that presuppose either agency or structure; the shopkeeper's view is one of methodological individualism, what Archer (1995) might call downward conflation. On this analysis, individual agents create wealth by working, and take the value that they generate to the market, where, by trading, they create a medium of exchange which comes to be recognised as money. The sum total of individual actions, through the market, generates money. The alternative view of money is one of structure, what Archer might call upward conflation. The society as a whole generates money as a way of regulating and managing the market; because money exists, individuals can operate in a disciplined and agreed way. Society creates the money and the money creates the market, no individual's action being essential to the process. These are two very different ways of conceptualising social processes, but even if the distinction is highly abstract, it may still have important consequences. The rise of monetarism in the 1980s, a theoretical view that money was simply another commodity traded in the market, and an increase in supply would necessarily result in a fall in price, as though money were no different from beans or sugar, seems to have been more easily and swiftly adopted by those who were methodological individualists. In comparative education we can never stray very far from important methodological questions.

It precisely because there is this interplay between the methodological choices one makes and the way that one describes concrete situations that I think that we should impose on ourselves, as comparative educationists, two particular constraints, as I have tried to do in this book. The first is to be aware, and to include reflection on, how our methodological position impinges upon our perceptions and descriptions of what we see. This in turn implies including a level of self-awareness, and self-disclosure in the work that we do. And the second is that we should aspire to an understanding, and to theoretical models that bridge those various different levels.

Returning to the ideal typical model of the USA, and moving away from the Constitution, it is less obvious exactly how the elements of an ideal typical model can be seen as operating or not operating in the national psyche. I have already mentioned Henry J. Perkinson (1995) and his book, *The Imperfect Panacea*, which suggests that again and again the pragmatic Americans come back to the notion of educational reform as a way of creating the basis for the nation to compete economically with whichever country appears to be in the ascendancy at the moment. What I am proposing is that ideal typical models be interpreted as those crucial points around which the nation's institutions, and at a larger scale the nation itself, circle in terms of discussion and debate. These are the assumptions and the points of contention to which they keep coming back in their non-random walk of self-development.

Identifying the content of the national ideal typical model is difficult for countries like the United Kingdom which has an unwritten constitution. To be more specific, it might be a good idea to start with a more specific national entity, as Holmes himself did, and examine an ideal typical model for English education, rather than for the whole of the United Kingdom. There are reasons for specifying England separately from other nations in the United Kingdom, and I will come back to those later.

Holmes suggested a number of documentary sources when he applied his method to identify the English national character. He suggested the Bible and the philosophy of John Locke. The question of using the Bible is a difficult question that goes directly to the heart of one of the important points about the selection of these ideal typical models. The Bible used to be a document that, at least in parts, was fairly well-known and English people of my age or older would have known several stories and certain passages in the Bible quite well. They might even have known some passages by heart. However, I think that there has been a development in our national literary heritage and what we are passing on to young people which means that young people are not so familiar with pieces of the Bible as children once were.

But this question of whether a book is consciously familiar raises an important point as to whether a literary source has to be consciously known for it to be included as part of the national ideal typical model. It could be argued, for example, that a work of literature might have just as strong an influence on the national psyche by diffusion. Indeed, the work of literature and the attitudes captured might be all the more influential for operating at a subconscious level.

To take one example, a resource like the plays of Shakespeare might enter the national psyche even though individuals profess to know very little about the actual works of Shakespeare. There is the no doubt apocryphal story of the person who on first seeing the play Hamlet asks why Shakespeare, when he wrote it, used so many clichés. Many turns of phrase in the play have become so familiar to speakers of English in England that they know substantial parts of the play without ever having necessarily seen the play. Among such elements, one might well speak of there being method in a person's madness, without necessarily knowing that the remark is first made of Hamlet. Nor does one need to know the exact exchange between Hamlet and the clown to have an idea that English people value eccentricity and are fond of their "characters":

"Why was he sent into England?"

"Why, because he was mad: he shall recover his wits there; or, if he do not, it's no great matter there."

"Why?"

"'Twill not be seen in him there; there the men are as mad as he."

We English people take considerable pride, if not in our mad people, then at least in eccentrics and people who devote themselves to eccentric activities.

In this sense we might be able to argue that the Bible or Shakespeare's plays form an appropriate source for the ideal typical model of English national character, even though the majority of English people are not consciously aware of them being the source of their thinking, or of seeing the direct links between those sources and many of the things that they assume and take for granted.

Holmes offers the selection of English culture which includes the selection of a philosopher as a representative for the national character. This is more difficult, as very few will have read even a little of the work of John Locke. But Holmes argues that Locke represents a particular form of empiricism which chimes well with the English character and, for example, is represented in a love of practical empiricism and trusting that which can be demonstrated physically. Thus, even though few people are familiar with the works of Locke, English people will be familiar with common, everyday sayings such as, "Seeing is believing," or "It is not money unless you can scratch a window with it." This latter phrase may already have largely disappeared into the annals of history, as our attitudes towards debt and abstract forms of money have been undermined by credit cards and bank loans.

But these common sayings and the work of Locke share an underlying approach which is typically English, of not liking theoretical abstractions and mistrusting people who are too comfortable with theoretical abstractions. That attitude persists.

Of course, one might well make the case for the inclusion of other works in the canon of things that are represented in the English national character. If the Bible and Shakespeare and the philosophy of John Locke are part of the national ideal typical model, then why not the novels of George Eliot, with *Middlemarch*, for example, representing an insight into the class system and the way in which English people react to class? It is certain that in any question relating to English life it is fairly difficult to understand the nuances of debate if one has not first got an understanding of class. This is not quite the same thing as saying that England is a class-ridden society; it just means that class will be always be in the background in the framing of important debates, whether they are about state education and private education, or about examinations and access to higher education. There will always be an undertone of class sensitivity in any discussion in an English context.

The actual content of any ideal typical model is open for discussion. However, what I am arguing here, in my interpretation of Holmes approach, is that the ideal typical model of a nation should be seen as those anchor points to which development keeps returning. The extent to which the actual behaviour of any individual, or even the whole nation, is accurately represented by the ideal typical model is small. In any complex system, the strange attractors produce an infinite number of paths through space, depending upon the starting point of the motion, so that predicting the outcome in a specific case is impossible.

But what I am claiming is that there is a body of English literature, comprising both philosophical and literary giants, that forms a collection of reference points as to what is acceptable for an English company, an English person or the English nation as a whole. I remember very well my father reminding me that there were some things that "a gentleman does not do," although, of course, it is also true that a gentleman would not need to be told.

In this discussion I have been interested in how I wish to present myself in terms of being English and exactly which of the possible elements constitute the strongest pool of reference points to which I am pulled. But I am also aware that how I think of myself, in terms of being English, changes with the circumstances in which I find myself. I tend to be less strictly aware of being English when I am in England and become more aggressively English when I am abroad, and confronting different elements of other people's cultures. I venture to suggest that this is a phenomenon that affects more people than just me, and is one reason why the English abroad are more unbearable than the English at home.

I remember the first time that I went to Istanbul being surprised to think of myself as European rather than British when confronting a culture which I found so strange and so different. I needed to reassure myself by seeking out the company of other people from western Europe and making increased efforts to speak with them, whether in French or German or English. I would make exceptional efforts to communicate with people whose cultural background was more similar to mine. One of the fascinations of comparative studies is that by confronting different cultures one can become increasingly aware of our own unexamined assumptions and prejudices. Every now and then, occasionally, one has the opportunity to glimpse how and why a social practice which makes no sense to you makes sense to those who practice it. Even more rarely, one catches a glimpse of how and why a social practice which enjoys our unthinking acceptance looks ridiculous or illogical to outsiders. Those few and fleeting moments make the effort required to conduct comparative studies worthwhile.

I found that first engagement with a new culture, before I started studying comparative education, quite threatening, and it unsettled my individual identity. Since then I have found the insights offered by comparative education more entertaining, more liberating and much less threatening. I would go so far as to say that one of the major points or purposes of comparison in education is exactly that relief into which it throws our own existence, to see that other people naturally think of things in different ways and regard different solutions to problems as the obvious ones.

When I travel to Wales, or when I am working in Wales, I think of myself as more British than English, and I make some more effort when I describe things as English or British to differentiate between the two, and not to claim ownership for the English of a tradition that is British – a full British breakfast, for example. On very rare occasions, when considering the educational systems of Wales and those of England and the reforms that have taken place over the last twenty years, I am inclined to think of myself as more Welsh than English.

So one person's individual identity is a reaction to the circumstances against which one struggles to maintain that identity. As it happens, the Welsh national character is very literary and the highest values are based on the notion of an Eisteddfod, which is a festival that celebrates poetry and song. Poetry and song are inescapable parts of the Welsh ideal typical model, and it may well be an advantage for an Englishman who wishes to feel Welsh that they have a love of words and an interest in literature, including Welsh literature. So I have a head start from my school days in feeling Welsh.

But I have also acquired more recently the opportunity that is created by a Welsh separation from the United Kingdom, at least in terms of the political system, to see more clearly the differences between the English and the Welsh. The purpose of drawing up an ideal typical model for either the English or the Welsh is, as I now understand it, to create a background and map of those sites around which people gravitate when considering and reshaping their own identity and the identity of the nation.

In trying to draw together these ideas of what can be done and what cannot be done, what an English gentleman or gentlewoman considers proper or improper, into a national ideal typical model, examining what is approved and what would be considered beyond the pale, it would be well to remember that this is a moving target. Different people react in different ways in different settings and there will be a slow transformation as people create a national character through their activities and their interpretations. So if we can take a term from the current vernacular, individuals will react to key elements of the literature and philosophy that surrounds them, and will "re-tweet" some of them, especially those that they approve of, on to their friends and colleagues. In so doing they will influence other people and cumulatively build up an idea of what it means to be English.

In England we have recently seen some spasmodic attempts by politicians to create a conscious discussion and deliberation about what it means to be English. Whether such a move as teaching Englishness or having an examination of nationality can be effective or not is still an open question. In this particular case it arises from a rather extraordinary circumstance of worrying about immigration and the effect that immigration can have, which inevitably influences the national ideals that are emphasised. I think that the activities of politicians are less likely to have an impact on our sense of national identity than the glacial movement that occurs spontaneously.

In this chapter I try to give a brief but comprehensive tour of the issues related to national ideal typical models. The model is not a stereotype, nor even a kind of average produced empirically. It is a good, but possibly contested, selection of literary and philosophical sources that can guide our analysis of debates in a national context. Any model is fairly arbitrary but the selection must be justified, at least as I understand it, by whether it is useful in methodological terms. The ideal typical model can help us to frame discussions, and to order the evidence we find, so that it can be marshalled to tell a plausible story. If an ideal typical model does not do that, then it does nothing of value and should be discarded.

One further point follows, which may be more difficult for the comparative educationist to swallow; it is possible to look for an insight into the national character in literature, just as much as in schools. The reading *Middlemarch* or *Hard Times* may well tell one more about English approaches to education than conducting a survey of attainment among 16 year olds. While that is compatible with the Popperian notion that one can learn something of theoretical value from a single observation, while a million observations may tell one nothing of theoretical value, this may be seen as an eccentric approach. I have to say, however, that I am quite comfortable with the idea that teachers can build up professional insights without conducting Research (with a capital "R"), and that it might be wise to extend that courtesy to other observers of the human condition, including novelists.

So while there is scope for seeking objectivity, and I think that Holmes was definitely looking for objectivity when he insisted that ideal typical models should be based on an explicit literature or explicit sources, nevertheless it is not the objectivity implied by the randomised controlled trial. What we seek is an objectivity where others can be aware of the foundations of our arguments, and they can contest those sources or substitute others. Our purpose is always to indicate quite clearly what our assumptions are, and what follows from those assumptions, or what we have chosen explicitly, and what follows implicitly from our starting position. This is not a crude scientific approach based on counting and the removal of meaning. It is an effort to understand the framework of education in terms of the thinking of the people involved. This is not necessarily the explicit thinking of individuals, but an underlying current that can be identified in the literature they love and revere and in the trends in their political debates.

Holmes offered four fully developed ideal typical models of national character: England, France, the United States of America and the Soviet Union. These four models were fully worked out in his books, but I will say something here about each of them, in the following sections, since my argument is that they are useful tools in the process of comparative analysis, and I offer my interpretation of them here, and commentary on them in that spirit.

Holmes also suggested that there might be other ideal typical models, an Islamic model for the Middle East, and a Confucian model for East Asia, for example, but he never really developed those fully. I will offer some limited comments, especially on the latter, in the hope of illustrating how this continuing work might be pursued.

2 Forming a National Character

As it happens, Bereday gave me a book. I think it was simply chance that Bereday had to hand the books in the series of which he was the editor, and this one happened to be the book he gave me. The book was Charles E. Merriam's (1966) *The Making of Citizens*. So, although I think that the gift of the book was a happy accident, I have since had many an occasion to think about the content of that book.

Merriam's main thesis is that the nation state is too large for a person to feel a direct association with. We become citizens by becoming part of small units. Those small units can be built up conceptually into the nation state. The child is first aware of the class they join in school, and their class teacher. Then they are introduced to the idea of the school that they attend, and through their attendance at the school they become aware of the district, and county, and state, where certain events bring schools together, such as sporting events or competitions. And through the building up of different levels the child becomes conscious of being part of the nation state.

Reflecting on Merriam's theme, I do not think that I spent a great deal of time as a child learning to be English. I did spend a great deal of time, for example, learning to be a Boy Scout, and before that a Cub Scout. I do remember many of those stories that taught me what it meant to be a Scout. I remember with fondness here the influence of Jack Chapman, or, as I knew him at that time, Akela. He used to sit us down in a group circle of thirty boys between the ages of eight and eleven and give us a talk about the values that he thought important. Jack was very principled man and wanted to impress upon us, I think, with something along the lines of Thomas Edison's dictum that genius is one per cent inspiration and 99 per cent perspiration. One of Jack's favourite words was "stickability," the ability to stay determined and committed to a cause and to see it through to a finish.

But from the Scouts I also learned a number of things that might be thought to have a direct bearing on my relationship to the nation state. I certainly learned about the national flag, the stories behind the different symbols that made up the national flag and how they represented the parts of the Union of Ireland, Scotland and England – Wales not being directly represented in the Union Flag. We learned the stories of the national patron saints, of the national flowers, and various aspects of the national history, in a peculiar mishmash of biblical stories of saints, religious history, national history and national pride, which makes up that sense of nationalism.

However, that sense was primarily associated with what it meant to be part of that particular pack or what it meant to be part of that Scout troop. As I grew up that sense of belonging to something gradually grew beyond the immediately local, so that the intense pride in belonging to a particular pack was replaced by a growing awareness that various packs and troops constituted the district, or the nation, or even an international movement.

I should, perhaps, stress that an important part of those values was linked with a sense of nationalism and a sense of religion. The opening words of the Scout promise are, or were then, "On my honour I promise to do my best to do my duty to God and to the Queen…"

In terms of what it means to be part of national character, let me speed through the years until I reach a point, around the age of twenty or twenty one, when I entered a republican and atheist phase, and could no longer take seriously the traditional meaning of that promise. I had, by that time, grown up through the Scouts, had been a Cub, and then a Scout and eventually a Cub Scout leader, and played a number of different roles in the Scouts. At that point, I decided that I had to leave the Scout movement, because I could no longer say the promise and mean it. One thing that I do not want to make a lot out of is whether that was the right or the wrong decision. I am sure that there are many honourable and decent Scouts who came to the same kind of crossroads in their lives and decided that, as republicans and as atheists, they could not take seriously the initial words of the Scout promise, but neither would they need, as republicans and atheists, to take the promise too seriously. They could therefore continue to be Scouts in good faith on the other side of that crossroads. I took a different view and decided that the values which I had been brought up on were so important to the Scout movement, that by rejecting them I had to leave the Scouts.

Consequently, I think of myself as having left the Scouts, but in a way that conformed to the values I had learned in the Scouts; on a matter of principle. And I expect that those who made a different decision also made their decision in the light of values they had learned in the Scouts. There are some influences on our values which are so strong, that whether we accept them and conform, or whether we reject them and rebel, they remain as guiding influences in our lives. This is most obviously the case with the things that our parents try to impress upon us, but may also be true for organisations with which we have a strong emotional attachment, such as a school, or in my case the Scouts.

So there is not a simple dichotomy between accepting or rejecting a set of values that are instilled in us at an early age. There is a kind of accepting through rejection that can happen, or possibly a kind of rejection through acceptance. I think that is very important in terms of the dynamic of the non-random walk and strange attractors, that an attraction and repulsion can be held simultaneously.

Most people, I imagine, at one time or another face the dilemma of rejecting one of the major influences in their life, whether that is school, or parents, or an association, or a political party. And in such a case, doing the exact opposite of what the person knows is required by that significant other, whether an individual or an organisation, the person realises that we are as much controlled by the opinions if we reject them constantly as if we accept them constantly. There is a difficult transition here to a point where one actually is in control of one's own destiny, rather than being controlled by other people. And the Scouts, for me, was such a major source of values that are directly linked to national import and promoted nationalism.

Other bodies which had a strong influence on me were the schools that I attended. Attending school, one learnt first what it means to be associated as a member of class, and then as a member of the school, and as one moves from primary school to beyond primary school one has broader social experience to see oneself as part of longer tradition, with institutions working to develop a consciousness of ourselves as opposed to the other. And through that process one comes to have a sense of belonging to certain traditions, which eventually build up to a national tradition.

It is worth looking in more detail at the way in which there is an accretion of sentiments that gradually builds up to be a sense of citizenship. Before I am English I am a Londoner. I am very proud of the city where I grew up, and I am very happy to show people some of the features of the city that I have come to know and love. Of course, being a Londoner, and London being in England, a Londoner is English. But a Londoner is English in a slightly different way from a native of another city such as Birmingham, Nottingham or Liverpool. Each different location will give a slightly different flavour to what it means to be English.

And a Londoner is never quite a Londoner. The most striking geographical feature of London is that it is divided into two parts by the River Thames. There is London north of the river, and London south of the river. And Londoners are always peculiarly aware of which side of the river they are. I was brought up in south London and as a result I am a south Londoner. I went to school in south

London, if only by a few metres, and the first twenty years of my life are associated with the south of London.

Each year, once a year, my mother would take us on a venture into foreign territory; we would go into north London, by taking a trip across the river on a wonderful old paddle steamer that was the Woolwich Ferry. And our venture into north London involved passing a site which once would have been a huge pile of waste from the Beckton coking plant. Just beyond the north terminal of the Woolwich Ferry was, and still is, a huge spoil tip of spent coke. At that time it was a black and dusty eyesore. It is still very much in evidence, but no longer black. It has been covered with grass, has had an artificial ski slope added, and it now rejoices in the name of the Beckton Alp.

My first teaching job was in Barking, just north of the river. I said to my first head of department that I had been brought up in south London, and that my vision of travelling to north London was of having to pass through an industrial desert that was dominated by a huge slag heap. And he said how strange that was, because it was his vision of travelling south of the river, that they had to go through a wasteland. And in spite of having worked most of my life in, and now living in north London, I never will become, or I have not yet become, a north Londoner. I remain a south Londoner in sentiment and in that sense of attachment, which can be quite local.

This concept of how one's sense of attachment to a place gradually builds up into something that one might describe as "Englishness" and membership, or citizenship, of a nation, strikes me as quite ironic in the context of the debates about Englishness that are currently going on in the British Parliament. The premise of that political debate is that it should be possible, indeed that it might be thought necessary, to identify Englishness as a sense of commonality. But in building up a sense of being English, a person from Newcastle and a person from Brighton would both be considered English but they would have a very different concept of what was involved in Englishness, because they were attracted to different geographical points, different sites, and different senses of what it means to be part of the nation.

What I am driving at here is that these points of attraction, around which the nationhood of individuals evolves, can be quite distinct from one individual to another. They act in quite paradoxical ways, and operate in the formation of the person so that each person is unique. The national character does not reside in what those individuals have in common, but in a constellation of points of attraction, issues or discussions, around which their sense of identity is formed, and towards which they are continually attracted back.

I do not want to think of national character as something that is held in common by all members of the nation. There are however key points to which members of the state, members of the nation, are pulled back to, or repelled from, and which form the personality of individuals. What they have in common is not that they answer specific questions in a particular way. What they have in common is that hidden, unobservable fact that they share a common strange attractor, even though each segment of the strange attractor is unique. It is the strange attractor that helps to define what it means to be a good English person, what kinds of actions are appropriate or inappropriate for an English person to do or say.

Every Englishman or Englishwoman is first an inhabitant of a particular city, is the product of a particular school environment, is a graduate of certain organisations, or the employee of an organisation, some of which actively promote nationhood and some of which do not. The people of a nation share certain concerns, so that it makes sense to talk about national character as some of those key anchorages around which the multiple non-random walks of millions of people circulate. Of course, I do not mean to say that a person can only be an Englishman or an Englishwoman if he or she is born in an English town. Migrants also carry the experience of their schooling with them, and arrive in their new home with concerns and expectations, which fit in with or conflict with the mores of their new home. It does not make sense to talk of national character as that which is held in common by all people in a nation.

In order to develop some of these points about how I wish to conceptualise national character, let me make a detour into an approach which has been suggested as a replacement for national character. In discussing comparisons between different cultures, Mark Mason raises the difficulty that, if there is such a thing as a cultural or a national character, then it has to be something that is recognisably held by all the members of that culture or nation (Mason, 2007, pp. 176–177). Mason's argument is that, if we are to use national character to explain the difference between, say, the French system of education and the English, then there must be clearly identifiable cultural characteristics that all English people share and no French people exhibit, and conversely, traits that are universal among French people but completely absent among the English.

I want to assert that this is not the case. In fact I would say that that is a very Newtonian, very mechanistic view of how culture could operate as an influence. It is reminiscent of Mill's description of scientific method of similarities and differences, which was developed at the end of the nineteenth century, and may have been a reasonable summary of the state of science at that time. However, I want to introduce the ideas of complexity theory and insights from science as it is developing at the beginning of the twenty first century, and in particular, the concept of the non-random walk and the strange attractor.

These notions provide a background or setting for national character as being a number of background influences which are experienced differently by different people, and can be examined. In order to understand what a nation is doing, one has to understand some of those key reference points on which the strange attractors of behaviour are fixed, if "fixed" is the right word, or anchored. This concern over complexity and interest in complexity theory is common ground that I share with Mason.

However, in practice, Mason suggests that, because there are differences in national sentiment between individuals, one might do better to discard the idea of a cultural or national identity, and instead use something like Hofstede's analysis of different elements of culture, such as power-distance and collectivism-individualism (Hofstede, 2001). In that way, national character would be replaced by national characteristics. This seems to me to be a backward step, or at least no advance, because it is based upon the idea that one can construct a kind of national average by statistical methods, an idea that I have criticised elsewhere as "single-centredness" (Turner, 2004, pp. 11–12). Single-centredness assumes that all individuals cluster around some kind of central position, and that any fuzziness or ambiguity about defining that central measure is a technical matter of improving measurement. This leaves the basic problem of diversity unresolved.

Because the mathematics of the normal curve is relatively straightforward, we are used to assuming that most people in a population will gather around the average and that individuals who are different from the average will become increasing rarer as we move further from the average. We are not used to thinking about populations with two or more distinct peaks. So we tend to think that if we define a scale, such as Individualism, it should follow the normal curve, with most people being averagely individualistic. But if the people of London are more individualistic than the people of Liverpool, or if the people of north London are more individualistic than those of south London, then the curve might have two or more distinct peaks. I call this phenomenon, that there may be distinct groups who are hidden by the mathematical search for an average value, "multi-centredness." And there may be structure to the idea of national character so as to make it a multi-centred phenomenon.

In addition, the transfer of attention from national characteristics to Hofstede's dimensions does not overcome the difficulty that all people within a culture are assumed to share those characteristics. Instead of assuming that all English people share something that might be described as "Englishness," they are now assumed to share several different things, namely a score on power-distance, a score on individualism-collectivism, and so on.

Ultimately, the key theoretical assumption behind Mason's critique of national character is that it assumes that homogeneous groups that will behave homogeneously. Earlier I have argued that this is wrong on both counts; it is possible for homogeneous groups in identical circumstances to behave differently, but it is also possible for heterogeneous groups to produce identical outcomes for at least some of their members (Turner, 2007, p. 27). What is required is not the rejection of national character, but a re-conceptualisation of national character along the lines I have suggested here, to overcome that sense of a mechanical relationship between input causes and output results.

I am trying to develop a more complex and fluid understanding of what it is like to have a specific national character, which millions of people share while retaining their individuality and unpredictability.

To reflect upon the question of Englishness further, it would once have been the case, and to a certain extent still is the case, that to understand anything at all about the English, it was necessary to understand social class. Of course, that is not to say that every Englishman or Englishwoman has an identical experience of social class, because that would, itself, be to diminish or dismiss the notion of class. It is to say that every person who was born and raised in England has a consciousness of their position in the social class order. They may have accepted that class position as part of the natural order of things, or they may have rejected it and aspired to leave it behind, but it was one of those anchoring points around which social interactions were constructed.

And having said that this was the case for all those born and raised in England, that is not to say that immigrants were immune from the impact of social class. They may well have encountered inappropriate class assumptions, such as the idea that a person of south Asian descent could not be (or must be) a doctor, or an afro-Caribbean could not be a professional. Stereotypes relating to social class, and a lack of well-defined positioning in relation to class, may well have been more of an obstacle for immigrants than it was to those inducted into the social class system from birth.

Nor is the idea that social class remains important in England a suggestion that social class is somehow frozen in a period television drama of the 1920s, with clearly defined boundaries between he landed gentry and their employees. Social class itself is on a non-random walk which changes its nature over time, even if reference back to 1920s period dramas is a continuing fascination and a necessary anchorage point.

Like locality, social class is one of those facets of national character which is experienced differently by different members of the nation, while remaining a potent force in the lives of all of them. I think that this is one of the ways in which the Americans and the English misunderstand each other.

Because social class and racism are present in both societies, inhabitants of each believe that they understand those elements in the other society. But, I would argue, while social class is the more powerful attractor in England, race and racism are much more powerful in the United States. It actually requires a comparative effort to comprehend how each mechanism functions in the alternative society.

The understanding of how the individual and the national intersect can perhaps be advanced by adding here Vygotsky's distinction between history and science. We each have a personal history that is unique. However, our goal is the development of a science, in his case of psychology, in mine of comparative education. The science will consist of those generalisations that apply to all cases, while the histories will each be unique and unrepeatable.

If I set out my personal history, it will be made up of unique experiences which are peculiar to me. The first influence is within the family setting. My father was English, and so I naturally learned what it was to be English through him. I say "through him" rather than "from him," because, although he was a teacher, his exemplification of what he meant by being English was never presented didactically, and only rarely explicitly explained. Some of that was an unconscious adoption of values through observing him, and learning by his approbation or disapprobation what was expected of me. I used to work with him, sometimes when he was doing woodwork, but more often when he was repairing our car. I would pass him tools as he needed them, or would shine a torch on some part of the car that he was working on. The latter, incidentally, is a very interesting exercise in understanding what another person is thinking, since one has to know what the other person is focusing their attention on, has to be able to shine the torch on it, and has to recognise that it is their seeing it, and not one's own seeing it, that is important to the success of the enterprise. And through learning to think what he was thinking, I came to be able to anticipate his actions so that I could know what tool he would need next.

In this informal way I came to learn how to mend my own car, but I also learned many other less specific attitudes, such as the importance of sticking at a job when it not going too well, or the importance of having a cup of tea now and then, so that one could review progress and plan the next course of action. Some of those attitudes I have internalised, and others I have not.

But there were also lessons, which if not exactly formal, did involve the conscious expression of the attitude on his part. One example I remember was the habit of always, when walking with a woman, making sure that one was between her and the traffic in the road. I am not as consistent as he was in this habit, but I still sometimes feel uncomfortable if I find myself walking with a woman between me and the traffic on a narrow pavement.

And then, of course, there was the attitude towards work, and the importance of taking work, especially work that had an aspect of public service, seriously. My father was a woodwork teacher, and as part of his preparation for teaching each year he would prepare printed sheets of instruction for his pupils, to show them the rudiments of technical drawing. I think that from about the age of six I used to help him with this preparation in the following way.

He would draw the master copy of the worksheets on large sheets of translucent paper. When I was a child photocopiers had not been invented, and the process for producing copies photographically involved placing the master copy over a sheet of relatively insensitive photographic paper in a wooden picture frame underneath a sheet of glass. Then my job was to take the frame out into the garden, hold it up toward the sun, and count slowly to twenty (perhaps thirty if a cloud passed in front of the sun, or fifteen if the sun was particularly bright – this was the skilled part of my role). I would then take the frame back into the darkened living room to my father where he would take out the photographic paper and immerse it in developer. Then he would put a sheet of fresh paper in the frame and we would repeat the process until he had enough copies for all of the classes he taught.

We thought it a great technological advantage when the school obtained a contraption consisting of a fluorescent light inside a glass tube, so that we could wrap the master copy and the photographic paper around the glass tube, and turn on the light for a fixed number of seconds, which removed all of the skill and most of the physical labour of the printing process.

All of this is history, and no other individual will have a history that is exactly the same. But through that personal history, I acquired certain attitudes to work, that a person has a responsibility to work for a living, that not working is dishonourable, and so on. Other English people will have been confronted with similar attitudes in the course of their own personal histories, so that one can abstract a science of experience that says that most English people have been confronted with, and many have adopted, a rather puritanical attitude to work, and a sense that anybody who is not working is not meeting their social obligations. Whether individuals have internalised that attitude or have rejected it, one can see the collective impact of this as a focal point of discussion in public debates about welfare and social services provided by the state. Especially since the 1970s, there has been a dominant strand of thought that has argued that poverty and unemployment are the responsibility of the individual who suffers them, rather than a failure of policy or a natural outcome of running the economy in the way that it has been run.

The core methodological question which remains, even if one accepts the idea that national character should be interpreted by analogy with a strange attractor rather than as a mechanical determinant, is how to identify it for the purposes of comparative study. How can individual histories be summarised and summed to make something that is a plausible science of the collective that is the nation?

Holmes' method for identifying national character is to insist on grounding it in written sources, in the case of England, in the Bible, the essentialist philosophy of Plato, and the philosophical empiricism of John Locke. This seems to me to be a good start, but one needs to recognise that any such selection from the culture in order to typify the whole nation is bound to be arbitrary and incomplete, and therefore contestable. What Holmes' method does is to make that discussion more concrete, and therefore more manageable.

I think that we will have to accept the incompleteness of any account of national character, as we accept the incompleteness of any science. The development of science rests upon abstractions, and as such can only proceed by omitting or glossing over those individual characteristics that make up individual histories.

However, beyond the elements that are omitted by necessity, there will also be elements that are omitted because they are too subtle or insubstantial to capture. Let me tell you about the English sense of humour. I can perhaps explain this by telling you a typical English joke... But of course, there is no such thing as a typical English joke. Once a joke is known by everybody, it is no longer funny. Once it has been told on national television, comedians have to go and look for new material. The national sense of humour is always moving on.

And then there are the elements that cannot be included in national character, because they do relate to characteristics that are truly supranational. Here I am not thinking of great British composers, such as Beethoven or Strauss, or great British novelists like Proust or Tolstoy, who might make us feel European, but of attachments that cut across national boundaries as though they were irrelevant.

I have more of an attachment to the community of comparative educationists around the world, people that I think of as my colleagues and peers, than I have to colleagues in my own institution, even to some of the other specialists in education in my own institution. Shared interests, and even collaborations, can span national boundaries. They may inspire reflection on national character, or they may simply ignore national barriers, but they generate a sense of belonging that may not be limited within a single national setting.

I have tried to present my sense of national character, as something fluid and contested, linked to the experience of individuals, but neither determining nor determined by those personal histories. I have also tried to illustrate how individual and collective notions of national character are experienced. I do this because I think that some sense of national and cultural difference is essential for comparative studies, and that a formal approach to defining national character is a useful tool for the comparative educationist. Consequently, I go on to examine Holmes' four ideal typical models of different countries in a little detail. Those four models are Essentialism, Encyclopaedism, Pragmatism and Polytechnicalism.

3   Essentialism

I have devoted a good deal of time and attention to the development of English national character as it applied to my personal case. In this section I will look at Holmes' attempt to formalise that process by basing it on clearly identified sources.

The essentialist curriculum model is based on educational thinking in England and, according to Holmes, is based on the Bible, the philosophy of Plato and the empiricism of John Locke.

Plato thought that astronomy was the highest of the sciences. But we should not be deceived by this into thinking that he had in mind anything like modern astronomy; he did not want to look at the stars. He was interested in abstract terms, the movement of the celestial spheres, and the eternal truths that are hidden behind the appearances of actual physical objects. The purpose was to improve the mind by contemplation of the eternal truths.

So, if we look at the selection of the curriculum for English schools, and I stress English, because the traditions of the Scottish and Welsh people are different, it is intended to develop the mind. It does not matter what one studies, so long as one studies in great depth, and that will sharpen the mind. Initially, the curriculum of English schools was the curriculum specified by Plato, but later, as the work of Plato was only accessible by those who could read ancient Greek, Greek and Latin became the most prestigious subjects for deep study.

And even though some of that prestige attached to Latin and Greek has gone, as late as the 1960s, when I went to university, being able to read Latin was a requirement for entry into Cambridge and Oxford Universities. The idea that the content of study is not directly useful or applicable to one's career takes longer to erode. When I was at university, a friend of mine studied Arabic for three years, and at the end of that time he went to work in the diplomatic service in the Foreign and Commonwealth Office. One would therefore imagine that his knowledge of Arabic, given the importance of the Middle East in political affairs, would have made the next step quite predictable. His first posting was to Moscow.

This attitude, that what was studied was not important, and that there was no necessary or direct connection between the whetstone against which one chose to sharpen one's mind and the use to which one put that mind later, was widespread, to the extent that I was really quite surprised when I first encountered, in 1971, the idea that applications to engineering courses in the American University of Beirut fluctuated according to the perceived rewards paid to professional engineers in different branches of engineering.

I can perhaps illustrate the English (and coincidentally British) concern for sharpening the mind, by looking at the difference between British crossword puzzles and American crossword puzzles.

My father completed the crossword in the newspaper on a regular basis. On most days, but particularly at the weekend, or when we were on holiday, he ran the crossword as a social event. He would read out the clues, and anybody in the room could volunteer a solution, or in difficult cases make some suggestions about how they were looking for the solution. So, Dad might say, "Six letters, and the letters are C blank R three blanks C" (C_R_ _ _C). 'After king, say, I cut ace of hearts.'" And then anybody could provide their guess, and possibly be asked to explain why their proposal was a suitable answer to the clue.[1]

And as the youngest in the family, I learned about competition. My father answered most of the crossword, while my mother, who had also had years of practice at crosswords contributed a lot. Then my older brothers, who were well read, contributed the more than occasional answer. And finally, I would count my contribution a great success if I could answer one clue in the whole crossword.

I learned a great deal from that process, about losing in competitions, and about judging one's own performance in isolation from what other people were doing, and also about patience. I also learned a lot about spelling, and something about a community where people were equally free to contribute suggestions, or to ask for justifications of the suggestions made by others. But although this is clearly formative, it does not make up part of the national character, because I cannot suppose that all over the country every family was sitting down to solve crosswords.

However, I think it is worth saying that even here there is a link with what is most valued in the national curriculum model. An English crossword is strikingly different from an American crossword, even though they are in the same language. A typical American crossword has clues that are straightforward definitions of the answers. An English crossword has clues that are cryptic, puzzling and only obliquely connected with the answers. (The example above was from an English crossword.) There is perhaps a connection here between a crossword that is designed and intended as a way of improving one's vocabulary, and is therefore of practical use, and one which is designed as an abstract puzzle, with no particular value except to provide a work-out for the intellect. Similar comments might perhaps be made about television quiz shows in America and television and radio quiz shows in Britain. Although with globalisation the distinction is fast disappearing, quiz shows which are direct questions with unambiguous answers where the format originates in the US might be contrasted with British formats, such as University Challenge or Round Britain Quiz.

So, although I understand the language, I would only occasionally be tempted to try an American crossword. And this personal development process is curiously connected with something which is evident at national level, even if it has only a tenuous link with the national model of the curriculum.

Where one stops constructing a national curriculum model of what knowledge is most valued is therefore somewhat arbitrary. One needs something that is complex enough to shed light upon the specific issue which one is addressing at the time, and that will often be something that is acknowledged as a central plank in the national curriculum. At other times one may simply be trying to tease out a puzzle about why a task is routinely tackled in a particular way, and that might require drilling down into aspects of the culture that are not so readily available to the outsider.

Holmes created his curriculum selection models on the basis of published and available documents which could therefore be used by anybody to check what they said and to form their own evaluation of how particular texts contributed to the national approach to education. Consequently, he limited himself to identifying three or four key texts which would define the central national debate. In the case of England these included the Bible and the philosophy of John Locke as well as the philosophy of Plato.

4 Encyclopaedism

Encyclopaedism is a tradition based in France, although it has been influential across continental Europe and beyond. Again, it has its origins in ancient Greece but draws more from Aristotle than from Plato. Unlike Plato, Aristotle definitely was interested in what is going on around us in the world. He was an avid observer of nature and provided descriptions of biology and the living world.

The archetypical French philosopher is Descartes, who was famously completely disinterested in physical things, and applied his system of doubt, where he tried to doubt everything he could until he arrived at a firm basis on which to build his philosophy. When he arrived at the question of whether he could doubt that he was thinking, he thought himself to have arrived at that basis, since it was necessary for him to be thinking in order to doubt his own existence, providing him with his "Cogito ergo sum," and the firm foundation on which he then proceeded to reconstruct everything else.

His other most well known contribution to knowledge is Cartesian geometry, a system of geometry that is based on algebra. Although algebra is clearly not French in origin, as "algebra" itself is a word taken from Arabic, algebra is the most highly prized branch of mathematics in France.

As a slight aside, this is in sharp contrast with the attitude in England, where geometry is seen as the pinnacle of mathematical achievement. When we look at the PISA tests, and their pre-cursors in the studies conducted by the International Association for the Evaluation of Educational Achievement (IEA), international comparisons very often involve tests of mathematical ability, probably because most people mistakenly assume that mathematics is culture free, the international language of science.

In fact, the early IEA mathematics studies included, among the few participants, students from Canada, both from Anglophone and Francophone areas. And the results quite clearly show that Anglophone students achieved much better scores in geometry, while Francophone students did much better in algebra. This should be borne in mind by anybody who thinks that maths scores in PISA can be taken at face value.

In fact, over the years the IEA studies became ever more sophisticated, looking more at curricula, what teachers intended pupils to learn, and what was highly valued in practice in the classroom, as essential elements in understanding attainment outcomes, and the discussion was less naïve in terms of resisting simplistic comparisons on the basis of raw scores. At which point PISA had to be invented to provide simplistic grist for the political mill.

The French Revolution was a key event in French history, involving the overthrow of the ancient regime. Around the time of the Revolution a group of philosophers called the encyclopaedists came together, including Diderot and d'Alembert, who decided that the way they would mark respect, not only for the high culture of the elite, but also for the culture of the people, was to collect everything that was known at the time into an encyclopaedia. They would write an encyclopaedia that would contain all of the knowledge that was worth knowing. And that would include the knowledge of the farmers, the knowledge of the artisans, and the knowledge of the army. Every sphere of life would be included, and not only "fine" arts or "high" culture.

So they started writing this huge project, but as can easily be imagined it was never completed. They wrote a few volumes, but in fact new knowledge was being created faster than they could keep up with it, and eventually they died with the project still incomplete. Notwithstanding the fate of the literal project to write an encyclopaedia, the insight that inspired the encyclopaedia persisted in French curriculum theory, in the sense that the curriculum of the French school was designed to be an introduction that would give every child access to everything that is known. The result was an extremely broad curriculum.

Now in England, I went through my last three years in secondary school, or high school, studying only 3 subjects: mathematics, chemistry and physics. And my career in school before that time had been marked by my eagerness to reach the points at which I could drop my least favourite subjects. Now that could not have happened in France. At that time in France, everybody took a curriculum to the end of secondary school that led to the baccalaureate, and to pass the baccalaureate the student had to pass an examination in French language, mathematics, a foreign language, a social science, political science, and a natural science, and they all had to be passed at the same time, in a single examination season.

More recently things have changes somewhat on both sides of Le Manche; in England we have realised that such specialisation does not produce good results, and that people need a breadth of subjects, including Personal, Social and Health Education, and Education for Citizenship. To be honest, people always knew that a narrow focus on science was not a good education, but a narrow focus on the arts or humanities was supposed to be acceptable well into the 1970s. Conversely, the French realised that nobody can study absolutely everything, and have started to develop specialists, allowing some specialisation within the baccalaureate, with an emphasis on modern languages, on science or on humanities. But "some specialisation" in the French context is still not as narrow as the broadened offering of the English schools.

There is, however, associated with this different stance on curriculum design, a rather marked difference in approach to equality of educational opportunity. Offering a restricted curriculum is seen, in France, as an obstacle to the student's subsequent ability to study at higher levels. Narrowing the curriculum was therefore seen as being equivalent to reducing access to higher levels of education.

This might best be seen in conjunction with Ralph Turner's (1960) distinction between contest mobility and sponsored mobility, with university entrance being determined in England by specialist tests, and the provisional acceptance by university academics that the student is "one of them," whereupon the student is sponsored through their study by the care and attention of the academics, who in turn take on a measure of responsibility if students later drop out of university.

In contrast with this, in France, passing the general examination for the baccalaureate traditionally gave access to any university scheme, yet access did not guarantee, or even suggest, eventual success. Oversubscribed classes and teachers who did not yet feel any obligation to support the students personally led to high drop-out rates and periods of study to attain a degree which very often exceeded the nominal length of the course.

Both systems produced certain logical inconsistencies, and as access to higher education has broadened from an elite system into a mass system in both countries the systems have grown more similar, with France introducing limits to class sizes in university and England introducing more general degrees and tolerating drop-out rates which formerly would have been thought quite intolerable, but which, nevertheless, might be the envy of many national systems of higher education.

A further development of the French education system is due to Napoleon. I say the French system, but of course Napoleon's introduction of bureaucratic systems and codified legal structures had an influence way beyond France, and eventually influenced the educational systems of most of continental Europe and beyond, whether by friendly persuasion or invasion. Sadly, due to its separation from continental Europe by a narrow strip of water, the benefits of the Napoleonic legal code did not reach England, which has remained as something of a political backwater ever since.

Under Napoleon's influence, France very early on experienced the intervention of government to establish an education system that could provide the educated elite that was needed by the country. In particular, the state established schools of mining and engineering, schools for professional administration and schools of veterinary science. And that has been typical of state intervention that followed the Napoleonic model; mining and veterinary science were of primary importance.

Actually, if one considers Napoleon's other interests, this focus on mining and veterinary science is easily explained. "Mining" has the dual meaning of digging holes in the ground to extract raw materials, and of digging holes under the defences of the enemy to make them collapse – undermining their positions. The latter could, of course, be rendered still more effective if the earthworks were filled with high explosive devices or mines, yet another meaning of the word. As for veterinary science, it has only to be remembered that at that time armies moved on horseback, were pulled by horse drawn carts and carriages, and horses provided the basis for highly manoeuvrable forces that could strike suddenly and effectively. Until the invention of the machine gun, horses were crucial for an army's success, so state intervention in higher education was designed primarily to meet the needs and priorities of the modern state, an important one of which is waging war.

It is a sobering, and not particularly pleasant, thought, that higher education has often been stimulated for its ability to promote destruction, from Napoleonic times to the Cold War, and probably beyond. One might also look at those occasions when educational reforms have followed closely after wars, since wars that involve mass recruitment draw the attention of generals to the shortcomings of the pool of potential recruits from which they draw, whether those shortcomings are physical, mental or manual.

I finish this account of encyclopaedism by emphasising once again the sense, which the French have, and so do those the French have influenced, that the breadth of the curriculum is related to quality and access. Everybody has to have access to higher education in a range of possible subjects and therefore everybody has to have a basis on which to build. It was this sense that inspired the encyclopaedists, but it persists in many attitudes to equality of access.

5   Pragmatism

Pragmatism is a relatively new and typically American perspective on things. The new country was established as a Christian country by dissenting Christians who could not find a peaceful, restful place in Europe. They left Europe to establish the colonies in North America, where they hoped to gain their independence and they developed a uniquely American approach to philosophy that is called pragmatism. From the perspective of education, the most prominent pragmatist was John Dewey.

In the book *How We Think* Dewey (1910) sets out in simple terms his schemata of how all people think in a problem-solving way. Dewey was a prolific author, and if you have several years to devote reading philosophy books, his works will repay attention. Lacking that time, *How We Think* is a good place to start. Starting from a state of confusion, the learner first formulates and defines the problem, and identifies the source of discomfort among his or her confusion. Having done that, the learner generates as many possible solutions to the problem as possible. Then, reviewing each potential solution in turn, the learner picks the one that seems to be most likely to succeed. This solution is the one that is implemented, after which the learner enters the next round of problem-solving, the next bout of confusion, armed with more knowledge than before, specifically knowing whether the supposed solution to the previous problem worked or did not work. The key criterion for success is, therefore, whether a positive and useful practical outcome is produced.

Dewey was a member of a group of philosophers, who developed pragmatism, according to which the knowledge which is of most worth is that which is of practical use. John Dewey was the specialist in educational theory. William James was the psychologist brother of Henry James the novelist, and wrote about psychology principally from the point of view of how people operate in practical circumstances. Oliver Wendell Holmes focused on jurisprudence and constitutional law, and was a Supreme Court judge.

Oliver Wendell Holmes was a very young Supreme Court judge. He claimed that when he was first appointed to the bench, he used to listen to the cases and then go home at night and write up his judgement from the case. And he delivered his judgement in the case the next day and everybody said that those decisions that he produced so quickly could not possibly have been properly considered. So what he did was to continue to listen to cases carefully, and then he went home and wrote up his judgement. And then he would put the judgement in his desk drawer and leave if for three weeks. After three weeks, he took it out and published it. Now people said they were wonderful judgements because he had taken such time deliberating. Holmes (Oliver Wendell Holmes) described this process as "maturing in the wood," and students might be well advised to consider this approach, rather than leaving assignments to the last minute.

Of all the pragmatists, I find C. S. Peirce the most difficult, as he insists, in a traditional philosophical way, on drawing fine distinctions. In particular, he described himself as a pragmaticist, in order to distinguish himself from pragmatists. But to my mind the real philosopher of pragmatism, besides Dewey, is George Herbert Mead.

When I am not behaving, if you like, like a comparativist, which is to say, when I am not trying to juxtapose competing theories in an even handed way, I resort to a limited number of theorists whom I take as a foundation for what I believe, my working approach to practical issues. First among those theorists are John Dewey and Lev Vygotsky. But I have a colleague with whom I have done some work, and he used to counter my references to Vygotsky by referring to the work of Mead. I think that they have a lot in common. Vygotsky was working in a framework of materialism, but building on that materialist base developed a theory of social learning. Similarly, Mead described himself as a social behaviourist, again emphasising a social construction on a physical basis for psychology. Mead provides an account of physical science which I find more convincing than any other.

Of importance here, is Mead's approach to education. He argues that in order to learn how to play a game, one has to learn how the other players will react. This means that playing a game is primarily social. In cricket, a good batsman must not only be expert in batting. He or she must also understand the bowler, what they are trying to achieve, and the techniques that can be employed to attain those ends. And in order to enter fully into the other person's perspective, we must, naturally, understand how they think about us. Mead argues that this activity, understanding how other people see us, is our first approach to understanding ourselves.

A similar argument can be made for any sport, and for many other social settings, so that games and sports are both a metaphor for how we develop self-knowledge through the eyes of the people around us, and a useful educational tool for supporting and facilitating that process. I think that there is a fruitful and under-explored area here, of how children's toys and games are used in different cultures to manage the earliest interactions of children as they learn how to think about themselves.

Although Dewey called his book *How We Think*, the theme of the book is normative, in the sense that what it actually proposes is how we ought to think, rather than how we do think. In the first place, Dewey notes that most people, in their eagerness to find a solution that works, pay too little attention to the stage of generating potential solutions to the problem in hand. Faced with the problem of getting across town as quickly as possible, I am unlikely to think of a taxi as a potential solution. (This is a personal foible of mine, and other people will have different dispositions which will cut short their search for possible solutions.) This happens simply because I have infrequently used taxis in the past, and consequently it comes to mind less readily. So Dewey's supposed descriptive account of how we think smuggles in a proposal that would help most people to think better. I readily accept that in my case, at least, starting to review potential solutions with a more open mind might certainly lead to better outcomes.

However, there is a more pressing problem, in the sense that Dewey's proposed method works, or is supposed to work, for both good and ill ends. If we start from a different problem, we might consider how to rob a bank. The problem is that the cashiers in banks, together with the money, are behind glass and therefore protected, to a greater or lesser extent, from our influence. We could then generate as many and as varied potential solutions as possible, as to how the money could be extracted, and then, having picked the solution that we thought most plausible, put it into practice. At the end of the day we would know whether that solution worked or not, and that would make us better bank robbers. That is obviously not a solution that Dewey is particularly comfortable with. Therefore, he adds a separate criterion, that what we learn should be that which is conducive to our future growth. Learning arithmetic or a foreign language opens me up to wider and more diverse experiences in the future, whereas becoming a better bank robber does not. Through this rather arbitrary and *ad hoc* addition to his theory, Dewey addresses the issue that education is necessarily a moral concern, and the idea that what works is what is right is subtly modified.

As noted above, Holmes includes the United States' Constitution as an important source for the curriculum model of pragmatism. The United States' Constitution describes and defines what the Federal Government in Washington can do and the Constitution does not mention education. Anything that is not mentioned in the Constitution is not the job of the Federal Government, but is delegated to state governments. And as education is not mentioned in the Constitution, education is the responsibility of the individual states.

The problem is that the (federal) state needs education, especially higher education, to provide the elite that will govern the country. Napoleon set up the modern state with its army and its veterinary colleges, and, in order to be a force in the modern world, America needed its education and its veterinary colleges to support its army. And it needed its agricultural colleges to help farmers to work more effectively.

While education was not the business of the Federal Government, the defense (sic) and welfare of the country was. To secure the defence and welfare of the country, and also to make the nation and establish higher education and continuing education, in the 1860s the Federal Government used its powers to secure the welfare of the nation by establishing the Land Grant Colleges. That is to say, the Government made available tracts of federal land, and gave them to the individual states on the condition that they were used to establish colleges of higher education. The actual detail of the educational plan was left to the state government; they could build a college on the land, or sell the land to raise funds to establish a college, or take whatever other measures they thought necessary to establish higher education. Many of those Land Grant Colleges are now major universities, like the state universities or Massachusetts Institute of Technology.

This is a pattern that was repeated, with variations, at various points in history, where federal intervention in education was justified in terms of the defence and welfare of the country, the Federal Government provided resources to the state, and then the state made the necessary decisions to implement the educational development.

For example, in 1919 at the end of the First World War the American generals came to the conclusion they had had to fight the war with a generally poorly educated army, in rather a similar vein to the comment by Wellington: "I don't know what effect these men will have on the enemy, but by God, they terrify me." Not for the last time, educational reform has followed a major war, war being an opportunity to see the population *en masse*. The adult males were discovered to be undernourished, sick and feeble and uneducated, and in an effort to improve education in 1919 the Federal Government made provision that war veterans should be able to use federal resources to return to education. In 1945, after the Second World War, the GI Act enabled soldiers to take grants so that they could go to university or school and pay their fees to the school. In this way government money is fed into education by the Federal Government, but the Government is giving money not to educational institutions, but to individuals.

This has become a common way for the federal government to circumvent the restrictions imposed on it by the Constitution, and its lack of reference to education. It is also a formula that overcomes other constitutional difficulties. For example, the First Amendment states that the Government shall make no law in respect of establishing a religion, which is generally interpreted as meaning that there should be a wall of separation between church and state, making it impossible for the Federal Government to provide funding for church schools. On the other hand, all citizens have equal rights before the law, and a child in a church school has as much right to support from the Government as any other. This particular circle is squared by providing support to the individuals, not to the schools.

Then in 1957 the Soviet Union launched Sputnik I, an Earth satellite, and many in the education establishment used this as a basis for a critique of the education system. How could it be, the critics asked, that the Russians could launch a satellite, but the education system of the US had failed to produce engineers and scientists who could match that feat? The outcome was the National Defense and Education Act which provided generous funding for the reform of science curricula in US schools. Again, the provision made under this Act was for the Federal Government to provide matched funding for initiatives that were controlled by the individual states.

The interesting part of this, from the comparative education perspective, is that there is a simple story here about educational reform; the Russians provided better scientific training and so developed a technological advantage which the Americans responded to by reforming their education system.

However, there is a competing narrative, which, although less often heard, also accounts for the sequence of events. That alternative account posits that the US had a technological advantage, and could have launched an Earth satellite before the Soviet Union, but held back for political reasons. A satellite in low Earth orbit must necessarily pass over the territory of many other countries, and it would be very hard to imagine an orbit that did not cross the territory of the largest country on Earth. A US satellite would probably have raised all sorts of objections from the Soviet Union had it been the first such vehicle. Once the Soviet Union had launched a satellite, thereby implicitly accepting the right to overfly other sovereign nations, the way was clear for the Americans to take advantage of the same presumption.

As in so many instances, such competing narratives, especially historical narratives, exist side by side, and the comparativist has to take them into account, without necessarily deciding which is "true" or being able to reconcile them. Like so much in the Cold War, space exploration was highly politicised. There is a wonderful museum of space exploration in Moscow where the equipment sent into space is displayed. And a more splendid collection of Heath-Robinson equipment is hard to imagine. The Soviets launched extraordinary machines into space and landed them on the moon. And the fact of the matter is that they could, because they had the most powerful rockets. The Americans, with less powerful rockets, had to be more thoughtful with their projects, using their technological advantage to make their machinery more compact, and make better use of smaller payloads. So, when the US was arguing for a convention that would prevent the use of nuclear energy in space, and the Soviet Union resisted it, it is tempting to see the US as the party with the conscience about environmental risks. In practice, however, the USSR needed substantial sources of energy to run their complicated contraptions, and the US could manage with conventional batteries. There was nothing particularly altruistic about the renunciation of nuclear power in space by the US.

The story is often told of the investment of the US agencies in the development of the ball point pen that would write in zero gravity, while the Soviets used a pencil instead. But this difference in approach, between high tech and low tech solutions to similar problems, permeated the whole space race, and much else besides.

From an educational perspective, however, the model promoted by the US is one of authority being devolved to individual states, and emphasis being placed on what works.

6 Polytechnicalism

Although the Soviet Union no longer exists, there still seem to me to be good reasons for examining the theory of the curriculum that was developed, principally under the direction of Krupskaya, Lenin's wife. This system was known as polytechnicalism, and the most practical reason for studying it is that it had, over the seventy years that the USSR existed, an enormous influence, not only within the territory of the USSR, but also in other regions of the world. Moreover, in keeping with the idea that national character takes the form of a non-random walk, with constant references to or away from historical elements, it is likely that this historical heritage still exerts considerable influence, either through a conscious nostalgia or revulsion for the past, or unconsciously through unexamined assumptions.

But the second, and perhaps more important, reason for studying polytechnicalism is simply that it serves, as I believe comparative education should, to focus attention and scepticism on one's underlying assumptions, simply by being so different. I remember very clearly going to a school for the deaf run by the Academy of Pedagogical Sciences in Moscow in 1981. Polytechnicalism included a very strong assumption that the environment could shape and stimulate the development of the individual, and while the debacle of Lysenkoism was well and truly over, teachers still retained strong environmentalist assumptions.

In the school for the deaf, we observed a class in which the children were instructed to remove their hearing aids, and the teacher gave a dictation, while covering the lower part of her face with a plastic shield (something like a spread fan in size and shape). The teacher then asked questions and took responses, and explained to the visitors (who could not understand the interchanges for themselves, as they were in Russian) that the children's hearing improved substantially over months. She cited the case of one boy, who six months previously had been unable to hear if a very loud noise was made directly behind him, but now was (evidently) able to conduct a conversation with the teacher, when she stood behind him where he could not see her. This the teacher explained in terms of the improvement in the children's hearing brought about by putting them in an environment where they were obliged to develop their hearing.

For an English observer, who has been brought up believing that inheritance is a substantial influence, if not the dominant influence, in child development, this was difficult to understand. The teacher, if not actually presenting evidence that would persuade her audience, was clearly sincere, and had no obvious reason to mislead the visitors. On the other hand, I would certainly have expected to see the children encouraged to lip-read or in some other way compensate for their deafness, not be forced to put aside even the limited technical aids that they had.

So I explained it to myself as being the case that the children had at least some residual hearing, and that the exercises that obliged them to rely on that hearing helped them to develop discernment and attention. That way I did not have to believe, as the Russian teacher obviously did, that their hearing had actually improved. In practical terms there may be no difference between improving hearing and improving discernment, but they fit into quite distinct intellectual schemas. But, notwithstanding my scepticism about teaching methods for children with special educational needs in Soviet schools, I came away with the very firm view that the faith in the plasticity of children exhibited by the Russian teacher was preferable to the opposite attitude I saw exhibited by many of my English colleagues, that a child's maximum "potential" was limited by genetics, and that there was little to be gained by extending education to those who were unable to benefit from it.

The basis for polytechnicalism was the writings of Marx, although there was also an obvious influence of the French, in that polytechnicalism shares with encyclopaedism the requirement that there should be a very broad curriculum and everybody has to learn everything. That is a question of equal access; you do not have access to the curriculum at higher levels of education if you have not been given a sound preparation at earlier stages of education.

Marx was not really a political activist. He sat and wrote in the British Museum, writing his books and supported in his work by the money that he got from the industrialist Engels. He thought the nature of the capitalist system was such that it would eventually collapse without needing anything in the way of special intervention. But he predicted that collapse would happen first in England and Germany, where the historical development of capitalism had reached its most advanced state. It was not part of Marx's own thought that Russia would become a communist country, because Russia did not have the industrial and economic base that he thought was a necessary precursor of communism.

However, a key concept in Marx's account of economic development is that all social structures are related to the means of production. It follows that this must necessarily be true of education also, and more particularly, that one of the main functions of education in a communist system is to highlight the link between the curriculum and the means of production. Consequently, in the polytechnical education developed by Krupskaya, a core principle was that, in education and learning, what we know must be related to the means of production. Value, in Marx's view, is produced by human labour, and we should therefore value anything that people have produced in proportion to the amount of labour it took to produce it.

There is an implicit critique of English educational thought here, where "high culture" and the intellectual were more highly valued, and the role of manual work undervalued. In communist thought, manual labour was precisely that which was to be highly valued, and the intellectual was only to be accorded its proper place, which is to say respected in proportion to the amount of physical labour it incorporated.

One of the beneficial side effects of this approach to historical development was a recognition of the historical place of artefacts, and therefore, for the most part, a willingness, even a keenness, to preserve palaces, buildings and things of historic interest. I was surprised, for example, on first visiting Leningrad (now St. Petersburg) to find that flowers had been left on the grave of Peter the Great. How could such a tyrant and despot be honoured in a communist society? To understand this one has to recognise that Peter the Great was thought of as a man of his time, and the best that he could have been in the circumstances, the promoter of a strong Russia and a strong foundation on which the USSR could be built. That he was not a communist when communists did not exist was not to his discredit. Such an approach to historical development is in sharp contrast, for example, with the iconoclasticism of the Cultural Revolution in China.

In the USSR, the close link between the school curricula and the means of production was very often evident in extremely practical links between schools and industrial enterprises. I remember going to a high school in Leningrad that belonged to the Metro system. The school was run by the Metro system, the Metro system provided resources to the school, and many of the graduates of the school would go on to work in the Metro system.

The physics laboratory was a large room, roughly square, with each wall about the length of a Metro carriage. And along one side of the laboratory was a carriage of a Metro train. So, you could go into the classroom and you could learn about electricity, and then you could go and check the application of those principles to the circuits used in underground trains. The curriculum was very specifically oriented to a range of vocational applications that were closely linked with the school.

I also remember going to a technical vocational school that was devoted to training tailors. To understand the impact of this experience on me, it is important to understand that English education is very abstract and very impractical, and that if one goes into a sewing class in England the sewing machines are the kind that might be used at home, and the children might be making a garment for themselves. In Leningrad, the school employed professional cutters to cut out the material for sewing, and the young students were using industrial sewing machines to manufacture garments for sale, on the occasion that I witnessed winter coats for the Russian winter.

I have to say, I was equally stunned the first time that I went to the United States and for very similar reasons. At that time, if one went to a computing class in a secondary school in the UK, the pupils would have been learning computing through a language called Basic, which is really good training of the mind, but completely useless. Nobody ever uses Basic, but the premise in England is that one teaches the principles of computing. When I went into a secondary school in the United States they were learning Cobol, which was then the business language of computing, and they were learning how to program computers for handling the details of company processes in a very practical sense. In both the Soviet Union and the US the education was, from my perspective, stunningly practical in relating education to work.

The Soviet school provided a commercial environment, in which children would learn about manufacturing, and developed the children for a variety of future employment, ranging from tailoring to working in the retail outlet where the garments were sold. To the English observer, these practices were redolent of child exploitation and child labour, practices which it had been the purpose of compulsory education to consign to history. But from the Soviet perspective, child exploitation as I understood it was impossible, since the means of production were not owned by a capitalist, and nobody was expropriating the value created by the children's labour.

We might still have a concern about whether the state was appropriating that value, and whether it was right for it to do so, but in comparative terms it is important to recognise that there was more than one way to interpret what was going on. We might also recognise that this contrast between the views of the capitalist and the views of the communist can be valuable in interpreting discussion in China about what can and cannot be done in schools as the country adopts a more liberal approach to trade within a communist framework.

I do not want to leave the question of polytechnicalism, however, without looking at a more general interpretation, which is possibly closer to the original intent of Krupskaya than this strictly vocational model. I owe my understanding of this more liberal view of polytechnicalism to my brother, who was a committed communist, and who worked for most of his working life as a lorry driver, although he did teach English in secondary schools for some years. He was also the most widely read person that I have met, so it is, perhaps, not surprising that he had an intellectual interpretation of polytechnicalism.

In polytechnical education, there is a need to relate knowledge to its social and historical context, and in particular to the means of production. So, if I teach children about plays by Shakespeare, they should be studied with a view to understanding their historical place and function. Take *Richard III* as an example. *Richard III* is ostensibly the history of the end of the War of the Roses. Richard, as described by Shakespeare, is a hunchback. In addition to his physical deformity, he is an unpleasant man who imprisons and then murders the king and subsequently murders anybody who might have a better claim to the throne than he does, including his two nephews. In the end he achieves his ultimate goal of making himself king. In short, he is morally corrupt, physically repugnant, manipulative and embodies everything negative that you could imagine.

In order to understand that Shakespeare play, it is important to recognise that Shakespeare was writing history at the time of Elizabeth I, and that the history he was writing was propaganda in support of Queen Elizabeth. Richard III was defeated and killed at the Battle of Bosworth, whereupon Henry Tudor became Henry VII, King of England, although he had only a rather slender claim to the throne. However, Henry VII was Elizabeth's grandfather, and Elizabeth needed his claim to the throne to be recognised as legitimate in order to secure her own position, and what better way could there be to do that, than for her propagandist to write a play about the base character of Richard III?

In addition, Henry VIII, Elizabeth's father, is generally recognised as the founder of the modern English state. He created the circumstances in which power was taken away from the barons, and destroyed their power base by knocking holes in the walls of all the castles around the country, so that nobody but the king should own a castle. In so reducing the power of the hereditary landowners across England, Henry also increased the power of the bourgeoisie, and in terms of the communist interpretation of history he is important precisely because this was the first revolution that led to the industrialisation of the country, and its eventual readiness for the socialist revolution. Shakespeare, therefore, attains a special status as the promoter and propagandist for this movement, as well as ensuring popular support for its continuation. Shakespeare wrote at a time when merchants were taking over economic power from the landowners, and some themes in his plays can be interpreted in that light. An alternative view of Richard seems to surface periodically which discounts the work of Elizabeth's propagandist, as exemplified by *The Daughter of Time* (Tey, 2009). The mercantile spirit of the age may also have been captured in the *Merchant of Venice*, while other histories address other themes of importance to Elizabeth's government.

After the death of Queen Elizabeth, Shakespeare continued to work as propagandist for his royal patron, but in this case it was James I of England, James VI of Scotland, who had ascended to the throne. In *Macbeth*, Shakespeare vilifies Macbeth, and extols the virtues of Duncan, thereby giving an account of James' ancestry which is, of course, favourable in terms of James' claim to the thrones of England and Scotland. Although a timeless and magical play about men who listen to the predictions of witches, and are misled when the letter of the prediction is fulfilled but the spirit is not, the play has a particular meaning when provided with its proper historical context of the reign of James I.

In Soviet schools one could occasionally find traces of this broader interpretation of polytechnicalism, where literature was seen in its social context, but it rarely extended beyond the more obvious interpretation of Charles Dickens and Mark Twain as critics of capitalism. One favourite for such an object lesson was Twain's *The Pauper and the Prince*, in which a prince and a pauper exchange places. The point of the story, for both Twain and Soviet educators, was the corruption of western society. And, lest that should be lost on anybody, we saw children in classrooms in Leningrad responding to questions, as good pupils in Soviet schools did, by raising their right hands just so far, and when invited to do so by the teacher, answering the question.

"Could this story happen in the Soviet Union?"

"No, because in the Soviet Union we do not have any princes/paupers."

"Could this story happen in the Soviet Union?"

"Yes, because in the Soviet Union everybody is a prince."

It might be of comparative interest to add one insight that the same class offered as to what it meant to be English, teaching the language in its social context. The following exchanges were used as a class exercise in conversation:

"Today is Wednesday," or some equally true and obvious statement.

"Yes, it is. I agree with you about that."

"Black is white," or something else obviously false.

"Excuse me, but I believe that you may be mistaken."

Sophistry, confusion and obfuscation are clearly deeply rooted in the English culture.

7 Other Ideal Typical Models

I offer the previous four ideal typical models more or less as they were developed by Holmes. I have embroidered them a little with my own personal experiences and interpretations, but essentially I hope they are as Holmes described them. They are everyday tools which I have found useful in understanding why some things seems obvious to people who are immersed in one national culture, but completely incomprehensible to people who are immersed in another. They are a valuable way of highlighting and structuring an understanding of intercultural exchange.

Although I have tried to report Holmes' view of these constructs, there are some obvious points where I differ from him. On the negative side, I think that I am probably less disciplined than he was in interpreting these ideal typical models as models of the curriculum, and I have allowed myself some liberty in using them to interpret cultural phenomena more broadly. But on the positive side, I think that I am in a position, by including them alongside the concept of non-random walks, or perhaps as exemplifying four concrete examples of non-random walks, to emphasise some points about the use of ideal typical models. I do not think that Holmes would necessarily have disagreed with any of those points, but the use of concepts from complexity theory make a language available for expressing those points which was not available, or at least not widespread, in the 1960s.

First and foremost, an ideal typical model is a model; it is an abstraction that may be helpful in describing, classifying and understanding actual events, but it is not supposed to be an account of those events. The extent to which actual events differ from the model, and the ways in which they differ, may be as important and as stimulating as the ways in which they agree with the model. While it is clear to me that the expression "ideal typical model" carries this sense, it is also clear to me that the expression itself may be an obstacle for some people to understand what is intended. That the model is "ideal" signals to some people that it is being put forward as some kind of norm to which actual events should conform. For me, and I think for Holmes too, with an understanding of how ideal typical models are used in physics, as in the case of the ideal gas law described above, this sense was never intended. Ideal typical models are "ideal" in the sense that they are not real, are potential rather than actual. As I drive around the UK, I will often see signs that tell me that it is so many miles to London. London being a large place, Charing Cross is arbitrarily chosen as the reference point to which those road signs refer. We might say that Charing Cross is the ideal typical location of London, without implying that all of London actually is at Charing Cross, or that the whole population of London has an obligation to crowd round Charing Cross. But from a good way outside London it is convenient to have a single point that can be used as the basis of measuring the distance to London.

I think that the word "typical" may be as misleading as the word "ideal." And it may help to clarify that there are two possible roots to the word "typical," and therefore two possible groups of associations with the word. "Typical" can mean the usual, the normal, the average value. But it can also mean that it is of a type, that it typifies something. Perhaps I can illustrate this with an example. In the 1960s, when there was a severe threat of bombs being left in London buses and trains, the authorities sometimes had campaigns to raise public awareness. One such campaign involved billboards that urged commuters to "Be Alert." On one billboard somebody had added, in felt tip pen, "London Needs Lerts." I would describe this as typical, in the sense that it typifies a particular kind of humour that is native to London. It is clearly not typical, in the sense of being normal or usual, as one could see hundreds of such posters, but very few that had been defaced in this way. But it does define a type of humour which one can see in London graffiti. It is a play on words, and it pokes fun at an official announcement.

Occasionally I will regret not carrying a camera with me, when I realise, usually with a substantial amount of hindsight, that I have missed the opportunity to take a photograph which is typical in this sense. I can think of two occasions when this happened in Japan.

I think that Japan has more backhoes per head of population than anywhere else I have been. (A backhoe is, according to the dictionary, a tractor with a mechanical arm in two parts, with a digging bucket at the end.) These are pieces of working equipment, and I presume that, in addition to use in building work, they are also useful to rice farmers. That was the only explanation I could think of for there being so many. As building/farming equipment they are routinely painted in bright but simple colours. On one occasion I saw a backhoe that had a giraffe painted on its side – the body of the giraffe on the side of the tractor, the neck of the giraffe on the two-piece arm of the backhoe, and the head on the side of the digging bucket. The reason that I regret not taking the photograph is because it was typical in the sense that I mean here. It was not, of course, typical insofar as I saw literally hundreds of backhoes in Japan and only this one had a giraffe painted on it. But it typified a rather whimsical sense of humour, a love of the cute, and an approach to everyday objects that sometimes verged on the surreal, all of which were discernible in other aspects of life in Japan. And in many ways it is those typical insights that the comparative educationist has to rely on to make sense of the cultural gulf that stands between them and the events they observe.

The other photo I regret missing, and on this occasion I share the regret with my wife, was on an occasion when we were walking on a narrow footpath and a small schoolgirl (I would guess aged between eight and eleven) sped past on a unicycle, talking into a mobile phone. There is something about the use of the unicycle (which can be found in all the Japanese schools that we visited), the traditional values of formal school uniform and the modern dependence on technology which encapsulates an experience of Japan, in all its contradictory themes.

So for me, the ideal typical model provides a framework for examining diverse experiences, and identifies debates around which national culture orbits, rather than presenting any kind of average, normal or acceptable picture of what one might find in a particular location. I think that was also the spirit in which Holmes advanced his four ideal typical models. Needless to say, that means that their application leaves a good deal of scope for interpretation. Tying them to specific texts helps to make them more specific and renders them open to critical examination, but does not entirely remove the artistry that must be used in applying and interpreting them.

Incidentally, I think that there is an interesting comparative study here in how the citizens of different countries use aspects of their culture to make political statements that would otherwise be impossible. I am thinking, for example, of the stacking wooden Russian dolls that I have, the outermost of which is Gorbachev. Inside Gorbachev is Breshnev, and inside that Krushev, and then Lenin. These are clearly not typical matryoshka, but they capture something that is typically Russian in the form of expression, of one doll inside another, and possibly also in terms of a certain cynicism over the nature of power.

One obvious area where there is need for interpretation is the question of whether more ideal typical models are needed. Why are four models presented, and not more? Should there be 200 or so ideal typical models, one for each nation? Or is it possible to say that the model of encyclopaedism influenced most of continental Europe, and so it is not necessary to have a separate ideal typical model for each European country? Or could all Latin American countries be covered by one ideal typical model? Or all Islamic nations?

There can be no hard and fast answers to such methodological questions, and an appropriate response will depend upon the purposes for which a study is being conducted. An ideal typical model of Latin American education may be of less value when comparing Argentinian and Chilean education, than when comparing Argentinian education with education in Spain. In the former case, more detailed models associated with each of the countries might highlight points that would be overlooked if one used a generic Latin American model.

The four models that Holmes developed, and which I have presented here, have some claim to being universal models, in the sense that they are probably the systems of education that have had the greatest influence worldwide, through their association with powerful nations that have been in a position to influence others. So, for example, China shares some of that Marxist Leninist tradition that has been set out under the heading of polytechnical education. There is, of course, the question as to whether there is a need for a distinctively Chinese model, perhaps a model based on Confucianism, or whether the polytechnical model of education can be used to illuminate at least some aspects of Chinese education.

Similar questions might be raised as to whether a distinctively Welsh or Scottish model is needed, or whether some variation of the English or French model might be used to create a framework of analysis, with appropriate riders and reservations to label clear differences. This might suggest that combinations of the various ideal typical models developed here might be used to extend their practical use to other settings.

I have to say that I was greatly encouraged some years ago when staying in Kuala Lumpur. The first night of the stay was in a back-packing hostel, an old and rather run down establishment, but one which gave me ample opportunity to indulge in my hobby of comparative plumbing. I discovered that the internal workings of the toilet cistern were of British design, a design, incidentally, that is quite distinctive and rarely used where there has not been British colonial influence. Subsequently we moved to a more luxurious and modern hotel, where the toilet cisterns proved to be of American design. It would therefore be possible to give a fairly clear description of the plumbing in the capital of Malaysia in terms of the historical influences, first from Britain and later from the US. Might it not be possible that an analogous process would also work in terms of analytical frameworks for the educational system?

I forbear from answering that question at this point, but continue briefly on the plumbing line, noting that, so far as I am aware, the world has only three or four distinctive designs for the internal workings of the toilet cistern; the British, the American cheap model, the American deluxe model, and the Swedish model.

There are important variations in cistern design in Japan and Australia. The Japanese cistern typically pours the incoming water into the cistern from a small height above the cistern, where it can be used for hand washing or watering a plant – a modification at one and the same time intensely practical and aesthetic, and therefore appropriately Japanese. The Australian variation, or at least the variation that I first became aware of in Australia, involves a double flush that can conserve water. Again, this is highly appropriate for the context in which it was first employed, although it is now becoming ubiquitous, even if, in Britain at least, it is often installed so that it does not work properly, and therefore does not save water. That may be another cultural influence.

So with models of education, it might similarly be possible to work with four or five ideal types, adding detailed accounts where national systems diverge from the ideal model. I think that it was in this spirit that Holmes offered his four curriculum models, although he was clearly open to the idea that further models might well be necessary in the case of Islamic education, Confucian education and possibly Japanese education.

I think that it is a matter of judgement when to discard one of the stock models that has already been developed, and when a new one is needed, and that will in large measure depend upon the educational issue that is being examined. An Islamic country may well have adopted a scheme of education in one area, for example in mathematics education, that was strongly influenced by another country. For example, it might use text books imported from France, or translated from or inspired by a French original. In that case it might be appropriate to analyse what happens in classrooms in terms of the encyclopaedist model. Encyclopaedism might be much less helpful, however, in supporting the analysis of religious education in the same country.

Therefore, it will be a matter of judgement whether a particular model is close enough to the theory and practice in a particular country to be useful, or whether a new model will need to be developed. However, the existence of a range of curriculum models, rather than only one, draws attention to the fact that there are irreducible differences between the ways that education is conceived in different countries, and that these differences need to be accommodated in some way. Problems that arise when cultural differences of this kind are ignored are not hard to find, and this might be illustrated by a case where the lack of an Islamic model of education is highly problematic.

Recently, the OECD has advocated the promotion of education for financial literacy. The OECD is promoting the idea that every child in the world should be introduced to the basics of how to manage money, so that we do not have another economic crisis. By and large, the previous financial crises have not been created by children, so it is not absolutely clear where this faith in the prophylactic effect of financial literacy comes from, but like other forms of universal panacea, it suffers from a lack of cultural contextualisation.

The OECD illustrates the kinds of questions that a financially literate child might be expected to answer. One example offered by the OECD is of a simple choice in the market place, where the potential buyer is faced with a choice between 10 kg of tomatoes for £7.00 or 2 kg of tomatoes for £2.00. The logic of the argument is that by buying 10 kg for £7.00, or 70p per kg, one makes a more astute purchase than by buying 2kg for £2.00, or £1.00 per kg. Of course, there are other things to take into account, such as whether I want to eat 10 kg of tomatoes before they go bad.

In fairness, the OECD does take such contextual issues into account, although it is not clear that they have taken all such variables into their evaluation. Is it early summer, when I might reasonably expect the price of tomatoes to fall before I have eaten 10 kg, or is it autumn, when the price can be expected to rise? Are alternative crops, or crops that complement tomatoes, coming into season, or going out of season? If we take all those different contextual issues into account, the actual price per kg pales into, well if not insignificance, then at least something close to insignificance.

The problem is rather worse when the person setting the curriculum, or the learner exposed to it, is less familiar with the context, as is presumably the case with buying stocks and shares on the stock market (OECD, 2014). When, the illustrative question from the OECD asks, is the right time to buy shares when the price changes as depicted in Figure 5.1?

This obviously invites the answer, presented as it is in this abstract form, that the best time to buy is in April, when the price is lowest. However, if we consider what a potential share buyer would know in April, the only evidence that they have before them is that the price has fallen sharply over the previous two months. If they invest heavily at this point it indicates extreme rashness, or insider knowledge that should get the trader a substantial prison sentence. The traditional wisdom of the stock markets is that you buy on a rising market and sell on a falling market. That would make the best time to buy May. How should the economically literate child interpret this context?

But in the cultural context, the real deficiencies of a universal approach to financial literacy emerge. The Islamic rules of sharia prohibit the charging of interest. This would make many of the calculations that are supposed to form the backbone of economic literacy – calculating compound interest on a loan, comparing different mortgage rates and so on – completely irrelevant for a major segment of the Earth's population. And incidentally, it would also make the buying and selling of shares beyond the pale, as investments where the risks and benefits are not shared fairly between the different stakeholders are also prohibited by sharia.

Of course, it was not so very long ago that the charging interest was also prohibited by the religion of Christians, since the Bible says that one should not charge interest. This seems to have been largely forgotten nowadays, but there was a time when only Jews could lend money for interest, and this is one possible explanation of the resentment felt by an indebted Christian population to moneylenders who were necessarily Jewish. Thus, four centuries ago we have a Shakespeare play that deals with a usurious Jewish moneylender in

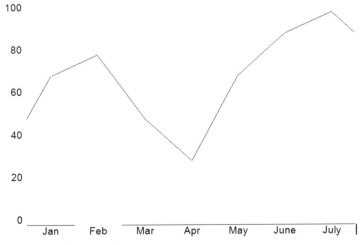

FIGURE 5.1   The price of shares over time

The Merchant of Venice. But that takes me back to another theme of seeing Shakespeare's plays in their historical, social and economic context.

The importance of comparative context, and I would say of national context, is highlighted by another of the illustrative questions from the 2012 cycle of PISA (OECD, 2014). The question presents an invoice for three T-shirts, a pair of jeans and a scarf, and states that, "Sarah receives this invoice in the mail" (OECD, 2014, p. 4). The question then asks, effectively, what role an invoice plays in a transaction – does it mean that the company is going to or has paid Sarah, or that Sarah is going to or has paid the company. The challenge of the question would appear hardly to be financial at all, but depends on imagining a world in which a teenage girl is invoiced when buying a small quantity of clothing. Perhaps one could imagine a world where all teenagers have Internet connectivity, and many of them purchase clothing on line. It might also be a society which routinely used invoices and receipts to reclaim expenses from any official body. (My students in China report that the first word of Mandarin they needed to learn was "receipt" so that they could claim out-of-pocket expenses from the university.) So it is perhaps not so much of a surprise that, according to the OECD website, 99.8 per cent of those tested in Shanghai knew what an invoice is.

On the other hand, if one was looking for a context where students would perform less well on this question, one might look for a country with less Internet connectivity and which is a heavily cash-based economy. That is less Internet connectivity than Shanghai, which, as an urban setting, is by no means typical of the whole of China. So finding a less connected country should be fairly easy. So it should be no great surprise that only 70.6 per cent of those tested in Colombia knew what an invoice is. I might perhaps add, in relation to what amounts to a vocabulary test, to check whether the young people know the word "invoice," I know a fair number of adult native speakers of Spanish who do not seem to distinguish very sharply between "factura" and "recibo" ("invoice" and "receipt"), which is crucial to answering the question correctly.

These various examples show the importance of taking into account the context of the education that is being discussed, or assessed, when coming to any kind of conclusion at all. Moreover, the detail of the cultural aspects that can be involved in an explanation, whether linguistic, religious, experiential, commercial and so on, suggest to me that it will never be possible to reduce these national differences to simple traits such as individualism or power-distance. It is barely possible to anticipate what aspects will be relevant in any setting, never mind codifying the whole range of possibilities in a few variables. This confirms me in the view that national character, in some form or other, will long persist as a cornerstone of comparative studies.

There is one very obvious area where Holmes' four ideal typical models could be supplemented, and that is the absence of China. With the population of China amounting to roughly a quarter of the population of the world, not to mention the influence of Chinese culture in Japan, Korea and other parts of south east Asia, there seems to be good reason for including an ideal typical model that reflects the roots of Chinese culture.

That is not to say that a Chinese ideal typical model will always be needed to examine Chinese educational phenomena; if one wishes to examine how Chinese education is responding to the challenges of opening the market and increasing entrepreneurialism, one might do just as well with an ideal typical model of a centrally planned Marxist economy and another of a free market economy, to examine which aspects of education were best adapted to which kind of economic setting.

However, as the second largest economy in the world, understanding China and Chinese education are likely to be important, and increasingly important, to all comparative educationists in the future. This is a quite radical change from the past, when China was largely ignored by scholars in the West.

I think that does need some explanation, or at least comment. In many aspects of political ideology, China followed the Soviet Union in adopting a Marxist-Leninist analysis. As I have noted before, this analysis was based on the assumption that all social phenomena were mere superstructure, and that what was important was an understanding of the base, or the relationship to the means of production. Thus a school where children made objects for commercial sale in the UK would be exploitative, because the school was located in a capitalist society, whereas a school in the Soviet Union where children made objects for commercial sale could not be exploitative as there were no capitalists who were in a position to exploit. This theoretical position makes it virtually pointless, and certainly not instructive, to compare schools in benighted capitalist countries with schools in advanced socialist countries.

It follows that a strictly Marxist-Leninist framework does not provide fertile soil for the growth of comparative education. What little comparative education was conducted in China between 1949 and 1980 conformed broadly to a pattern of knowing what the "enemy" were up to, which may have been highly valued by the state authorities but was not likely to produce independent comparisons of the kind that I envisage here. As a result, I would not regard the field of comparative education to have been very vibrant in either the former Soviet Union, or in China, until relatively recently. However, with the collapse of the Soviet Union and the opening up of China, that situation is now rapidly changing. Comparative education is flourishing, and at the same time much more educational information of all types is much more accessible to western scholars. It would therefore seem to be a major mistake to ignore models of education in east Asia, and it is for that reason that I attempt to sketch an ideal typical model of Chinese education here.

8 Confucianism

I am deeply indebted in attempting to sketch an ideal typical model of Chinese education to Gu Mingyuan (2013), and the many scholars who have worked hard to make his work available in English. And I follow Professor Gu in giving a central place in that model to the thought of Confucius. I do that with some hesitation, however.

Nobody will really need to be reminded that China has a long and noble history, and an equally rich cultural heritage. And although Confucius may be said to stand out in that tradition, he hardly stands alone. Other schools of thought have flourished, and the interpretation of the work of Confucius has changed over time. And consequently there may be other candidates for the position of founding philosopher of Chinese education. Among those, the most prominent might be Laozi, the founder of Daoism, and a contemporary of Confucius. In connection with the unbroken civilisation of China, it is worth remembering that both were roughly contemporary with the pre-Socratic philosophers in Greece, but while only fragments of ancient Greek thought remain, we have whole books by the Chinese philosophers.

Laozi's teachings included the rejection of worldly honours. He is reputed, in some traditions, to have withdrawn from the world and lived as a hermit. This is in sharp contrast with Confucius, for whom service to the nation, and particularly a position in government, was regarded as an admirable goal, if not the principal goal, of life.

For me, this raises the obvious question, namely, to whom does Chinese traditional culture owe more, to Confucius or to Laozi? I mention this point, however, mainly to emphasise that it is the wrong question, even though it is one that I find hard to ignore. Confucius, hardly less than Laozi, provides a philosophy where balance is a crucial principle, and the co-existence of opposites is welcomed. Laozi and Confucius had their differences, the explanation goes, but Confucianism is not dogmatic, and can incorporate into itself an interpretation of Daoism that makes an amalgam which can all be understood as Confucianism.

I still find this difficult. If Confucianism can incorporate anything, then what is it, and equally important, what is it not? But intellectually I know that what is required of the comparative educationist is an effort to put aside the preconceptions that he or she brings with them.

I think of Laozi as a sort of parallel of Diogenes, as one who eschewed official position and who had no regard for official position or for power. In contrast with that, Confucius is a sort of parallel for Plato, whose concerns were with statecraft, and creating a well ordered society, in which people settled to the position to which they were entitled by virtue of the talents with which they were born. (I do not particularly approve of this habit of identifying "the Chinese Plato," "the Chinese Diogenes" or "the Chinese Tycho Brahe," especially as the Chinese part of these comparisons generally precedes the European part by several centuries, but the linking of ideas in this way does serve two useful purposes: for me it serves as a kind of shorthand, so that I do not need to start from scratch in describing the concerns of Confucius or Laozi, and it also serves to highlight a number of universal concerns with which everybody is familiar, such as how to organise society.)

So perhaps I should start with the guidance of Gu Mingyuan (2013), who says that the primary feature of Chinese culture is that it is moral. But although Professor Gu offers very little in the way of guidance, I think that some guidance is necessary if that simple statement is to be understood, because, at first blush, China does not seem to be a particularly moral society. I do not mean that it seems a particularly immoral society, in the sense that people do a lot of dishonest things, or that they do a lot of things that I disapprove of, like spitting on the street. I mean that, to me, Chinese society seems fairly amoral.

Of course, I have been brought up on European ethics, and particularly Kant, so, for me, being moral normally means following a general principle, such as telling the truth. In that context, Chinese society seems to be able to tolerate a very high level of untruths or hypocrisy. In the autumn of 2014, for reasons that I need not go into, the official Chinese television programmes in English, CCTV, devoted a great deal of time to government statements about the importance of "the rule of law." However, it is fairly clear that the Chinese concept of the rule of law is not the same as mine. For me, the rule of law covers the notion that the law must apply equally to everybody who is subject to the law, and in particular to all citizens of a country that has adopted the law. It may, in certain circumstances, and particularly if the law is unethical, be necessary or moral to break the law, but the consequences of breaking the law must then be accepted, and must apply equally to anybody who breaks the law.

The Chinese concept of the rule of law is that the lawmakers make the rules, and that the rules must then be followed by everybody. The law has failed if it is broken, or rather the law breakers are at fault for having broken the law. So, for example, the Chinese Government seems quite comfortable with two positions that seem to me to be incompatible; "one country – two systems," which necessarily means that the laws apply differently, or different laws apply, to some subset of the citizens of the country, and "the rule of law," which implies that the laws should apply equally to all citizens. In fact, the Chinese Government seems not only to be comfortable, but seems to be proud of adopting both principles at the same time and making propaganda out of them.

So for Professor Gu to be right that the main principle of Chinese society is its moral character, then the term "moral" needs to be examined carefully, and history might offer some help. Confucian societies lived in splendid isolation from the developing civilisations of Europe for centuries. One driving force behind such isolation was the belief that Europe could not possibly have anything to offer which would be of any value. China (and/or Japan and/or Korea) had culture, art, music, refinement, artisans, philosophy and political sophistication; what more could possibly be added? This is an essentially static view of society. The ideal society is well ordered, and not in need of change.

The other aid in understanding the Chinese sense of morality is arithmetic; in whatever area of interest, in China, the numbers are huge. There is an earthquake in a western province, and the casualties are in the hundreds of thousands. There is a problem over school enrolments for children moving from rural areas to the cities, and the population involved is in millions. There is a scandal over adulterated food, and the number of people affected is measured in thousands, perhaps tens of thousands. Every aspect of communal life is regulated on the basis that hundreds of thousands of people might turn up and expect to take part.

I do not, of course, mean that all life is regulated. A person is free to walk about, cycle about, get on a bus or take a taxi without restraint. But go to a railway terminal or a bank, and one is immediately engaged with a system that is designed to handle people in quantity. A ticket-holder cannot wander through a major railway station in China as one would in the UK (or, indeed, Japan; there are variations in the way that any Confucian model can apply). One is herded into the waiting area that is appropriate for one's train, tickets carry the passenger's name and are checked at the barrier, which only opens to allow access to the platform thirty minutes before the train arrives. There is an imposed order, a concern for ensuring conformity that goes far beyond that which is strictly necessary. But on the other hand, as one can see from Chinese history, any disruption to order, any weakness of central control is often followed by war, pestilence or famine which can end the lives of millions of people.

Consequently, the highest principle is order, and a society in which everybody knows how to behave, and where the desirable behaviour may be very context specific. That is to say, Chinese culture is moral, but it is the morality of order, and of everybody knowing how to behave in a way that is appropriate to their position. Confucius encapsulates this concept in the notion of the "gentleman" or "superior man," who roughly corresponds to Plato's philosopher king. As a government official, the superior man knows how to order society, as he knows how to order his family life and his personal concerns, although different conduct may be appropriate in the different spheres.

As I have mentioned, my father was also a "gentleman" in the English sense, and keen to instil a sense of gentlemanliness on his sons, and although there are differences between the Chinese and the English concept, they also have something in common, which I hope helps me to grasp what Confucius meant. This is a sense of morality that goes beyond following a rule in a conscious way (as with Kant) or of conducting some sort of reasoning about the best possible outcome (as with Mill), and instead involves some sort of inner equilibrium, and inner certainty about what should be done. So my father would say that there were things that a gentleman did not see, or did not hear. This was not a question of knowing how to react if one saw something – say a friend doing something questionable; one had not to see them.

I do not mean to imply that the concept of a "gentleman" is owned exclusively by the English and/or the Chinese. It seems to me that Atticus Finch in *To Kill a Mockingbird* (Lee, 1963) is certainly a gentleman. But in his case, as in the English case, being a gentleman involves a personal code of honour that comes from inside the individual, and is expressed as a particularly immovable kind of moral judgement. It extends to his personal relationships and his conduct of his profession, but it does not, as in the Chinese case, extend to a principle of social organisation, much less government.

That exemplifies, in my view, the reason why a sense of national character is so important, and why any attempt to break national character down into component parts is bound to fail. Very similar components will, nevertheless, be interpreted very differently in different national settings. What one needs to look at is not the concept of a "gentleman," which may occur in different places and at different times, but at how it is interpreted in England, China or the United States, to become an idiosyncrasy of that particular national character.

It is curious that, as I have set my goal of seeking coherence across different aspects of theorising about comparative education, I should occasionally come across links that I had not expected. One of the models that I have introduced to facilitate theorising is Stafford Beer's viable system model. However, while working on this section I came across his book (again) where he sets out the basis of his theory; its name is *Think Before You Think* (Beer, 2009). The idea, as I interpret it, is that each of us both follows and constructs his or her own strange attractor as we live our non-random walk, so that we can eventually only think the things that we have constructed ourselves to think. And in a curious way that has echoes in Confucius, that the gentleman acts in accordance with the feelings of his (or her) innermost heart, while the lesser man is blown hither and yon by more immediate or materialistic motives.

Confucius was very fond of arguments of the kind:

> For want of a nail the shoe was lost.
> For want of a shoe the horse was lost.
> For want of a horse the rider was lost.
> For want of a rider the battle was lost.
> For want of a battle the kingdom was lost.

So an inner kind of peace means that an individual will not attach excessive value to material things. And being indifferent to material wealth, the person will be both able to order his or her personal relationships well, and be incorruptible as a government official. In this way, for Confucius, personal morality and social order were intimately linked, with family duty and filial piety being at the foundation of personal character.

At one level I find this quite attractive, in the sense that it has overtones of complexity theory. A tiny change at a personal level can have huge implications at a societal level, and patterns of behaviour have echoes at all different levels of societal organisation. However, it is an approach to complexity that I reject, in the sense that it responds to the butterfly effect by trying to control for all minor disturbances, which, as I have noted before, is impossible.

At a practical level the Confucian approach also creates difficulty, by making it impossible to offer a critique of an organisation without it being taken as a personal attack on the individuals who work in that organisation. I feel no particular personal engagement if somebody chooses, in the course of conversation, to criticise the UK Government, the University of South Wales or the city of London, In fact, on many occasions, I will be as vocal a critic as anybody else. But such a detachment would be impossible in the Confucian worldview. A complaint about the way an organisation works is taken as a personal complaint about the person to whom it is reported.

It seems to me that the Chinese and the Japanese have come up with very different ways of resolving this difficulty. Within the Confucian framework, it is impossible to propose that institutions be reformed without it being interpreted as a personal critique of the people involved. In the Japanese case there is certainly a devotion to order and bureaucracy, but that generally means that the people involved have internalised the values of wanting a smoothly running institution, and therefore try to anticipate criticism, so that it can be avoided before it arises. The Chinese, by contrast, seem to be content with some terribly inefficient institutional arrangements.

It was something of a surprise, when I was a visiting scholar at a Japanese university, to be asked to stamp (or sign) the time sheet every day to indicate my attendance. Any UK scholar might interpret that as a curtailment of academic freedom, when it was, in fact, only part of a smoothly running bureaucracy.

It was more of a surprise, however, to find in a Chinese university that there was no centrally organised post room, and therefore no system of sending a note to another department, or of putting a letter into the external mail. When I asked how I got a letter into the post, it was interpreted as a personal request to take it to the local post office.

In the next chapter I talk about the video of a Japanese school, Children Full of Life.[2] In connection with that video, and to emphasise how much it goes against Japanese sentiments to make an outright stand against authority, I tell my students the story from history of a family that was dispossessed of its land, as the head of the family thought unjustly, by the head of the clan. To correct the injustice, the head of the family appealed to the Tokugawa, over the head of the head of the clan. The judgement of the Tokugawa was delivered in two parts; the actions of the head of clan were unlawful, so the land would be returned to the family, and the actions of the head of the family were inappropriate (going outside the normal chain of command) for which the head of the family would be executed.

After I had told this story in class, my Chinese assistant came up to me and told me that it had reminded her of a story. In the period of the Warring States, the Emperor had gone out on a hunting expedition, with a large entourage of servants – a servant to look after the Emperor's coat, a servant to look after the Emperor's shoes, a servant to look after the Emperor's hat, and so on. They camped out for the night, and in the night it turned cold. The emperor awoke to find that he was warm, thanks to the thoughtfulness of somebody who had spread an extra coat over him in the night. He enquired who had performed this kind act. First he asked the servant who looked after the Emperor's coats, but he denied having done it. Then he asked the servant responsible for the Emperor's hats, who admitted that he had done it. At which point the Emperor ordered that the servant who looked after the Emperor's hats should be executed, for making a decision that was outside his sphere of responsibility.

I have to say that I have found this story most helpful in coming to terms with my experiences with large corporations in China, especially banks and telephone companies, that there is no penalty for failing to make a decision, but there is a penalty for making a decision that is outside one's remit. So long as one deals with an official who feels empowered to accede to one's request, things progress perfectly, but as soon as the official feels that the decision required is beyond his or her pay grade, one meets a brick wall, and the customer is expected to "appreciate" the difficulties that the organisation faces.

What one is trying to do in creating an ideal typical model is to identify the nature of this body of folklore that is passed on from generation to generation and helps to explain the behaviour of the people who have, to a greater or lesser extent, bought in to that way of seeing the world.

The methodological problem we face as comparative educationists is twofold; how do we select the stories that we include in the characterisation of national character, and how do the individual stories and anecdotes fit together to make a more or less harmonious whole. These are questions that I will return to in detail in the next chapter, when I revisit the scheme for comparative education set out by Hans, with the benefit of hindsight. But I want, here, simply to draw attention to some of the obvious difficulties.

I do not even know where I found the Japanese story that I have related here; in a novel, a tourist guide, on the wall of a historical monument – wherever it was, I remember the story but not the source. Worse than that, I have since tried to trace it in the usual ways, by searching the Internet and asking Japanese friends, but I have failed to confirm that it is a Japanese story at all. But it remains in my mind as capturing something that typifies a Japanese approach to authority. Similarly, I have no idea how widespread the Chinese story is, or whether the majority of Chinese people know it. Indeed, I am not sure that it is important.

As a child I was taught the importance of not taking oneself too seriously, or of, as we would have put it, "putting on airs" and presenting oneself as grander than one actually was. There are, of course, very many vehicles that might be used to convey that lesson to a child, stories from the Bible, snippets from Shakespeare, fables from Aesop or from Uncle Remus. It is not necessary for every child to know the same story to ensure that every child knows a story that carries the basic message. Indeed, as those examples make clear, the stories themselves are not necessarily native to the country where they form a part of the national character. So selecting stories as illustrative of national character is a thorny problem in its own right, which comparative educationists have solved in different ways.

Edmund King, for example, simply offered anecdotal evidence that seemed appropriate to him, an approach that the reader may have concluded that I favour myself. Brian Holmes tried to restrain his choices, and make the process more amenable to discussion, by drawing on specified historical sources. While I actually find that approach intellectually more attractive, I am not sure that it escapes from the arbitrariness (which sources to choose) or from the essentially personal nature of the selection (the sources do not really appear to be comparable across countries). So it seems that the idea of the national character is itself used in the selection of supporting evidence, which creates problems for those of us who at least aspire to be scientific.

NATIONAL CHARACTER

The same stories will be used in different countries as typifying something in the national character, and it may be more important to see how those stories come together to produce a coherent (or contradictory) whole, rather that worry about how to select the components. I will, as I say, return to this in some detail in the next chapter. But I also want to emphasise here why, despite the obvious difficulties, understanding national character, and indeed the study of comparative education more generally, is important enough to devote a large amount of effort to.

We have a tendency to think that the stories that we have been handed down by our parents and ancestors are the natural way of seeing things. We have a related tendency to dismiss and laugh at those who see things differently. But as communication makes the world an ever smaller place, and we all come with increasing ease into contact with people who see things otherwise, we need the tools that help us to accommodate and empathise with difference, without necessarily cutting us off from the world that we feel most comfortable with. In my view, comparative education lies at the core of this more general sociological enterprise of making the strange familiar and the familiar strange. And national character is one of the most potent weapons that we have in contextualising different ways of framing the world.

I do not want to be too dogmatic about the need for the difference to be recognised at a "national" level. Cultures cross national boundaries, and Chinese culture may be as influential in parts of Malaysia as Italian culture is in parts of Switzerland. Similarly, Shanghai may be as different from Beijing as Liverpool is from London. The units of analysis may be bigger or smaller than nation states. But if we give up the idea of national character altogether, we put aside a valuable tool which could help us understand the position of others in the world, and, through their eyes, our own position.

I want to acknowledge that people from different cultures can take very different things for granted, and have very different expectations. These things are not completely arbitrary, and one can see patterns in how they fit together. Ideal typical models can help to bring order to those various experiences and in that sense are useful. However, as noted in this case, there can be divisions within those models, and a general Confucian model may, on the one hand, be useful in interpreting the collectivism that is common to China, Korea and Japan, but on the other hand may need to be differentiated between those three cultures when looking at other aspects. Confucianism may be common to all three, but has been overlaid by more recent events in the history of all three cultures. How the comparative educationist uses ideal typical models is likely to remain an art rather than a science.

This present sketch is little more than an outline of how I use Confucianism to make sense out of my experiences in east Asia. A fuller development of such a model will need to wait for the attention of a scholar who is much more fully acquainted with Confucianism.

It is worth noting, however, that the use of ideal typical models raises the old and thorny methodological dilemma of whether it is legitimate for an "outsider" to impose their own conceptual scheme on the behaviour of others. My argument has been, and is, that it is legitimate, so long as the use of such ideal typical models is seen, as I have tried to portray it here, as a dynamic and flexible interpretation of key "anchor points" of national behaviour, and not as a stereotype of behaviour that can be applied crudely to any individual or individuals. Moreover, as I hope the present case makes clear, the "insider/outsider" dichotomy is not as sharp as might be supposed. Any outside observer, in constructing an ideal typical model, would be foolish to ignore the perceptions of those who are being studied, and would be wise to draw on whatever resources are available, whether they are constitutions and legal documents, literature, or, as in the case of work by Gu Mingyuan, works that are specifically designed to help the outsider gain some insight.

In the end, any methods for understanding another person's lived experience is bound to be partial and faulty, but the alternative to using partial insights is not to attempt cross-cultural understanding, and that must be much worse.

Notes

1 The solution is 'cardiac,' meaning 'of hearts.' The rest of the clue makes up the answer in parts: 'a king, say' is an example of a card, followed by 'i' and cut ace 'ac,' producing card-i-ac.
2 http://www.youtube.com/watch?v=1tLB1lU-H0M

CHAPTER 6

Nicholas Hans Revisited

1   Hans' Factors

Since the work of Nicholas Hans (1967) was my point of entry into comparative education, it is perhaps appropriate that I should return to his work on my non-random walk, and offer my current reflections on the major factors that he identified as shaping a nation, both in terms of the specific content of those factors, and also in terms of methodology. As Hans presented them, the key factors that make a nation a nation are race, religion, language, history and territory.

However, this is not merely a matter of nostalgia, of a revisiting of past mistakes. I want to make several methodological points. Most importantly, I wish to reflect further on the question of scientific method, and what it means to make a science of comparative education. Erwin Epstein (1983) argues that there are two contrasting approaches that have been taken to comparative education over the last sixty years and more: an approach that aspires to a general science of comparative education, which he calls "positivist," and an approach which is more susceptible to the influences of specific cultural conditions, which he equates with "relativism." I want to argue that the methodological choices that we face are much more complicated than that, and cannot be reduced to simple dichotomies of positivist/relativist, any more than they can be characterised as quantitative/qualitative. I have already argued that "positivist" has at least three distinct meanings, and that there are many ways of being scientific, not all of which are positivist on all three meanings. Similarly, there are distinct ways of taking account of the specificities of individual events and circumstances, and not all of them imply cultural relativism. And most certainly, there are ways of being scientific that are compatible with concern for the specific character of one-off events. So my purpose in reviewing the work of Hans is to find ways in which the methodology of the area can be advanced.

That is not to say that Epstein's analysis is uncommon, or not accepted by many comparative educationists. I have heard Andreas Kazamias complaining, or regretting, that comparative education has moved away from its humanistic origins, presumably to be found in the works of Schneider and Hans, and moved towards being a social science. The implication is that, thereby, the field has lost its sense of history, and one naturally can understand, even sympathise, with that sentiment. My purpose, however, is not to try to turn the clock back to embrace humanistic values, but to seek a way in which a social science can be simultaneously humanistic. My chosen route for that development is to take concepts and methods from the latest developments in science, especially from complexity science, and show that this framework is not positivist in any kind of mechanical sense, but can be truly humanistic. And hence comes my interest in non-random walks.

I had survived the first twenty years of my education without developing any interest in history, which, as I understood it at that time was "one damn thing after another." Hans was an eye-opener because he did not present history as one damn thing after another; he sought to abstract general principles and to point to a generalising science of history. Vygotsky drew a distinction which I find valuable, namely between a history of development, in which each of us passes through our own inimitable and ineffable series of experiences, and a science of development, in which we draw together those features. In this sense (if not in Kazamias') Hans was providing a science of educational development, not a history.

The exact boundary between the two, between the science and the history, is not a simple matter. Twenty one people are sitting in a room. As soon as we start describing the situation with generalising nouns, we start imposing culturally and socially defined norms on the situation. The teacher addresses her class of twenty pupils. The accused faces a jury of his peers (in the presence of a judge and several other officers of the court). The conductor checks the tickets of the passengers.

That is to say, as soon as we start to talk about situations, by applying language we start to highlight certain features, and to presuppose certain relationships. Following an argument from George H. Mead, if I walk across a room in the dark, I may find that certain brute facts obtrude, as I trip over them. But as soon as I start talking about the stool, chair, cat, or rock that I have tripped over, it stops being a brute fact, and starts to be a socially constructed artefact. In this sense I am a realist, that there is a substrate of hard facts that we can trip over or bump into, but that as soon as we start applying language we need to start recognising that the world we are discussing is socially constructed, and therefore influenced by the culture of the speakers.

Not everyone will agree with me, and others will allow that a scholar may move further in the application of language before they wander into the socially constructed. They can talk about facts, and only stray into social science when they engage explicitly with theoretical constructs and hypotheses. I suspect this is what Epstein and Kazamias mean when they draw the distinction; social science eschews the artistry of the historian in favour of the rigour of the randomised controlled trial. But, as I say, I think that one slips away from the unique and uninterpretable nature of atomic facts very much earlier than that. So my first fascination with Hans was that he was a scientific historian; he sought those common and driving factors that would explain a wide range of disparate phenomena in many different countries.

But if Hans was a scientist in terms of method, he was very far from being a scientist in terms of content. On my reading of scientific method, even (or especially) the concepts of science are socially constructed. Electricity is not, in my view, a force of nature. It is a theoretical construct to account for many phenomena that are forces of nature, but which, for obvious reasons, I cannot discuss. It is the worst kind of mistake to take the concepts of science and treat them as facts of nature.

Nowhere is this error more apparent than when race is treated as though it were a naturally occurring phenomenon. The supposed science of the late nineteenth and early twentieth century developed that idea, that the races were distinct, natural categories, with inalienable properties. Subsequent science has shown this to be mistaken; there is only one race and it is the human race.

On the question of race, I would recommend the theme of a book by Ivan Hannaford (1996), *Race: The History of an Idea in the West*. At least twenty years ago I was on the executive committee of the British Comparative and International Education Society, and Ivan was also on the board. At that time he was, I think, pro-Vice Chancellor at Kingston University, or whatever the institution was called in those days. He was a charming man with a very low opinion of academics – we ran several conferences together, and he was of the view that, at an academic conference, you had to expect academics to walk into the exit backwards so that they could avoid paying, which, of course, meant that the conferences he ran operated at a surplus. He subsequently, and very soon later, died of motor neuron disease. But he was working on a book. If that were not extraordinary enough, a preface to the book notes that in spite of having an elevated position in the institution, he said that he "carried on teaching clandestinely, to stay sane."

Hannaford's obsession was this historical work on the genesis of the concept of "race." His thesis was that race is a modern concept – post renaissance – which scholars then projected back onto antiquity. So we think of the Greeks as having a particular racial ideal, as shown in their sculpture, but he argued that their view of people was not informed at all by what we would understand as race. In fact, the Greek ideal of the city state stood in contrast to the family/clan (and by implication what would have been race if they had had the concept) by stressing links of citizenship as opposed to links of blood. A person was a citizen because he (and sadly normally only he) accepted the protection of the city state and its political processes and obligations, rather than because he was born into a particular status in life. So Hannaford opposes a racial view of the world to a political view of the world, and suggests that the Greeks made an incredible invention before they invented democracy, and which was necessary for the invention of politics, namely a separation of the public and the private, and a distinction between ties of citizenship and ties of birth.

He then goes on to argue that, starting with the persecution of the Jews in Spain in the 15th Century, we converted to a view of a person as an essentially physical being rather than a political being, and started trying to account for people and their behaviour in terms of their physical origins, their heritage, and so on. And in doing so, we have devalued the concept of the political and the polis and the cultural. This new approach led to the conclusion that a person's views are determined by birth and upbringing, and consequently there is no possibility of converting him or her through persuasion, with the tragic consequence that the only effective way to oppose those that you disagree with is to kill them.

I would add a rider to Ivan's work, that in the last twenty years we (meaning society in general) have gone further than he saw, mapping the genome, looking for genes for this and genes for that, and insisting that, in order to understand who you are, you must "know your roots," and that we are victims of the way our brain has evolved. And of course, in the process we have undermined the idea that politics is important, and notions of citizenship. This has an interesting, but in my view rather corrosive impact on our view of rights. Hannaford argued that rights arise out of one's engagement with the state, accepting one's obligations to the public arena, whereas we have come to see them (like race) as a natural phenomenon that does not have a political context.

I find Hannaford's arguments persuasive, and have come to the conclusion that the importance of race and gender have both been very much overstated in the comparative context. Both are socially constructed, and one needs to understand their meaning in relation to the social context in which they are set. As a consequence, I tend to downplay the physical inheritance of people and concentrate on constitutions and policies as forms of social structure, as I think Holmes did also. In this context, Holmes never referred to a "right" unless its origin could be identified in a document, such as a constitution or the Universal Declaration of Human Rights, which conferred that right. If that discipline were universally adopted a good deal of loose assertion about supposed rights might be avoided.

Race and gender are, of course, important, but as social facts, not as biological or physical facts. It cannot be repeated too often that there is no biological basis for the idea of race, when all people are 99.9 per cent the same genetically, and share more than 95 per cent of their DNA with chimpanzees. When I taught science in secondary schools to 11- and 12-year-olds and I liked to tease them with the physical similarity, or supposed biological differences, between boys and girls. If you start a session with the question, "What is the difference between boys and girls? When archaeologists find us in two thousand years time, how will they be able to tell which of us were boys and which girls?" Now, of course, 11- and 12-year-old children think that they know the difference between boys and girls, and they think that they are going to have some fun. They are invariably surprised, and not a little disappointed, to be told that the skeletal differences amount to no more that some minor quantitative differences in the width of the pelvic girdle and the carrying angle of the elbow.

Mercifully, it is now no longer acceptable to use race as a major category in comparative studies, but gender is frequently used, and rarely with enough attention paid to the way in which gender is socially constructed. Gender, or more correctly sex, can relatively easily be determined with a question as to whether a respondent is male or female, but that does not necessarily mean that it is an important category for understanding educational phenomena, unless it is given its proper social context and meaning, which certainly will vary from country to country.

Like all aspects of sexual orientation, I do not understand why such minor differences, often irrelevant to education, should be seen as a major category for examining differences, much less the major category divisions to create a lens through which all human endeavour should be viewed. I am more interested in whether a person can read and write, loves mathematics or feels strongly about art, than I am interested in whether he is he or she, and whether she is gay or straight or any combination of the two. For these reasons I also reject the idea that race should be an important category for understanding national difference. Of course, Hans never suggested that gender was important to national character, since it is impossible to imagine a nation composed of only one sex. But I have to say that in this case, also, I am not sure that these distinctions which are fundamentally physical in their basis are as interesting as differences that are purely cultural, and I think that gender is less often of interest than one might imagine if one simply considered how often it occurs in comparative studies as a variable of interest.

I would go further than that, and assert that reductive reasoning that depends on our physical inheritance, whether real, as in the case of DNA or brain structure, or imagined, as in the case of evolutionary psychology and the environmental context for which evolution is supposed to have prepared us, is always damaging for a comparative understanding, any physical effects being swamped by cultural effects. This is an issue that I will return to in my conclusions, when I consider what I think are the major threats to comparative education in the immediate future.

So, in terms of Hans' first factor, race, I have come to reject entirely the view that he took, that race could be an explanatory variable in explaining cultural outcomes. Indeed, I tend to think of things in the exact opposite way, that attitudes toward race are what need explaining, and that this can best be done in the context of cultural settings that make racism more or less acceptable.

I have taken an extended look at Hans' use of the factor of race because it has been, for me, a useful way of exploring what it means to try to construct a science, especially a science of history. It also offers the opportunity to examine how it may be desirable, and indeed necessary, to reject some of the central concepts that have been used to construct the field of comparative education. And, lastly, it provides an interesting reflection on how ideas can be valuable, even if, in the end, they provide only negative stimulation to development.

I will examine the way that Hans developed the other factors at slightly less length, and then return to the question of dividing national character into factors in general.

Hans' second major factor was religion. There is almost nothing that I would want to say about religion. I have already mentioned the possible insights that sharia might have when considering financial literacy, as well as familiarity with the King James Bible, as literature as much as religious text, and the impact on English national character. But I think that we should be extremely wary of going beyond the analysis of specific religious texts and the insights that they can offer, especially if that involves confounding religion and culture in a more general way to arrive at a "clash of cultures" thesis. It is worth remembering Hannaford's tracing of the origin of the concept of race to the religious conflicts in 15th Century Spain, and the fact that the rigidity of that framework of analysis led to inter-communal strife, persecution and ultimately violence. Any scheme that does not leave room for a person to change their mind is likely to damage something, if only intellectual integrity and not actual physical violence.

Hans' third factor was language. That language does not ensure national unity is clearly illustrated by the case of the English language. Winston Churchill said of the United States and England that we are two nations that are divided by a common language, and it is in a sense true that two native speakers of English, albeit different forms of English, are mutually intelligible, and can understand every word the other speaks, and yet still not able to understand each other.

It is often a struggle for English people to understand the American mentality, particularly in relation to the events we have seen on university campuses, where people have been shot by heavily armed gunmen. Incidentally, despite thinking that Americans are rather brash, I have nevertheless been very impressed by the polite way in which Americans drive. I happened to mention this to an acquaintance in North Carolina, and he said, "Oh yes, we are very well-mannered when driving. But then we have a lot of guns."

One of the sources of mutual incomprehension between British people and American people is that Americans cannot understand why we put up with the Queen, since they regard the monarchy as anachronistic; why be subjects of the Queen rather than citizens? Although a growing number of us seem to be coming to a similar opinion, there is also the fact that the Queen, or her father before her, is a part of what we learned about in the context of learning what it means to be British. States have to have a head of state, and a figurehead of no great importance may be no worse than a politician who wants to be elected president. So the Queen becomes a symbol of what it means to be British. She may not symbolise the same thing to all of us, and for many becoming a republic would be a wonderful way of symbolising that Britain had moved into the modern world. But our debates about national character continue to be couched in terms of our attitudes to royalty, the church and other institutions through which we have learned to be British.

Coming next to Hans' fourth factor that defines a nation, a shared sense of history, I want to make a slight diversion to set the context of what I have to say. One of the resources that I have been using lately is a video called Children Full of Life.[1] The video shows a year in the life of a class in Grade 4 in an elementary school, with their teacher, Mr. Kanamori.

As an aside, I note that I first came across this video on the recommendation of a teacher from California who I happened to be sitting next to at a display of traditional dance at Shuri Castle in Okinawa. So coming across this video was something of an international experience. Actually, my wife and I only spent a long weekend in Okinawa, but we were fortunate to happen upon a cultural celebration.

Okinawa is part of Japan, but it is a group of islands that lie well south of the main archipelago. Historically, Okinawa was an independent nation which, standing between China and Japan played an intermediary role, and managed to maintain its independence by communicating between the two, and no doubt playing one off against the other. By the middle of the 19th Century Okinawa was partially independent as a vassal state of Japan. Shortly after the Meiji Restoration and the civil war that followed, the good people of Okinawa decided it might be an opportune moment to assert their full independence from Japan. As it happened, the Emperor had an army of battle hardened and rather unruly soldiers who he did not know what to do with, but decided it might be a good idea to send them off to a distant island. The solution of these two problems came neatly together, with Okinawa asserting independence, and then being invaded by an army from Japan, and being fully annexed to the state of Japan. Ironically, Okinawa is now something of an intersection between Japan and the USA, on account of the airbase which dominates the largest island.

Anyway, at the time of our visit to Japan in November 2009, the Okinawans were celebrating their culture, which looked something like a celebration of their own independent culture, and a harking back to the glory of Shuri Castle. This, again, is a reflection of national character, that there will be competing strands which are simultaneously accepting of that national culture, and a show of resistance to it. Okinawa as a whole is very different from Japan, in terms of weather, in terms of diet, and, as we saw, in terms of history and culture.

Yet in other ways, Okinawa is very typically Japanese. As we entered Shuri Castle, we collected a map of the castle which marked the twelve or fifteen key points in the castle where we could see some important defensive feature or reflect upon some point of history. Arriving at each point in turn, we found the site illustrated on the map, and to one side a small lectern-like stand (with a perspex cover to protect it from the rain, which threatened on and off all day). On the stand were an ink pad and a rubber stamp, so that we could record the fact that we had visited the site by stamping in the appropriate space on the map. This is not an idiosyncrasy of Shuri Castle; we had a similar map, but with plants, at the arboretum. Our local railway station in Saijo, Higashi Hiroshima, also had a stamp so that visitors could record their visit, this time presumably in their diary, as no special map was provided.

I include these ramblings on the grounds that they relate to education. The system of collecting stamps was clearly intended for children, and designed to introduce them to the curious (to my eyes) notion of presence required by Japanese culture, especially in relation to historic sites. The adult version involved me marking the attendance record with my personal stamp each day when I arrived at the university, a measure that most of my Western colleagues regard as a gross infringement of academic freedom. So the observations are also comparative, in their way.

To return to the video, what I note is that when people who are not comparative educationists see this video for the first time, we might say as naïve observers, they tend to interpret it in universal terms. They see Mr. Kanamori as an extraordinary teacher, but immediately contrast and compare this with their own experience in the USA or UK. "I had an exceptional and empathetic teacher like that," or "I wish I had…" There are also the very negative postings on YouTube: "This teacher is a pervert the way he touches and hugs his pupils," although I have to say I have never seen that reaction among those I have watched the video with, all of whom have some connection with education, although occasionally they will note that the norms for teachers in their country would make such behaviour suspect. But the point that I am making is that naïve viewers rarely see this as an example that is typical of Japanese education, but comment on it instead as an example of good or bad education.

Of course, there is some merit in this perspective, since it not only supports reflection on how we might learn from others to improve our own system; it also highlights the fact that any observation we make of classroom practice is likely to be abnormal, simply because we are watching it, and all the more so if a television broadcasting organisation has selected it as the subject of a film. I do not have any doubt that Mr. Kanamori is in many ways exceptional.

But in contrast with this, when I watch the video, I am struck by how very typically Japanese very much of what is presented appears. There is a very special feel about the video that education is connected with the passage of the seasons. And this is one of the aspects of Japanese culture that is most striking to me, the way that the Japanese mark the passage of time, both the seasons of the year, and moving through different life stages, such as the progression from Grade 3 to Grade 4. One of the most wonderful events we attended in Higashi Hiroshima was at a sports hall where, on the Day of Youth, all the eighteen year olds gathered for a celebration of their coming of age. The young women were resplendent in their furisode (literally "long sleeves," identifying the style of the formal, colourful kimono, quite different from the yukata, the informal kimono worn by men and women at the summer celebration). The young men were mostly looking rather drab, in dark grey lounge suits, although a few of them wore more colourful traditional dress.

What was noticeable, however, was not so much the elaborate coiffure, the polished finger nails or the engagement with the event, as the sheer delight that the young people clearly had in just being together, in talking with their friends (including all through the formal parts of the ceremonies). And when the event was over, they all hung around in the car park, catching up on gossip, taking pictures with their friends and generally having a sociable day, extremely cold though it was.

This sense of time passing pervades daily life, with the seasons of the year being extremely evident in the fruit that is on sale in the supermarket, in a way which we have lost in the UK, and I think that is not particularly an improvement.

So, Mr. Kanamori enters the Grade 4 classroom, and marks the beginning of the year with a pep talk, though rather different from what I would have expected. "Why are we here?" he asks, "To be happy." This is certainly strange to British ears. I would expect an admonition to hard work in the coming year, to try one's hardest. But to be happy?

Of course, Mr. Kanamori is doing very little more than stating the Ministry of Education guidance for early years education. There are four general goals for kindergarten education, which include learning to be sociable and learning to communicate one's feelings. Primary education is more formal, with specified numbers of written characters that have to be learned in each grade, but one is not bombarded with a detailed list of transferable skills that have to be taught, and above all tested for. Affect is extremely important in Japanese culture.

I should perhaps insert a note here to the effect that emphasising the importance of the emotions is a double edged sword. It can lead to a culture of, "If it feels good, do it," as emotions can be attached to any end, good or bad, if there is not some sort of counterbalance. As I think Brian Holmes said to me on many occasions, "Sentimental people can be very cruel." Actually, I think he said it to me only once, because I can remember the circumstances in which he said it very clearly (and they had nothing to do with Japan) but I have come back to the idea again and again, in that non-random walk way, as I have tried to make sense of other experiences.

At one point in the video, three of the boys in the class are given the task of going to cheer up one of their classmates who is grieving the death of his father. So, of course, they go and buy some snacks for him. One of the few Japanese television programmes in English, and therefore one of the few programmes we could watch, was a programme called *Cool Japan*. A group of foreigners would be brought into the studio to make a short documentary about an aspect of Japanese life, and to discuss their findings. On one occasion the topic of one of the mini-documentaries was the local snack shop. The shopkeeper, a middle aged man, ran a small shop selling sweets, chocolates and other snacks to children. The children would come and spend time in the shop, gossiping, seeking recommendations on the best snacks, deliberating over spending their pocket money and generally passing the time. The British participant in the programme observed that a middle aged man who devoted himself to selling sweets to children would be viewed rather differently in Britain, but apparently this is seen as quite normal in Japan, which perhaps gives some context to the earlier comment that I mentioned about seeing those who do engage with young children as perverted.

I do not have any doubt there is "stranger danger" to young children in Japan, as there is in other parts of the world, but in Europe we certainly tend to overestimate the risk, and use this sense of heightened risk to guide the management of the lives of young children. Children in London today have much less freedom than I enjoyed in my childhood, and that seems very sad, not to say a lost educational opportunity. So I am always pleased to see a young child, sometimes even a very small tot carrying a very large school bag, making their way through the streets of Tokyo or Hiroshima and generally going about their business, or the groups of older children in school uniform cycling through the shopping area, chatting, waving, or posing for photographs when they notice I am trying to capture them going by.

But all in all the idea of using snacks to cheer people up seems to me to be a very Japanese notion.

But for me the most moving part of the video, and the part that is most typically Japanese in some ways, is when one of the pupils challenges the authority of the teacher. The teacher, stony faced and immobile, listens to the arguments put forward, first by one of his pupils and then, as he falters, others come to his aid. One of my students this year commented that Mr. Kanamori had been very insensitive, and had not encouraged the pupils to express themselves. Once again, I think this is a response in terms of the education he knew, without understanding the whole context. Japanese culture is replete with stories that underline the importance of duty and especially obedience, even obedience as being more important than life itself. Mr. Kanamori may be implacable, but he is no more than personifying a tradition which everybody in that classroom must be acutely aware of – challenging authority in the Tokugawa period carried the death penalty.

What is extraordinary in this case is the Mr. Kanamori allowed himself to be persuaded, and to rescind the punishment that he had originally decided on. Not only that, he takes a certain pride in the fact that his pupils have taken it upon themselves to defend one of their group. In that he may be showing himself to be a rather extraordinary teacher.

The point about watching this video is that one watches it with two grand narratives running in one's head at the same time, although of course, one or other of them may be prioritised at any particular moment. The first is a universal narrative; here is a good/bad teacher employing principles that can easily be understood without knowing anything at all about Japan. The second is a culturally specific narrative; here are practices that have a very specifically Japanese origin and setting, and which can only properly be understood in relation to aspects of Japanese culture. There may be other narratives, too. A British observer may be running a different universal narrative than a Chinese or American person watching the same video, and observers may have rather different ideas of what counts as "Japanese culture." This running of different narratives, without necessarily needing to make a definitive decision about which of them is right, seems to me to be at the heart of comparative education.

In *The Devil's Dictionary of Education*, Tyrrell Burgess gives the following definition of "intelligent":

> intelligent: (adjective) being able to hold opposing ideas in mind at the same time, enjoying it and not being paralysed

It seems to me that comparative education requires a good deal of intelligence of this type, and, indeed, that it is exactly this kind of intelligence, rather than content or method, that characterises the study. In terms of Epstein's (1983) dichotomy between the positivist and relativist approaches, the heart of comparative education appears to me to be, not a tension between the two, but a constant effort to bring the two together in some meaningful way.

An important element of specific, Japanese knowledge is an understanding of Japanese history, the code of the samurai, and traditions that are grounded in history. This brings us back to Hans factor of history, and its importance. However, as noted above, there can be different interpretations of history within nations, as well as between nations. For this reason a shared history cannot be presumed in any nation, and the fact of having passed through the same history of events cannot be a primary factor in creating the nation.

Nowhere is the need to manage competing constructions in a balanced way more apparent than in issues that relate to history.

The great mistake that the Japanese made in terms of history was to learn history from the Americans. The Americans believe that the Second World War started on December 7, 1941. If you go to the Hiroshima Peace Memorial Museum, which is a remarkable and moving museum for many other reasons, you will find that the history of the Second World War is portrayed exactly in those terms: it began on December 7, 1941.

From the American point of view, it makes sense to start history at that point, and to treat the attack on the Pacific Fleet in Pearl Harbour as an unexpected event, an event without, as it were, pedigree. To do otherwise is to take a longer perspective on history. If we push the starting point back to the middle of the 19th Century, then we would have to take account of the American use of naval force to open Japan to trade, and the entry of the "black ships" into Tokyo Bay in 1853. This intervention, to which Japan had thought itself immune, led to the overthrow of the established government and a prolonged civil war. It also led to a Japanese ambition to shape itself as a military empire that would be able to defend itself, and take on the power of the United States in the Pacific region. A prolonged love-hate relationship began at that point, and the US was not entirely innocent in its beginning.

On the other hand, it suits the Japanese very well to think of the war as starting on December 7, 1941. They wish to assert that the use of atomic weapons in 1945 was an act without moral precedent. The evil of atomic weapons is not, according to this argument, to be mitigated by any prior actions. No consideration of the lives that may have been saved, or of the atrocities committed before, should be allowed to blind us to the fact that the use of atomic weapons was in a different category, and an absolute evil, which should be eradicated from the Earth.

Now, I do not wish to be seen as an apologist for nuclear weapons. I believe that their use was not justified, and that in fact their use achieved relatively little, beyond the destruction of two large centres of population in Japan. I also think that the world would be a better place if all nuclear weapons were destroyed. But the official Japanese view of history serves a different purpose as well, which is to stop our backward examination of history at 1941, and to draw a veil across the occupation of Manchuria, the Rape of Nanking, the occupation of Korea and the invasion of Malaya, none of which affected the US very deeply. So the rather different views of history held in the US and Japan coincide in that particular point.

Obviously there are other people in the region who take a rather different view. The Chinese and the Koreans, to name but two, are unlikely to be satisfied with a history that does not take into account the earlier events that led up to the Second World War. Japan's neighbours want to see all those events in the context of the imperial expansion of Japan that took place prior to 1939.

This is a case which is both chronic and acute, but which in general terms is not particularly unusual, where there is more than one narrative competing for attention. There is no agreement about how events of the Second World War should be viewed. And, depending on which historical backdrop one chooses to interpret events, and that can have a very dramatic effect on what meaning one brings to those events.

In other settings we are quite familiar with the idea that there are competing narratives in the interpretation of history. In the Middle East, the date at which one chooses to start history can have a major impact on what one sees as appropriate policy in the present day. How one frames that history can have a major influence, can create what seems to be a natural backdrop, or the natural scenery, of the events, and that will lead almost inevitably to a particular interpretation. How one interprets current events may depend crucially upon whether one goes back 200 years or 2000 years to set one's starting point.

Controversy over the Second World War in the Pacific and the Middle East are emotional issues, very much alive in terms of realpolitik. But contrasting interpretations in history can occur anywhere, in those aspects of history which one has almost forgotten, but for which one is sure there is a simple story, and we learned it in school. I remember going with a French friend to Monmouth Castle. What could be nicer on a visit to Britain than to visit a historic castle? We stood in front of a plaque that recorded the fact that Henry V was born in Monmouth Castle.

"Do you know about Henry V?" I asked, ready to offer some history broadly based on Shakespeare's version.

"Of course," she said, "He burned Joan of Arc at the stake."

Nearly 600 years have passed, and nobody is likely to go to war over different interpretations of Henry V's role in history, but the sharp differences are present, nevertheless, in interpretation, and to each side their own account seems perfectly natural, unquestioned.

I can also remember a rather similar introduction to alternative histories on first arriving at a kibbutz in Israel. As a member of a party of young Britons travelling to Israel, the kibbutzniks had arranged a welcoming party in a large dining hall decorated with flags of Israel alongside the flags of the United Kingdom. As we went in I overheard one kibbutznik remark that he had never expected to live to see the day when those two flags would be seen side by side. My lack of comprehension of what that meant had its origins in the fact that the history of Israel/Palestine, and of the British mandate, was not a staple of the curriculum in London schools when I was a pupil. Things may have changed, with the current emphasis on more recent history, but I rather doubt it. However, at least one history of Israel/Palestine clearly was a major element in the formation of Israeli children of their understanding.

What I have presented here is, of course, a caricature, in the sense that there is not one monolithic view of 20th Century history in Japan, any more than there is in the US or the UK. There is a vocal minority movement in Japan that wishes to reform school textbooks to reflect other views of history, at the same time as there is a reactionary movement to make history text books more "patriotic." The debate is alive and well.

2 The Way Forward

And this raises the obvious question of how we should deal with such situations as comparative educationists. My own view is that we must struggle to be intelligent (as defined by Burgess), to suspend judgement about which is the right view of history, and to recognise that there are competing histories, each of which plays an important role in the development of different national characteristics. More importantly, we need to recognise that it is the presence of those competing historical narratives that constitutes an important element in the subject of our study. As people and as teachers we may have a strong commitment to a particular interpretation of history. Actually, quite frankly I doubt that. I have a strong inclination; whenever I hear an opinion being dogmatically expressed, my inclination is to present the opposite view, arguing evolution to the creationist and the argument from design to the atheist. That may merely be my contrariness as a person. But I am sure that, as comparativists, it is important that we recognise that sincerely held and contradictory beliefs are part of what we are interested in. And we can only come to a proper understanding if we do suspend judgement, and try to see all sides in the best possible light, and understand why they make sense to their adherents.

At the same time, we also need to recognise that "suspending judgement" is a counsel of perfection, and very few of us, if any, are actually going to achieve perfection in our lifetimes. That means that we never completely escape from the history that we learned as children, and for which there has as yet been no reason to challenge or question its taken-for-granted quality. A very small incident can draw attention to the fact that we have seen only one side of the story, and that we have assumed too much, as when my French friend drew attention to the fact that she associated Henry V with the burning of Joan of Arc, or when my mother in law referred to Sir Francis Drake, Sir Walter Raleigh and other national heroes as "pirates." And while those incidents have been enough to surface the occasional challenge to unconsidered interpretations, there necessarily remains a mountain of cultural baggage to which I have had no time to devote attention. Any move towards the cultural impartiality to which I aspire has been incomplete and leaves me with one foot firmly rooted in English/British/European culture. For this reason we have to involve ourselves in our studies, not as "objective" outsiders, but as people with history, and with history that shapes our perspectives and perceptions.

Besides, suspension of judgement can never be total, or at least never totally desirable. Any observer will wish to make moral judgements, will perhaps see it as their moral duty to make moral judgements. My understanding that there are two sides to any piece of history might nevertheless be followed by my conclusion that one party or the other was morally responsible for the outcome.

In the end our understanding will be partial and incomplete, but to me it is the effort to understand why something that appears so counter-intuitive to us should appear so obvious and natural to somebody else that distinguishes comparative education, and not the subject's content or its method. It is a disposition and intention that marks out the field of comparative education. In order to advance our understanding, we rely on helpful friends and colleagues who will explain how their idea fit together, even if our obtuseness in not seeing the obvious frustrates them. But above all, we have to start with a disposition to listen to all sides of the discussion.

However, this conclusion renders untenable the Hansian idea that there is a single, undisputed history that can be used as a factor in determining the character of a nation.

Similarly, considering the last of Hans' factors that I am going to look at here, it is interesting to speculate about countries that do not have integrity of national territory. One historical case of note in this respect is Pakistan, which after independence in 1947 consisted of two parts separated by thousands of kilometres. In the event that political entity did not survive, and Bangladesh sought separation from the country and independence. But again, it would be unwise to extrapolate this into an iron rule that countries that do not have territorial integrity cannot survive. The United States seems to do fairly well, and it is not at all clear how such a rule should be interpreted in an archipelago nation such as Indonesia, or even Japan or the UK.

Similarly, if Hans had been correct, Belgium could not exist as a political entity. So, while Hans may stimulate interest in developing bold theories in comparative education, I think that he is, for the most part, only of historical interest, and certainly not to be taken seriously as presenting a definitive answer about how to proceed in comparative education.

Since the 1950s there have been major movements of people, and most countries now have multi-ethnic populations, multiple religions and multiple histories. There may still be some homogeneous countries with only very small minority populations, but they are very few and far between.

However, even if one rejects the kind of sweeping generalisations that Hans made, I do not think that I want to go to the other extreme in terms of taking into account the cultural specificity of each system. According to Vernon Mallinson (1966), in order to understand the national/cultural context, one should immerse oneself in the language, culture and life of the system being studied for many years. To properly understand the comparative context, one would have to spend ten years immersed in the country. In so doing one would come to understand the patterns of thought, hopes and expectations that make up the fabric of national life. However, this imposes the very necessary limitation on comparative studies, that one would only be able to examine four or five countries in a lifetime.

Of course, there is no logical reason why one should limit Mallinson's caution to analysis at the national level. To understand, to really understand, the English, one would have to spend five years in Manchester, five years in Birmingham, and five years in Leeds, not to mention five years as a sheep farmer in rural Wales, and five years in a village in Norfolk. If we took Mallinson's admonition seriously, nobody would ever be qualified to make any kind of generalisation. But we all make generalisations all of the time. Indeed, it is part of the nature of speech that we use nouns that perforce imply the grouping of near-similar objects together in the same category. Anything that we say necessarily removes some of the individual and context specific from our account.

So I do not believe that one can take too seriously Mallinson's idea that in order to be able to say anything at all about a country one would have to live in it for many years. It is a notion that has its general counterpart in the political idea that only women can represent women, and only deaf people can represent deaf people, and so on, itself based upon the idea that only members of a sub-group or sub-culture can understand fully the members of that group. At one level this is a truism, that we can only have lived the life that we lived. But I think that the corollary that is often drawn, that in consequence no general theoretical perspective can be developed by an outsider, is a false one. Indeed, it is the outsider, who has no access to direct experience of a culture, who is most in need of a theoretical understanding, and comparative study is the continual effort of the outsider to gain insights, however partial, into the working lives of insiders. For me, that effort is at the heart of what it is to be a comparativist.

I do not want to overstate the idea that what I aim for is diametrically opposed to what Mallinson was seeking to achieve. I once sat in on a PhD examination, where Mallinson was the external examiner. My own approach in that situation is to start from some questions of general theoretical interest and then focus in to examine some more detailed points, and finally to end up with questions about typographical errors and so on. Mallinson's approach was, indeed, the exact opposite, to start from very detailed questions, rooted in the text, and gradually to draw back until he was looking at the overall theoretical scheme of the thesis. I came to the conclusion that the end result was very similar for both of us, even though we had arrived at it by different paths, he with his passion for detail and me with a desire to see the overall plan or "big picture."

I cannot pass over this without remarking that by setting the bar of experience so high, Mallinson's approach produces the collateral effect in comparative education, of suggesting that comparison is best carried out by linguists, people who have immersed themselves in the language of the countries being studied. Of course, understanding the language cannot do any harm, but there seems no reason to believe that a study of the national language is more important than an understanding of the technology, the art, the social relations or any other aspect of the culture.

So I think that we have to take Hans' view of what makes a nation, and what makes national character, with a very large pinch of salt. His idea that a country has unity of race, religion, language, history and social structures is now largely redundant in the face of so many nation states that are culturally diverse. Some interesting hypotheses remain, such as the different roles that religion has played between the Protestant north of Europe and the Catholic south of Europe. There are important demographic differences, with children in Scandinavia starting school later in their childhood. But there is a danger in developing this partial insight into a deterministic "clash of cultures" thesis.

Before moving on to some concluding remarks to end this chapter, I wish to reflect briefly on the overall question of dividing national character into factors, as Hans does. In a purely mathematical sense, if we wish to explain the differences between two hundred different nations, then we could produce an equally satisfactory explanation by including two hundred different factors. And by including two hundred and fifty factors, we could provide better explanations, in a technical sense. But whether we could devise names for those two hundred and fifty factors that are intuitively intelligible and meaningful is another matter. So we are probably left with whether the understanding of two hundred different national cultures can be reduced to an account in terms of a dozen or so factors.

And on that point I am very sceptical of the value of such analysis in terms of factors. Even if we take a small number of factors that are relatively easy to interpret, such as Hofstede's (2001) collectivism/individualism or power distance, it is not clear that they mean the same thing in different settings. Individualism in the US is different from individualism in France, and race in the UK is different from race in the US or Japan. So even to make sense out of factors in different national settings one is reduced to interpreting the concepts in terms of national approaches, or national character.

For me, the major merit of Holmes' method of characterising national characteristics in terms of specified documents, especially written constitutions, is that it makes broad stroke, impressionistic characterisations of a whole nation possible for the outsider. But by stressing that the characterisation is related to specific documents, it prevents it from becoming ossified into an essentialist national character; it can always be challenged, drilled down into, further explicated.

Of course, not having a written constitution, the British are perhaps more aware of the limitations of written constitutions. (In spite of the oft repeated idea that the British do not have a written constitution, insofar as a constitution is the legal framework that defines what the citizens of a country, including its government and government officials, can and cannot do, Britain has a written constitution. It is just not all written down in one place, and perhaps just as importantly, it is not read as a single document.) But just as Gödel demonstrated that no logical system can ever be complete, so no constitution can ever be complete; a written constitution cannot specify the necessary course of action to be taken in every possible configuration of future circumstances. And for this reason, written constitutions need to be re-interpreted from time to time, through a mechanism such as a supreme court.

And since written constitutions cannot be complete, and are especially vague when it comes to the conduct of people in informal everyday settings, such as the home and the school, scholars who wish to use ideal typical models to structure discussion of national character will need to supplement their model with other material. Holmes suggests religious texts, such as the Bible or the Quran, or the works of philosophers who in some way capture the national ethos. For example, for the English he suggests the Bible and the philosophy of John Locke.

Certainly, when I was a child, people learned in school certain tracts from the Bible, and could probably recite them word for word. To a large extent, the King James' version of the Bible was treated as literature as much as a religious document. The situation is very different now, with few people treating the modern English of the Bible with such reverence (in terms of literary criticism) and the decrease in churchgoing and increase in multiculturalism all contributing to the fact that the text of the Bible receives less attention in schools. But at the same time, it is not always necessary for people to have read, or even for them to be consciously aware of an influence, for a text to be valuable in an ideal typical national model.

For this reason, although very few people will have read the philosophy of John Locke, Holmes' proposal that he should be included in the English ideal typical model makes some sense. He does capture some of that basic distrust of theorising and an attitude of "seeing is believing" which characterises the attitudes of many English people to many aspects of science and society.

In much the same way, English people may be influenced by Shakespeare, without ever having read or seen a play. Many expressions or metaphors are used in everyday language, so that one can know a good deal of Shakespeare without being aware of its source. So, for example, it is not unusual when observing a devious or subtle person at work to comment that, "There is method in his madness," without tracing it back to a description of Hamlet. Indeed, my father would often use this as a third person commentary on his actions, with much the same sense as another person might have said, "I love it when a plan comes together." And with a similar source, it does perhaps capture something in the English psyche when Shakespeare has the clown tell Hamlet that a person's madness will not make him stand out from the crowd in England.

But this raises an interesting methodological question, since literature often does offer a unique insight into understanding the way that other people think, which is, presumably, why we encourage young people to read literature. When I lived in Japan for a year, I read a great deal of Japanese literature (in translation, which clearly may not be as direct a route) in order to have more sense of what was going on around me. And we know very well that what happens in a novel by Dickens or Trollope, Proust or Hesse, Melville or Tolstoy may be more true than what happens in a national census or an international study of educational achievement, in the sense that it captures a very local understanding. But how can we weigh the relative importance to attach to such understanding?

For example, is it legitimate to study the English educational system by reading *Hard Times*? The point that I want to make here in methodological terms is that teachers, like other professionals, learn in the course of their daily practice, and from one-off events. This made it particularly difficult when universities started to formalise ethical approval for research studies undertaken by teachers. If a teacher says he or she is going to observe the reactions of 30 six year old children to monitor their progress when given some new teaching material in arithmetic, then everybody would say that was part of their job. But if they say they are going to do exactly the same thing as part of a research project, perhaps for a part-time master's degree, then all sorts of mechanisms are put in place to check that children's well being is not threatened, and that their anonymity is maintained. If I tell an anecdote of an event that happened in a classroom where I happened to be, does that conform to the highest standards of ethical research? Or do I have to fictionalise it, at least to the extent that personal identities are protected?

The issue is that research through professional practice seems to me to be perfectly legitimate, and we should not allow it to be extinguished by heavy handed ethical controls. It seems to me, also, that this is perfectly compatible with a scientific approach; Karl Popper specifically points out that while no amount of confirmatory evidence is ever conclusive, a single refuting instance can be. It follows that a one-off incident in a classroom in the course of professional practice can be as telling as all the evidence gathered from a large scale survey with standardised tests. It also means that a novel, play, poem or film, any of which may similarly reflect a distillation of professional practice (though this time the professional practice of the author, director, actor or artist rather than the teacher) can be as telling as the large scale survey or the report of the teacher (which might be no more than the illustration of a truism borrowed from the literature of large scale surveys).

It is worth stressing, as I have done here, the "can be" and the "might." In some cases large scale surveys may be necessary. The classic cases will be those where effect sizes are so small that they may not show up in a small (or even a relatively large) sample. So on many occasions one meets teachers who are interested in gender differences in performance in reading or in mathematics. What we know about such differences is that they are consistently found in large scale surveys, but the differences are very small, so that the differences between males and females in a class of 30 children are purely a matter of chance. It makes no sense, although I often do it, to see an idle underperforming brother and a hard working achieving sister in the same family as an illustration of the national results indicating that girls perform better than boys in academic attainment tests.

I think that what this means is that, in building up a picture of a national education system, we can legitimately, indeed we must, draw upon the unrepeatable professional experience of individuals, the distillation of other people's experiences as represented in literature and art, and the results of large scale surveys. How we weigh each of those elements will depend upon the size of the effect that we expect to be finding, the size of the sample, and a range of other essentially human responses. There is no simple methodological lesson here in terms of how to construct what Derrida has described as bricolage. Or, at least, if there is a simple methodological message here, it is that we must not allow ourselves to be seduced by those who advocate the simplicity of supposed scientific method, and the idea that there is one "gold standard" in method, such as the randomised controlled trial.

So, for example, large scale surveys are crucially important when examining large scale social effects, such as the impact of race or class on educational achievement. But understanding the mechanism by which such social constructs operate cannot be derived from large scale surveys alone. The novels of Jane Austen or George Elliott may be just as telling in developing an insight into how social class operates in England as the work of Halsey, Bernstein or Rutter. The worst mistake that the comparative educationist can make is to assume that "social class" means the same in two distinct countries, and that therefore they can necessarily, easily, or as it were without thinking, understand the analogous phenomenon in another country simply because they understand it in their own.

I think that it is true to say that one cannot properly understand the English without taking class into account at some level. As Shaw said, "It is impossible for an Englishman to open his mouth without making some other Englishman hate or despise him." And this sense of class as part of personal identity is largely self-imposed, as when my mother went to great lengths to make sure that we knew we were of "working class stock," despite her consistent efforts to move us into the middle class by means of education. Her father had been a hard working, labouring sailor who had died too young for me ever to meet him. But I think that my mother would have regarded any attempt to forget that we were working class as an act of personal betrayal of her father and a lack of recognition of the sacrifices he made to send her to secondary school.

That kind of sense of class informs many transactions in English education at many levels. But there is nothing less edifying in comparative education terms than English sociologists looking at other societies and explaining what they see in terms of a system of social class that they presume to function in a similar way, or an American scholar who looks at England and believes that race functions in the same way as in the US.

But, again, it is worth stressing that in identifying the ideal typical model of a national character, I am not looking for anything that constitutes an essence of being English, American, Russian or French. The behaviour of people is dynamic and fluid in many ways, not least in that our senses of identity are context specific. People change the emphasis that they place on different elements of their identity according to the confirmation or challenge they find in their environment.

In England, I feel myself to be a Londoner, or a person from North London. I only become conscious of being English, or indeed of being British, when I cross the Severn Bridge into Wales, when I have to become deliberate and careful about ascribing the adjective "English" or "British" to anything; in England the words are used more or less as synonyms, but in Wales they most definitely are not.

Similarly, I first became aware that I had a European identity when I travelled to Istanbul and was confronted with that exotic, bustling and in many ways unexpected city. And I become increasingly attached to certain British habits, most notably letting passengers off underground trains and lifts before trying to get on, when I am in Beijing. And much of the time I do not think of myself of having a national identity at all; I occupy some kind of neutral or cosmopolitan territory. After all, as an academic with an interest in education, I share more with colleagues in California or Australia than I have in common with other academics in my own institution, or my next door neighbours.

So I am not looking to identify national character as something fixed. Rather, as I have noted before, the ideal type of a national character is merely the anchor points around which each individual, group and nation weaves its own identity, in a manner that is analogous to a non-random walk.

What impressed me in Hans when I first read him, when Holmes presented him as an appropriate introduction to comparative education, was the ambition that national systems of education were susceptible to some sort of comprehensive explanation. Hans' attempt to produce that explanation requires us to assume that we can step outside culture and history to become dispassionate observers. I do not any longer believe that such a move into objectivity is possible, as there is no neutral, culture-free pivot against which to lever one's observations. I think that the ambition may remain, but the best that we can hope to achieve is built on the foundation of our own cultural biases. And for that reason, self-reference must be included in any attempt to understand others.

Note

1 http://www.youtube.com/watch?v=1tLB1lU-H0M

CHAPTER 7

Holmes' Problem Solving Approach

1   Holmes' Taxonomy

The word problem appears to have some pejorative overtones, which may have lessened the attractiveness of the method to policy makers, who do not like to think of themselves as dealing with problems. And perhaps "problem" is an unfortunate word. "Events" or "Things worth comparing" or "Points of comparison" might be better, and would not carry the same overtones. The first step in Holmes' problem solving approach is to identify a problem, and this is simply a situation in which something of relevance has changed while something of relevance has not changed. In this technical meaning of "problem," as Holmes explained, the word carried no negative implication; it merely identified a point of possible friction, or time lag, in the educational system. I offer this account of the problem solving method on a similar basis, as a tool for analysing events that occur in the normal course of events, and one that I would commend to comparative educationists as a way of focusing in on a topic for study or research. It also provides, I think, a framework that allows the other aspects of comparative education that I have been discussing to be brought together.

I think that there is one other point that is worth emphasising before embarking, and that is that problems, or comparisons, are not found; they are created. The first part of any study is to develop a clear understanding of what the problem is, what the research questions are, and why the phenomena under discussion are of interest. It might also be worth asking for whom it is a problem, and how confident we are that the data really do indicate the presence of a problem. If we think about ubiquitous problems in the education system, we might think about teachers leaving the profession, skills shortages, and a mismatch between the skills of graduates and the needs of employers. But if we are prepared to take such problems, "off the peg" or ready to go, then we are likely to miss some important opportunities for understanding.

Skills shortages are notoriously difficult to pin down. A job advertised does not necessarily mean a job vacant, as an employer might advertise three jobs in related areas, hoping to find one person who could handle related aspects of a multidisciplinary post. And if young, well educated professionals leave the teaching profession after a few years of honing their communication skills and self-control in difficult circumstances, and take that experience from the education system into other sectors, we should probably celebrate their contribution to those new fields rather than complain about the retention of teachers in the schools. And if employers complain about the lack of readiness of graduates to join the workforce, we should at least wonder whether we want the education system to prepare young people to slot neatly into their first employment, or whether we hope that education provides a grounding that will serve them through life and many and various aspects of employment.

So, if we simply pick up the problems and research questions that are widely acknowledged, or are the focus of some current moral panic, we are likely to overlook some aspects that would benefit from closer scrutiny. And it is the merit of a more formal and explicit way of identifying problems, such as the problem solving method developed by Holmes, that it encourages examination of those questions a the outset.

Anybody who was a student of Holmes, or who attended his seminar, will be familiar with his seminar on critical dualism. He would take a polystyrene cup, or anything else that was roughly round, and draw three or four circles on the blackboard as shown in Figure 7.1. Since dualism implies a contrast between two elements, drawing four circles may seem an odd place to start, but it was the first two circles that were the focus of his attention, as they will be of mine.

The first circle represents the sum total of normative statements in a particular social environment. Normative statements are expressions of how things ought to be, and are normally expressed in the form, "Such and such a thing ought to be the case," although, confusingly, they are not always. For example, a normative statement might be, "All children between the ages of five and eighteen will attend a formal educational institution." Such a statement probably needs some translation to make sure that it is definitely a normative statement, as we often use a rather lazy form of shorthand in expressing such statements, especially if they are widely held and thought not to be in need of examination.

"All children between the ages of five and eighteen ought to attend a formal educational institution," would express the same norm, but is phrased to emphasise that it is a normative statement. Perhaps even better would be, "The parents of children aged between five and eighteen ought to ensure that

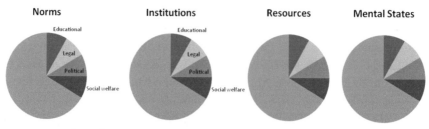

FIGURE 7.1   Holmes' diagram of critical dualism

they attend a formal educational institution." This last formulation makes clear who ought to be held accountable if the normative expectations are not met, and may even be coupled with a further normative statement indicating what ought to happen if a parent fails to meet expectations.

Normative statements, as indicated by the divisions in the first circle, can apply to any area of social life from the legal and public to the private. There are educational norms, but there are also legal norms, economic norms and political norms which may also have an impact on how education is organised.

The point about normative statements, insofar as they are the beliefs of an individual, can be changed at will. "Boys ought to play with toy cars and girls ought to play with dolls," is a (double) normative statement. But I might be persuaded to change my mind about it, and adopt instead the alternative norm, that, "Boys and girls ought to be offered the same toys to play with." Nothing is needed for me to change my normative value than that I simply change my mind. At eight o'clock in the morning, travelling to work through the Beijing traffic, I believe that capital punishment should be introduced for motorists who fail to stop at a red light. By ten o'clock I have reverted to my normal view, that no crime warrants capital punishment, not even parking a car in a cycle lane.

There may be an expectation that the normative values of an individual should be fairly consistent: "What kind of vegetarian are you if you wear leather shoes?" or "What kind of a liberal are you if you want to impose censorship on this medium of communication?" But the fact that one individual can hold combinations of norms which appear to another person to be incompatible is evident in political debates every day. This sharp separation, or dualism, between what is the case and what ought to be the case, has a long philosophical tradition, as I have noted before, and is directly connected to the idea that no amount of detail about what is the case can ever lead to a conclusion about what ought to be the case.

In the institutional sphere, the situation is very different. If some institutional changes are introduced, other institutional changes (although not necessarily unique or specific institutional changes) must follow. I think that the analogy here is with mathematics. Once you have accepted the axioms of Euclidean geometry, then Pythagoras' Theorem follows. The chain of deduction from the axioms to the conclusion may be long, but one is no longer free to choose, at will, between possible relationships between the sides of a right-angled triangle. Similarly, once one has accepted the basic rules of counting and arithmetic, then $2 + 3 = 5$, and one is not free to choose that $2 + 3 = 7$.

In an educational context, we might imagine a change in the institutional context having certain unavoidable implications. If we increase the length of compulsory schooling by one year, then either, (a) we will need to employ more teachers, or (b) average class sizes will increase, or (c) the regulation will not be implemented. In the institutional setting we are not free to choose the outcomes of our actions with the same freedom as we select our norms.

What that leaves as the major task for comparative education is identifying the rules that govern the links in the institutional sphere. Like the process of discovering proofs in geometry, can we identify the rules that will allow us to deduce the likely impact of a change in the institutional realm? Holmes' called those rules "sociological laws," and thought that they would be of the form, "If this... then that...." For example, a sample sociological law might be, "If we make our school system comprehensive (non-selective) up to the age of eighteen, then demand for tertiary education will increase." There may be some more work to do on this sociological law, like defining with more rigour what the terms "comprehensive" and "demand" mean, and how they can be measured. But the essence of Holmes' insight is that actions have consequences, and if we intend to run and manage institutions, we had best try to anticipate what those consequences might be.

I think that I have signalled fairly clearly *en route* to this point what my feelings are about sociological laws. In the first place it seems to me that it is actually essential to have some idea of such links between actions and consequences in mind, or planning is impossible. That means that I agree with Holmes that seeking sociological laws that allow us to anticipate what will follow from specific actions, or whether our chosen means are likely to lead to the desired ends, is of primary importance in any social science. I also hold, with Holmes, that, since any policy maker, armchair advisor or activist must have beliefs about how means link to ends, sociological laws, or at least candidates for becoming sociological laws, must be very common.

Where I differ from Holmes is in the form that I think sociological laws should take. For the most part, I regard laws in the form, "If this... then that," as being too simplistic and mechanical. While some situations may be amenable to treatment with such laws, generally speaking we need sociological laws which allow for the imponderable intervention of human agency, which means that sociological laws will be related to the behaviour of masses of people rather than individuals. They will deal with overall distributions, and provide a sociological arithmetic which allows us to work out how the actions of individuals will add up to make social movements (*pace* Game of Life or Day and Night in Chapter 2) or they will show how individual actions can be derived from the incentives provided to large groups of people. Elsewhere, I have indicated how game theory might be employed in modelling such processes (Turner, 2004).

That is to say, I agree with Holmes on his basic position of sociological realism, that the institutional world is to some extent "out there" in the world, and objective, and that if you push in on an institution in one place, institutions will push back somewhere else, in ways that might be anticipated, but in ways that cannot be wished away or ignored. In contrast with those features of the institutional world, my norms can be wished away as I choose, and so long as I am willing to accept my own failings, I can be the kind of vegetarian who wears leather shoes, or the kind of liberal who wants censorship to protect children for excessive commercialism. That distinction between norms and institutions is central to the idea of critical dualism.

Holmes also believed that the normative values of a society are embodied in legal documents and constitutions, religious documents and philosophical assumptions, and that these, like the normative values of an individual, can be relatively easily changed. And this is where things become both more complex and more interesting. In order to change a constitution, one has to engage with institutional arrangements that may be extremely complex. Raising social awareness of an issue to the point where a fatwa or an encyclical is produced to introduce a new interpretation of a religious document may take a great amount of effort. The normative values of a society are enshrined in institutions, so that a complete separation between norms and institutions is impossible.

Of course, in terms of introducing new philosophical values, I can make a start by sitting down on my own and writing a book, but I may then have to wait a long time before my work becomes typical of the English nation and replaces the work of John Locke. The activist who seriously wishes to change national normative values will also be engaging with institutions in order to have the effect they wish, which means that they will stand a better chance of succeeding if they have a sound grasp of some sociological laws. In England it will be easier to have a new normative value passed into law if it is first adopted as policy by one of the major political parties. So this sociological law may inform the line of action that I adopt in my political campaign. In a different institutional setting, such as the one that prevails in the United States, I may choose a different line of action and go to law to prove that opposition to my new norm is unconstitutional.

So at a national level it is not so simple to change a norm as it is at the individual level, and the separation between norms and institutions is more complex, but I still accept that the distinction is important. There is, in principle, no obstacle to the collective change of mind on the question of norms, and the importance of seeking sociological laws to manage the inevitable consequences of actions in the institutional sphere remains.

It is primarily to this circle of normative statements that the question of ideal typical models of national behaviour have been addressed, as set out previously. If we take one very concrete element of a national model, in the UK until 1965, the norm was enshrined on the statute books that if a person was convicted of murder they should be executed. In 1965 the law was changed, so that a person convicted of murder would instead serve a life sentence in prison. In that sense one can identify an unambiguous point, a specific day, on which the national norm changed. However, as made clear in the discussion of ideal typical normative models, that static view of norms is perhaps their least interesting aspect. One can also see this as a focus for on-going debate, and whether, overall, public opinion has changed over time. One might even question whether public opinion as a whole has ever been in favour of this change of norm, as opposed to the opinion of lawmakers in Parliament.

In general, I have been at pains to try to import into the framework that Holmes provided a more dynamic approach to our understanding of ideal typical models, informed by insights drawn from complexity theory. One can certainly identify moments at which specific norms change in terms of government policy, such as the length of compulsory schooling, the content of the curriculum in state schools and so on. But one can also recognise that not everybody is always in agreement with those norms. There may be, for example, as there is in England, a very long-standing debate about the form that the examinations at the end of upper secondary education should take. Put crudely, there were once high-stakes, specialised examinations taken by pupils in their final year of schooling, where the marks were dependent upon a period of intense examinations over two or three weeks in the summer. Reforms to those examinations led to the inclusion of more coursework and less dependence on final examinations in the assessment, and the curriculum was, to some extent, broadened. The matter has by no means been settled once and for all, however, with traditionalists (including occasional ministers of education) advocating a return to the previous format, and reformers advocating further broadening of the curriculum and evaluation that gives candidates the opportunity to show their abilities in a wider range of contexts than the examination room.

I am therefore suggesting that, while an overall approach that recognises that the most easily manipulated area of educational policy is the sphere of national normative values, it is better to see these values as an interaction between the non-random walks of elements in society, individual and institutional, than as either fixed features or as flags that blow to any passing breeze. The fact remains that it is relatively easy for governments and ministers to pass law and regulations that a specific feature change in an educational system, whether that is a change in curriculum or a new relationship between educational institutions, and rather harder to put in place all the institutional arrangements that are necessary to put those laws and regulations into effect.

In terms of direct comparison, it is important to compare like with like, and to compare either the laws actually in force or the state of public debate in different countries, but so long as these differences are borne carefully in mind, there should be no real difficulty in recognising the norms that prevail in a particular environment.

In contrast with this relative fluidity in the first, normative circle, it is much more difficult to produce changes in the second circle. The second circle represents the sum total of institutions. Again, the institutions cover the full range of social life. There are educational institutions, legal institutions, political institutions and so on. The key point about the institutional circle, however, is that changes cannot be introduced merely by wishing them. There are certain interconnections that exist independent of our wishes, so that if one wishes to bring about changes in the institutional circle, there will be certain aspects, certain consequences, that are beyond our control. In philosophical terms, this is a realist position; there is an objective world which imposes limitations on what we can do simply by changing our ideas.

It is the role of comparative education, in Holmes' view, to understand, explain and predict those connections, so that, even though they cannot be wished away, they can be handled intelligently. He described this process as the search for sociological laws. So, for example, we might posit the sociological law that if there are two separate educational institutions that provide education for similar groups of people, one will always come to be seen as superior and the other inferior. Or, following the judgement of the US Supreme Court in the case of Brown versus Topeka, 1954, separate provision is inherently unequal.

Under the influence of the philosophy of Karl Popper, Holmes preferred to turn this around into a negative format, such as, "It is impossible to create separate institutions that enjoy parity of esteem." However, it is important to understand that, despite the connotations that one might bring to the term "sociological law" this remains a hypothetical suggestion, held provisionally while properly tested, and even then a sociological law can never be fully confirmed or certain.

One might, for example, look at the specific case in the US, covered by the decision of the Supreme Court, which addressed racially segregated institutions. Or one might look at the parallel tracks of academic and vocational education in the UK, which were supposed to enjoy parity of esteem, but where there was never any real doubt that vocational and technical education was seen as a poor second choice. So far, so good, we have a hypothesis that seems to be working, and now we ought to go and look for more difficult cases, to see whether this proposed sociological law holds up. And our evidence will be more convincing (but never conclusive) if we deliberately seek out cases where we expect to find our expectations confounded.

This search for sociological laws is a controversial aspect of Holmes' work, and one that I believe has frequently been misunderstood. It is assumed that because Holmes argued that institutions are governed by sociological laws, he thought that institutions operated in a mechanical way, and consequently he has been labelled a positivist or a neo-positivist. I do not believe that this is either a fair or a sustainable description of his position. A sociological law describes our understanding of an institution, and not the behaviour of the institution itself. Certainly, institutions have links between their parts which imply that actions have consequences that are beyond our direct control; in that sense Holmes was a realist. But whether we could ever come to know that underlying structure was a moot point.

What needs addressing more urgently, however, is the fact that most other scholars, including those who criticise Holmes for being a positivist, actually have a much more mechanical view of how institutions function. Some years ago I was delighted to come across, in the art gallery in Gothenburg, Sweden, an installation called The Fountain of Prosperity. This is a wonderful construction with a tank of water at the top, and the water flows down through various pipes, over weirs, past valves and down into a sump where it is pumped back to the top again. Pipes, weirs and valves are labelled, "Imports," "Exports," "Income Tax" or "National Reserve," so that the whole represents a national economy. The artist, Michael Stevenson, claims, I have no idea with how much veracity, that he found the construction, derelict, in the basement of a national bank of a Latin American country, and that it was part of a programme supported by the International Monetary Fund to set up a network of such machines to plan and manage national economies around the world. That sounds to me like a story that owes more to artistic license than to historic events, but that does not make the story any less interesting.

Several things do seem clear to me however, perhaps the least of which is that the world might now be a much better place if economists spent more time fiddling with the valves on machines that model the economy and less time intervening in the economy itself. More important is the recognition of how pervasive such a mechanical model of the economy is. We speak of "cash flows," of "liquidity," and so on, and treat financial flows as being as well conserved as water, in such equations as "Savings = Investments." And most government policies have at their basis the simple truths derived from such models, that an increase in price will produce an increase in supply and a drop in demand.

It is actually interesting watching the UK Government (or most other governments, for that matter). They believe that they are in possession of such laws. Reducing the salaries of senior bankers will reduce the number of people wishing to become senior bankers, and this will reduce the quality of personnel available to the banks. Increasing the subsidy for the generation of electricity from renewable resources will increase supply. In most areas of life, governments assume that free market principles obtain. But when it comes to student fees for higher education, they deny that an increase in the price will lead to reduced demand. That is to say, the UK Government acts as though the sociological laws that describe the operation of the market are in fact norms, and one can, by an act of will, decide where they will apply and where they will not. Critical dualism should alert us to this difficulty, and suggest that there is a crucial difference between norms and institutions, in that institutions have an underlying structure that is beyond our grasp, and which proceeds whether we wish it or not. Sociological laws are merely our attempts to understand that underlying structure.

What I do think is the case is that Holmes was misled by the underlying links that are used by policy makers into believing that sociological laws would be simple, and have the form, "If this, then that": "If we introduce a unified school system (comprehensive education) then the average level of performance at the end of that cycle of education will be better/higher"; "If we select for entry to higher education on the basis of academic performance, certain types of people (personality types) will be systematically excluded." I have come to the conclusion that this formulation of the type of sociological law that was sought is excessively mechanical. I will return to the question of what I think sociological laws should be like, but at this point I will simply note that I think they should say something that is more related to the overall pattern of development. Social change, as I have explained, follows a non-random walk, and if that is the case we would expect a pattern of development that involves two steps forward and one step back, the kind of cyclical development that Mandelbrot has described in terms of the Joseph Effect. I think that a search for sociological laws that looks at the overall pattern of development rather than a single instance is more likely to be effective.

However, before I can get on to the issue of sociological laws in any detail, there are two prior concerns. The first is to describe the remaining two circles in Figure 7.1, and the second is to consider Holmes' conception of problems.

The third circle represents the natural environment. This is the sphere that is governed by the physical sciences, which is beyond human control, and which can impact upon educational issues. Finding oil in the North Sea has had a huge impact on the economy of Norway (and a smaller one on the UK), and hence has had indirect effects on education. Educational institutions will be open for a certain number of days each year, but snow or floods may prevent this happening, however hard teachers, parents and pupils try to mitigate the effects of the weather. So we can see that the natural environment can have an effect on the way that educational institutions operate. But Holmes had relatively little to say on the matter.

If pressed, his example was the rise of oil prices in the early 1970s, which led to a worldwide recession, with inevitable consequences for education. I happen to think that this is a poor example, insofar as it arose out of the change of norms among oil producers about how they should be compensated for selling their natural resources, and was mediated through economic institutions, which responded in a fairly mechanical way. So it is no easy matter to separate out the impact of the change in the physical environment and the changes in the institutional environment. However, since this circle did not play a huge part in Holmes' analysis, I think that it can be passed over with little comment.

The fourth circle did not appear in Holmes' original analysis, but became increasingly important as time went on. It represents mental states, which do probably need some comment. Holmes had been very impressed, quite early in his career, by the work of Gunnar Myrdal (1944), author of *An American Dilemma*. Myrdal distinguished between higher and lower valuations. A person holds higher valuations, or norms, at a conscious level, and if you ask a person for their attitude or opinion, then what you will gather will be their higher valuation. But a person also holds lower valuations, which they may be less conscious of, but which motivate their behaviour. So, for example, I may embrace the idea that access to university education should be more widely available, while bemoaning the fact that the standard of students entering the university has declined, and refusing to provide additional support for the new types of students who are now in the institution.

Myrdal's work was related to race, and so his example would have been along the lines that a person could espouse racial equality at an intellectual level, and yet still be motivated by less laudable opinions about living side by side with people from a different culture, or about intermarriage, especially as it related to his or her own son or daughter. This is mainly a reflection of the widely observed phenomenon, that interviewees are more likely to give a socially acceptable answer than an accurate answer about what motivates them. But according to Myrdal, lower valuations were more than that, in the sense that they might be unconscious, and they operate behind the back of the person who had them, so to speak. And last, but not least, they are much more difficult to change that higher valuations.

For Holmes, then, mental states provided some sort of inertia in the system. Difficult to change, and motivating action more strongly than the easily changed normative patterns, mental states grew in importance in his account of educational problems, and he sometimes equated mental states collectively with Mallinson's idea of national character.

Holmes suggested that there were ways of studying mental states, and that, for example, projective tests might be a better way of judging a person's mental states than a standard attitude test. So, for example, asking a person about how they thought that they would act in a given scenario might be a better way of testing their mental states than merely asking their opinion on a related topic, which would almost certainly elicit a higher valuation or norm.

Coming to Holmes' concept of a problem, a problem arises when something changes in one of the four patterns and something else does not change. Change need not be considered absolute in any sense, and a relatively rapid change in one area matched with a relatively slow change in another area would also create a problem. Asynchronous change is at the heart of problems as Holmes defined them. Beyond that, there were almost no limitations on the changes and lack of changes that could produce problems.

So, for example, a change in one norm might produce a problem when coupled with a lack of change in a related norm. "We ought to use examinations at the age of eighteen to select suitable candidates for higher education" is a long-standing norm in the UK as in many other countries. A more recent addition to national norms, and possibly only slowly adopted, is the norm that "More children should be encouraged to stay on at school until the age of eighteen, and to take examinations at that age." This produces a problem, in the sense that the increased number of suitable candidates for higher education means that the examination grades are no longer sufficiently precise to serve as a selection criterion.

On the other hand, a problem might arise as a result of a change in the normative sphere and a lack of change in the institutional sphere. In my first year as a teacher I was plunged into the turmoil that was produced by raising the school leaving age in England from fifteen to sixteen. As a normative change, this was relatively easily changed by the Minister laying an order before Parliament. Schools, however, were somewhat slower to change, not having a curriculum that was suitable for the majority of sixteen year olds, and therefore being faced with a new batch of students who found the prospect of being in school for the whole year distinctly unappetising. (That was probably compounded by the fact that they had been looking forward to this year as the year of their release from school, and they were disappointed.) The curriculum, and the qualifications which would cater to the needs of this new clientele, took longer to change.

As I have noted above, a change in the natural environment, such as a late harvest that occurs in school time, when children are both needed in the fields and expected in school, creates a problem if the school system is not flexible enough to change when the weather changes. And so, in principle, a change can occur anywhere, and produce a problem as a result of a lack of change anywhere else.

But in practice, if one was looking for a lack of change, the most usual place to find it was in the mental states of parents, teachers or pupils. Especially in the case of curriculum reform, everybody may welcome the introduction of a more frank and inclusive curriculum on sex education, but the parents may think that their own children are not yet ready for it, the teachers may find it takes them outside subjects that they have been trained to teach and feel comfortable with, and the pupils may find it intrudes into areas that they would prefer not to discuss.

So a typical analysis offered by the problem solving approach involves looking for a change, such as the expansion of secondary education, which has occurred at different times, but in similar ways in many countries. Generally speaking, quantitative expansion of institutions took place while the previous curriculum, designed for a minority of children, was still in force. Consequently, there was a problem produced by a normative change and a lack of institutional change, where more children were included in a secondary education that was designed to prepare them for higher education, but without any expectation that they would all continue to higher education. Ultimately, the inertia in the system could be traced to the relatively fixed mental states of teachers, pupils or university lecturers.

I have to say that I do not care for the idea of mental states. Not on the grounds, which I have heard expressed, that academics with an interest in education find it too easy to place the blame for any failure of reform on the teachers. I accept the merit of that argument, and it is a too often made excuse that this curriculum development or that failed because the teachers had not received sufficient preparation. But I do not care for mental states because they violate my first principle of theory, that, if I wish to apply it to others, I should be happy to see it applied to me, which, in the case of mental states, I am not. I do not like explanations of my behaviour which do not take into account my expressed opinions.

Generally speaking, appeals to unconscious motivation are invoked to explain why somebody else does not do what I think they should do, or what I would have done in their situation. I think that we would always do better to ask why the action that they take serves their purpose better than any other action. A change in scale – benefits in the long term as compared with benefits in the short term, or benefits for the community compared with benefits for the individual – can often show how something that seems not to be logical to me can seem very logical to another. And as I have commented in relation to the Game of Life, the connections between those changes in scale can be paradoxical.

I might illustrate my position here by considering two different approaches to an educational "problem." Over time we have changed our normative values, in very many countries, about equality of access to higher education. We have expanded intakes to universities, and we have monitored the percentage of different groups who attend higher education. We have also introduced policies that encourage more applications from under-represented groups, ranging from differential fees and scholarships to quota systems for admissions. And yet, despite all the changes of norms and institutional policies, many under-represented groups remain under-represented. If we are to bring institutions into line with our changing normative values, we will need to understand why those groups are not in higher education, so that we can introduce effective measures to increase their participation.

The first approach is to ask why, in the face of all the evidence that having a university degree increases lifetime earnings, do these under-represented groups choose a counter-productive course of action and leave the educational system after secondary education. And the conclusion is that there must be something irrational or non-logical that is motivating their behaviour. We, as outsiders, can see that there must be something that is operating behind their backs to motivate them to do what is not in their best interests. And the construct of mental states is designed to provide that explanation. Mental states explain why people do not take the logical course of action.

The second approach is to ask why the course of action that appears to me to be irrational actually serves the best interests of the under-represented groups. There is plenty of scope for such theories. The early years educational provision or elementary schools expose the members of under-represented groups to different, and prejudicial, educational experiences, so that they are not well prepared for tertiary education. The under-represented group face prejudice in the labour market after graduation so that having a university qualification is worth less to them than it is to the average member of the society. The emotional cost of attending an institution where the members of under-represented groups feel out of place and out of sympathy with the mainstream culture adversely affects the cost-benefit analysis of attending tertiary education, which means that it is, in fact, economically rational for minority groups to avoid university education. I am sure that I have only started to scratch the surface of possible reasons why it might make eminently good sense for an under-represented group, whether that is defined in terms of class, race or ethnicity, to avoid certain institutions. And mental states do not appear in any of these explanations.

So I think of mental states as a kind of catch-all, an explanation of why other people do not see the benefit in choosing to do what I think is good for them. I think that it is always preferable to ask, Why do the choices these people make produce benefits that they seek? rather than asking, Why do these people make choices that do not produce the benefits that I would seek? Of course I am not arguing that people never behave irrationally. I am arguing that they behave irrationally less often that we think, and that resorting to irrationality as an explanation ought, as a matter of methodological choice, be a position of last resort.

This has important implications for how we think about a range of educational issues. For example, the evidence is overwhelming that, on average, education is one of the best investments that one can make. So why do some groups in society choose to leave education early? The (sociological) laws of economics imply that they must stay in education, the facts say that they leave. We therefore resort to a kind of pathology, to explain why they do not do what is expected. They must be lacking information; if we just provide them with the right information, they will act in economically rational ways.

Of course, this argument stops short of the correct conclusion. If this information really is so economically valuable, then economic rationality dictates that this group of people would seek it out. So this really will not pass muster as an explanation. It is also noticeable that such explanations are always in the third person; they are irrational, or they are doing the wrong thing. I have never heard anybody say, "If only I had more information I would act rationally," although I have heard many explanations of why different courses of action are rational, despite appearances to the contrary.

Or, to take another example, we have introduced this new curriculum measure, but it has failed in the schools because the teachers are set in their ways, afraid of change, inadequately prepared to introduce the change in their classrooms, or did not have adequate support. We very rarely hear explanations that refer to the fact that the new curriculum measures were dreamed up by politicians who had no idea what it was like to be in the classroom, or worse still by academics who were pursuing their own theoretical agenda, the statutory provisions were half-baked and contradictory, and the teachers were following the only reasonable course of action rejecting a thoroughly bad change in the curriculum.

No doubt there are some teachers who resist change because they will no longer be able to recycle last year's lesson plans. But I think that we might entertain some other options before concluding that all teachers should be tarred with that particular brush.

So, in interpreting the problem solving approach, I prefer to omit mental states, and to deal with those elements that can be treated at the conscious level, namely explicit norms and institutional arrangements. Which is to say, I prefer to think of people, including myself, as rational agents, who weigh up their purposes and choose means that are appropriate to their intended ends. No doubt people do, sometimes, act irrationally or spontaneously, without conscious thought, but if such actions consistently produced terrible results, I do not have much doubt that those same people would bring their decision making processes to a conscious level and examine them. I do not need to believe that all decision making is completely rational to be persuaded that rational thought is the standard by which all decision making should be understood.

Even then, between conflicting norms and competing demands on one's time, I see plenty of scope for uncertainty over outcomes, which means that analysis in terms of problem solving can be fruitful. On balance, I have found Holmes' problem solving approach very fruitful in terms of analysing educational situations, some of which I have hinted at in this chapter.

One of the aspects that I have taken much longer to appreciate is that Holmes always claimed that the first step in applying his approach was to choose a theory of social change; one has to have a sense of how changes come about, or are brought about, in society, in order to apply any method. The methodological individualist will see all change as originating in the decisions of individuals, while those who see disembodied social forces in terms of "capitalism" or "class conflict," or who believe that the discourse speaks through us, will explain social change in terms of those larger forces. But, for whatever reason, changes happen, and if we aspire to understand them, we need to have an idea of which parts of society can initiate change, and how those changes are articulated subsequently.

Holmes himself was a methodological individualist, and he certainly saw changes as originating in the decisions of individual actors. There are some advantages in such an approach, most particularly in drawing attention to the fact that educational systems do not always function in the way that is anticipated. Holmes drew upon the work of Talcott Parsons to distinguish between the processes of policy formulation (which anybody can do, and unaccountable civil servants often do), policy adoption (which has to be done by somebody with a legitimate public position in the institution, whether minister, headteacher or lawmaker) and policy implementation (which can only be done by those who actually have to do the work). This analysis was linked in Holmes' work to a model of institutions that was divided into the public interest, the managerial and the technical, which are often, although not necessarily, linked with policy adoption, policy formulation and policy implementation respectively.

The main purpose of such an analysis was to render problematic a simple and mechanical interpretation of reform, which suggests that the minister of education decides upon change, and that everything else follows automatically from that. A great many supposed reforms have failed to be implemented, because ministers of education have failed to persuade teachers of the need for them, and those teachers have either ignored the reforms, or interpreted them in a way that fitted better with their workload. One need only look at the number of analyses of educational reform that conclude that the main obstacle to implementation is the lack of skills or poor preparation of the teachers to recognise that such a simplistic approach to reform is alive and well.

As I have noted above, a simplistic application of the problem solving approach would transfer the blame for eventual failure of reform away from the teachers' skill set and onto their mental states. I do not believe that this was what Holmes intended, and it is certainly not what I intend, which is why I intend to leave mental states to one side. There may be good and explicit reasons why teachers decide not to implement a specific reform, just as they may have good reasons for not expressing those reasons, but simply keeping their heads down and getting on with their work. The world may be a much better place because of the failure of those multiple attempts at reform.

Holmes thought that a wide range of theories of social change could be accommodated within the framework of his problem solving approach. As I have set out here, I am advocating a very specific theory of social change, which is attached to methodological individualism, up to a point. It starts by looking at change in the individuals who make decisions, but it recognises that those individuals have complex motivation and are following a non-random walk in a way that may limit the choices they can actually make, or the way in which they evaluate those choices.

So, for practical purposes I come back to critical dualism and the division between norms and institutions, and I follow Holmes in believing that problems arise when there is a change in one aspect and a lack of change in another. Perhaps "problem" is not the right word, but I offer this insight into critical dualism because I find it a valuable tool, and a helpful guide in analysing situations. The "situation approach" does not have quite the same ring as the "problem approach," and even Holmes added the word "solving" to produce the "problem solving approach." This overcomes some of the negative associations of problems, and makes clear that he wished to be understood as contributing to the solution of problems, not just creating them.

It is worth adding here, however, that problems, situations or whatever we choose to call them, are created and not found. Just as, in his method for how we think, Dewey made the second step the clarification of the problem of concern, so in any study the second step must be the clarification of what it is that we wish to look at. A predominance of female teachers in early years education is not, in itself a problem. It becomes a problem when I couple it with a changing societal norm about gender equality in all spheres of life. And then, by making the issue clear, I can focus attention on it exclusively (while perhaps leaving space to bring in ancillary issues as necessary).

Increasing the size of higher education institutions does not of itself produce a problem, a situation, or even anything that would interest us. But if we couple that with the expectation that higher education institutions will prepare specialists in certain areas of professional practice such as law, then we have something that looks like a problem, especially if more than half of the students who graduate in law go on to find employment which does not involve the practice of law.

Similarly, increasing enrolments in secondary education does not in itself produce a problem. But if we couple that with the idea that the curriculum of secondary education should primarily be designed to prepare students for university, then, unless the majority of graduates of secondary school do go to university, that might constitute a problem.

The great advantage of the problem approach is that it liberates comparison from constraints of time and place. If a problem is defined, then comparisons can be made between systems that are experiencing, or enjoying, the same problem. Expansion of secondary education takes place at different times in different systems, as does expansion of higher education. Systems can be compared at times in their history when they were undergoing the same process of expansion, rather than at contemporary points in their histories. Expansion of secondary education might even be compared with the expansion of higher education in the same system, so long as the lack of change, and therefore the problem, was similar in the two cases.

A further, if secondary, advantage of the problem approach is that it immediately leads to an understanding that there must be at least two ways of obviating the problem, namely to reverse the change in the changing element, so that both elements now match in showing no change, or changing the unchanging element, so that the rate of change is the same in both elements. There may be other solutions, too, but at the very least the problem approach should remove the temptation to fall back on the idea that there is no alternative.

Together with the overall concept of the problem-solving approach, Holmes incorporated a number of other models that were designed to improve analysis, and make examination of the problem identified more precise. These included, as noted above, a model of institutional structures which he derived from Talcott Parsons, showing the institution to consist, like a business company, of the public interest group, the managerial group and the technical group. Thus, in a school, the public interest group would be the board of governors, who are the body that can hold the school to account in the public interest. The management group is the head and his or her senior staff who are responsible for the day to day organisation of the school, and the teachers are the technical group in the sense that they perform the task that is the raison d'être of the institution. This parallels the shareholders, or the board of directors as their representatives, the management, and the shop floor in a business based on a factory.

In addition, Holmes drew a distinction between policy formulation, policy adoption and policy implementation. Rather than assuming that the minister of education does everything, as too many comparative educationists do, Holmes emphasised that anybody can formulate policy, from a junior clerk in the ministry to the World Bank. But then policy has to be adopted, normally by the minister or by some public interest group. And finally the policy has to be implemented, normally by a technical group, whose support for the policy can by no means be assumed. This provides a rich framework for examining where things happen inside institutions, without making any unnecessary assumptions that an institution must work in a particular way, even if it says to on its organisational chart.

Such tools may be useful, as may others, such as Peter Checkland's Soft System Methodology (Checkland and Scholes, 1999). My purpose is not to be prescriptive about the tools that may be added in to this overall framework. Each researcher will need to select the tools and instruments that fit their topic of interest. However, because of the importance of sociological laws in Holmes' problem solving approach, and because I want to emphasise that we should look at sociological laws differently, I will focus here on developing the idea of sociological laws in relation to Stafford Beer's viable system model and non-random walks.

2   Sociological Laws

At times I find Holmes' account of problems and sociological laws too mechanical, so I have tried to introduce metaphors from complexity science in order to make the view of educational systems that is presented less mechanical, more organic. In general, I do not feel that this contradicts the spirit of what Holmes was trying to do, as he always emphasised the provisional and hypothetical nature of anything that was implied in terms of a prediction.

At other times I feel I have gone too far in relaxing those mechanical constraints. In a system where the flap of a butterfly's wing can create a hurricane, we are in danger of simply accepting that anything goes, anything might happen. At those moments I try to reintroduce more formality to modelling institutions, using more constraining models such as the Game of Life or Beer's viable system model. And in that, too, there are echoes of the approach adopted by Holmes, in his assertion that we ought to be seeking quite specific sociological laws, albeit hypothetical sociological laws.

As ever, the challenge of comparative education is to walk a tightrope between generalisation and the logic of specific situations, between rigid formality and fluidity, between precision and uncertainty. Each scholar will have to make up his or her own mind about where he or she stands on this question. I have argued that it was around such central questions, and in particular how one could approach a generalising science of comparative education, that the methodological debates flourished in the field in the 1960s.

It is my contention that the field has suffered, not so much from getting the balance wrong, as from the fact that the field has stopped asking the question. One group of practitioners has moved in the direction of generalisation, theorising a world system that dominates local idiosyncrasies and makes study of local specificities more or less irrelevant. At the same time, the bulk of work that is actually conducted is highly descriptive, deeply embedded in the local conditions. The latter work resembles nothing so much as the early stages of Bereday's scheme, while never aspiring, or at least never achieving, the overall integration that was his goal.

My purpose in discussing sociological laws is to open up some of the middle ground in the field, to provide a path through which studies of specific cases that show proper respect for local conditions can nevertheless contribute to a more integrated vision of how educational systems work across the world. Generalisation is, as I have noted above, unavoidable once we start talking. Designating a building a "school" carries a whole range of implications and taken-for-granted assumptions. Of course a school in Rwanda is different from a school in Texas, but it is still a school. So at one level or another we have to address this question of how to balance the specific with the general. I wish to reassert that what we should be doing in comparative education is trying to understand why there are certain institutional regularities that are independent of what we believe. How is it that something works in one cultural setting, even though it is completely unimaginable in another?

Let me call the quest for understanding institutional regularities a search for sociological laws, as Holmes did. Like Holmes, I wish to transfer some understanding that has been gleaned from the physical sciences to the study of social institutions. I do that tentatively, as he did. And I resist the idea that what I am doing is positivist, although there will be many who regard it as positivist, simply because I have asserted that I wish to transfer something from the physical sciences to the social sciences.

Where I differ from Holmes is that I think that we should be looking at the whole distribution of outcomes, and not just average figures. One of his examples of a sociological law was, "If we introduce comprehensive schools, the average level of performance will rise." I want to say that this still leaves sociological laws within a Newtonian, mechanical framework, and I want to go a step further. I want to say that sociological laws should take a form something like, "When educational institutions change, they will follow a path that can best be described as a non-random walk." And that brings me back to the theme that I have attempted to use to integrate the whole enterprise of comparative education. But I have not given enough detail, up to this point, to explain exactly what such a law would imply.

I think that it is worth saying again that sociological laws of the kind advocated by Holmes are not hard to find. Most thinkers, even those who decry the idea of the law-like behaviour of social institutions, nevertheless hold many law-like opinions. I have suggested many from the field of economics that are commonly assumed by educational theorists and policy makers; an increase in price will lead to an increased supply and a reduced demand, is an example. The search for sociological laws is widespread. And the problem is not to find such laws, but to dig them out from the debris of background assumptions to make clear that they are merely provisional and open to testing. So in searching for appropriate sociological laws, I take it to be the case that my main task is not to search for hard-to-find laws, but to explain why the myriad laws that are already underpinning policy are inadequate, and why laws based on non-random walks are better. And that explanation hinges on the difference between random and non-random walks, because most of the assumptions that currently underpin policy are based on random walks.

The simplest metaphors that we use for interpreting our experience are mechanical. And the very simplest of those is the pendulum. We quite often conceptualise policy movements in terms of the swinging of a pendulum; "I am concerned about how it will be ensured that the pendulum that has now swung away from tyranny, corruption and oppression, and towards freedom, transparency and dignity, will stay where it rightly belongs. How to ensure that the pendulum will not swing back, nor be hijacked by movements with self interested or unconstructive ideologies" (Al-Nasser, 2012). Of course, if the metaphor is applied precisely, it is not possible that the pendulum should be held back. Pendulums swing backward and forward with the relentless regularity of, well, clockwork.

One of the prevailing metaphors in understanding human behaviour, especially aggregate or mass behaviour, is that of the random walk, or the normal distribution. These two concepts, the random walk and the normal distribution, may not be generally connected in people's minds, so some initial explanation is required.

In 1905, Einstein published one of his famous contributions to physics, which dealt with Brownian motion (Fowler, 2008). This phenomenon, first studied by Robert Brown in 1827, deals with the (observable) behaviour of large bodies (pollen grains, smoke particles) under the impact of the (unobservable) smaller bodies that they move among (water molecules, air molecules) (Fowler, 2008). These larger particles can be observed to follow a random path, moving first one way and then another. Einstein's contribution to the study of Brownian motion was to provide mathematical rigour, and a proof that the overall distance moved by a body is proportional to the square root of the time taken, or $d = kt^{1/2}$ where $t^{1/2}$ is an alternative notation for the square root of t, d is distance, t is time and k is a constant.

The connection with the normal distribution is that, like the normal distribution, in any particular time period, a movement to the left is as likely as a movement to the right, and small movements are much more frequent than large movements, so that, if we look at the distribution of moves over a long period of time, the result is the familiar normal curve of distribution.

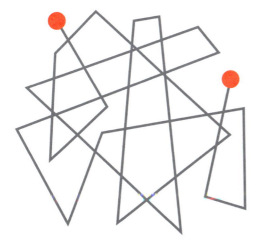

FIGURE 7.2   Path of particle in Brownian motion (from Lee & Hoon, 1995)

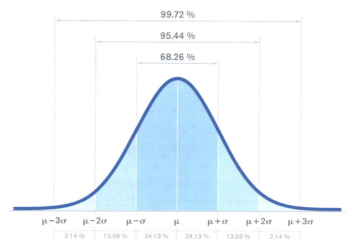

FIGURE 7.3 Normal distribution with percentage of cases in each standard deviation (Mean = μ, Standard Deviation = σ)

Very many physical attributes of human beings are distributed according to a normal distribution. So, for example, height, weight, IQ and many other simple measures of human qualities are found to fit to the normal distribution. This has led some theorists to suppose that all human behaviour, especially group or aggregate behaviour, can be described in terms of a normal distribution. For example, attempts have been made to describe the movement of stock markets in terms of a normal distribution – small movements are very common, larger movements are much less common, and catastrophic stock market crashes are very rare indeed.

Another characteristic of this kind of motion needs to be mentioned; the probability of any particular movement in a specific time period is totally independent of anything that has gone on before. Observers can watch the dancing pollen grain for as long as they choose, trying to work out patterns in its movement, but they will never find anything that helps them to predict what it will do in the next period of time. It should perhaps be noted that this is in sharp contrast to the way that we think about stock markets, where pundits believe that they can gain some insight into what the market will do from its earlier behaviour. It is true that such insights might lead to conflicting predictions, as in the case of an increase in stock prices yesterday, which may be seen by one pundit as likely to encourage investors into the market, leading to a bull market and rising prices, while another pundit anticipates profit taking by those who were in the market yesterday, and a drop in prices. So, in human behaviour we frequently think that yesterday should influence today, but in a pure random walk there can be no such influence; the particles in Brownian motion have no memory.

Finally, one last characteristic of time series like random walks is that they look much the same when looked at on different time scales. A chart of fluctuations of the stock market for the last ten years looks very much like the chart of the fluctuations of the stock market for the last six months, unless you look carefully at the labelling of the axes. Similarly, if you zoom in to look at fluctuations by the day, or by the minute, more and more detail can be seen, and the movement never becomes smooth and regular. This property of "hidden" detail, which becomes clear as you zoom in, is a quality that random walks and non-random walks share with fractals.

In the nineteenth century, a hydraulic engineer called Hurst, working on the River Nile, became fascinated by movements in time series that were almost random. His work has been made better known because of the account given of it by the mathematician Mandelbrot. Mandelbrot characterises the patterns that Hurst was interested in as $d = k.t^H$, where all the symbols mean the same as they did in the previous equation, but the exponent H, which Mandelbrot calls the Hurst exponent, is not equal to ½. The resulting movement, which might be thought of as a quasi-random motion, moves in a rather unpredictable way, first to the left and then to the right, but in aggregate moves away from its point of origin slightly faster (H > ½) or slightly slower (H < ½), than a particle moving on a pure random walk. There is, in a sense, a force of attraction (H < ½) or repulsion (H > ½) between the particle in its current position and its original position, and that can only happen if the system can remember what its original position was.

Therefore, quasi-random movements, of the kind that interest Hurst and Mandelbrot, are distinguished from pure random walks by having memories. It has to be admitted, however, that it is a rather interesting sort of memory. It is not restricted to remembering where the movement originated. A pendulum "remembers" its starting point, and always returns to that central position, the centre point of its swing. A non-random walk is attracted to or repulsed by its starting point, but does not necessarily ever return there. In addition, the starting point of the movement is not in any way special. In its motion, the particle will be attracted or repulsed by every point that it has ever occupied on its path, and by every point that it will occupy in its future.

That makes it sound very complicated, but Hurst and Mandelbrot tell us some very interesting things about the behaviour of non-random walks. Hurst, whose professional preoccupation was with the level of water in reservoirs on the Nile in successive years, noted that what happened in any year was strongly dependent on what had happened in the preceding year. That is to say, if the water level rose in one year, it was more likely to rise in the subsequent year. In fact, Hurst noted that he was likely to get a sequence of years when the water level rose. Mandelbrot calls this the Joseph effect, after the biblical character who prophesied seven good harvests followed by seven poor harvests (Mandelbrot and Hudson, 2004).

However, in between these more or less settled sequences of increase or decrease, there was a necessary sudden shift of fortune, which Mandelbrot calls the Noah effect, again after a biblical character. And this is a pattern of behaviour that is typical of non-random walks; apparently settled sequences of behaviour, interrupted by sudden and violent reversals. Moreover, very small changes are less likely than is the case in the normal distribution, while very large movements are more common.

The attractions of this analysis for examining human behaviour should be immediately apparent. Mandelbrot has used his analysis of non-random walks to look at the behaviour of markets. Markets are subject to unwarranted bouts of enthusiasm – bull markets and bubbles – followed by corresponding intervals of depression – bear markets and crashes – with sudden and unpredictable changes between the two. Violent collapses of the market price are much more common than is expected by market analysts who use the normal distribution to work out the likelihood of a rise or fall of a particular size. And the market looks as though it ought to be predictable, even if it is not.

Prediction occupies a very special place in the philosophy of Popper, who argued that one ought to make risky predictions on the basis of what one believes to be appropriate sociological laws, in order to provide the most demanding tests for those laws. What Hurst and Mandelbrot tell us, however, is that prediction needs to be viewed in a very special way. We may not know whether the next movement in the market will be a rise or a fall. We may not know whether a student's response to a direct instruction will be quiet compliance or a violent expression of resistance and rejection. Individual actions are unpredictable. But distributions of events are predictable, within specified frameworks. If we adhere to the Black-Scholes model of the market (that it performs like a random walk) then we will have a clear view that rises happen as often as falls, and large movements happen with a specific frequency (Bodie et al., 2008). Similarly, walking into a classroom and issuing a direct instruction, I may have a fairly clear expectation about the likelihood of being met with compliance or sullen rejection.

It is worth pursuing this a little further, and I will illustrate the point by considering the difference between a random walk and a quasi-random walk.

I remember hearing a geography colleague bemoaning, years ago, "We have spent so much money on researching the atmosphere and weather movements, and developing computer models of the atmosphere, and still the best weather forecast that we can produce is no more likely to be true than the prediction, "Tomorrow's weather is going to be the same as today's." Taken in isolation, "Tomorrow's weather is going to be the same as today's," does not sound like much of a prediction; it sounds like the sort of thing that my grandmother might have come up with, without the benefit of years of meteorology and computer science.

However, it becomes rather more remarkable if we recognise that it represents a non-random walk. Compare it with the true random walk model, "Tomorrow's weather will be like the average weather for this location at this time of year." Today, in late August 2020, in London, the weather is unseasonably warm, and the random walk prediction would involve an overnight drop in temperature of about eight degrees Celsius. "Tomorrow's weather will be just like today's" sounds a much better bet, even though I know that, in the long run, the weather must change and the heat of summer start to fade. In much the same way, "The performance of the stock market tomorrow is going to be similar to its performance today" sounds like a much better bet that "The performance of the stock market tomorrow is likely to be typical for 23 August."

There is the risk that this will sound obvious, so it is important to remind ourselves that the statistical methods that are routinely used in education make the opposite assumption. A normal distribution of outcomes is assumed, and any difference between an individual and the average is presumed to be in need of explanation: "In the absence of any additional information about this student, the best prediction that we can make of his or her performance is the average for the cohort." That is the standard assumption in educational research, and is so simple as to sound obvious. But, having reviewed some of the background, we might propose a different prediction; "In the absence of any additional information about this student, the best prediction of his or her performance is that it will be the same as that of the person sitting next to him or her in the test."

Am I suggesting widespread cheating and collusion on the test? Not at all. On almost any administrative arrangement that we can imagine for the test, the two students sitting next to each other are more likely to know each other than not. They may have been in the same class, where the enthusiasm of the one inspired the other, or where the more able helped the less able. They may have been taught by the same teachers. Their active curiosity may have spurred their teachers to perform better than usual. They may even have been selected to attend the same school on the basis of their similar ability. We can think of a dozen mechanisms whereby high levels of performance tend to cluster together in some places and low levels of performance cluster in others. Education abounds with virtuous cycles and vicious cycles, where learning creates confidence and confidence leads to greater dedication, and more dedication produces more learning. Or, sadly, the converse.

And this clustering, the educational expression of the Joseph effect, is the hallmark of the non-random walk, the system with memory. It may sound odd to say that the weather system needs a memory in order for tomorrow to be just like today, but it does not need a memory for tomorrow to be just like the average for this time of year. A pendulum has a memory of sorts, in the sense that it always returns to the same place, and oscillates about a central position. But a complex movement needs a memory that can be continually updated, so that the system knows where it was a second ago, and then, in a second's time, will remember where it is now. A memory that can remember only one fixed item is not much of a memory, when compared with a memory that adds new information all the time. And to follow the path of a non-random walk a system needs a memory that can add new information and update all the time.

In contrast with the metaphor of the pendulum, think of two fairly similar pendulums suspended from a not very rigid support, so that they can influence each other. If we set one pendulum swinging, the first pendulum will gradually transfer all its energy to the second pendulum, so that after a little while the first pendulum nearly stops swinging, and the second pendulum is swinging at its maximum amplitude. Then the process will go into reverse, as the energy is transferred back to the first pendulum. And so the cycle will start over again. Complex systems of the sort that follow a quasi-random pattern appear to oscillate, rather like a pendulum, but the period can change slightly. As a result, we may be able to predict which pendulum will be swinging more in the short term. And we may be able to describe the overall motion, with first one pendulum swinging more and then the other. But we will not be able to predict which pendulum will be swinging more even a relatively short distance into the future.

Earlier, I introduced John Conway's Game of Life. And I drew attention to the fact that the cellular automaton produces some areas of the pattern that are active, other areas that are inactive, and occasionally a small particle being fired off from an active area heading into an inactive area. Most often these particles hit a small static group, and the activity fizzles away, but sometimes they spark off a new area of activity in a region that had previously been static. These features are quite distinct and quite evident whatever the starting pattern.

But we can see in that pattern of clustering activity and inactivity, where activity breeds more activity, a pattern in time which is very reminiscent of the non-random walk with its Joseph Effect, and occasional Noah Effect when an area of inactivity can be prompted into activity.

The parallel between the Game of Life and a non-random walk should be clear. In both cases the next move of the system depends upon the route by which it arrived at its current situation, and its present configuration embodies the memory of that earlier activity. As a result, activity falls into vicious or virtuous cycles, with short term repetition of patterns, and rapid and abrupt changes between different states.

What should be very clear in terms of these abstract models is that the development of these virtuous and vicious cycles is closely connected with the existence of memory. Memory is also an inescapable, but often ignored, feature of learning. We often deal with education in a way that denies memory, so that we imagine that a student can "repeat" a year, or we can compare two different methods of teaching a topic. But meeting a topic for the second time can never be the same as meeting it for the first time; the second encounter will be overlaid with recognition and a sense of understanding or frustration. In a process of virtuous cycles, we pick out what we think we will be able to learn on the basis of what we have learned before.

In Conway's Game of Life we see that the history of the system creates a background of more or less static "resources" in the form of some areas that are "alive" but not doing very much, and other areas that are much more active. These more active areas fire off gliders, which travel across the more static background until they hit something, either producing a short-lived burst of activity that then fizzles out, or creating a new area that is active. This might be a metaphor for those active and enthusiastic individuals (active areas) who communicate (fire off gliders) enthusing other people around them, either temporarily (active areas that fizzle out) or permanently (more sustained areas of activity).

Alternatively, we might think of the Game of Life as a metaphor for educational organisations, which capture the imagination of a generation of teachers, and inspire them to reform practices, but the reform becomes institutionalised, and eventually the organisation becomes absorbed into the general ethos of mainstream education, or becomes settled as an area of inspiration to a small body of committed educators. In these terms we might think of the work of Pestalozzi, Froebel, Montessori or Steiner, each of whom has inspired a reform movement in education. While a small organisation remains faithful to the "pure" vision of the great educator, the influence that they have exerted on the general way that educational systems function has been adapted to the background of theory that the new ideas encountered, and innovations have been absorbed into the mainstream only in a modified or adapted form.

Or, again, we might think of the Game of Life as representing the body of learning, partial and fragmented, that exists in the mind of an individual.

Following a period of intensive learning in a specific area (an area of intense activity), the learner will start to make links to other areas (fire off gliders) which stimulate the revision and consolidation of other areas. So learning in one area, such as, say, chemistry, can prompt thoughts that feed in to the way that the individual thinks about biology, or history. And since each individual has a unique pattern of prior knowledge, the links and consolidations that are prompted will be different for each of us, leaving us once again with a unique basis on which new learning will be constructed.

Or in a more cultural and social sense, we might think of the Game of Life as a metaphor for the state of current knowledge, with a new discovery in genetics triggering unexpected and unpredictable inventiveness in medicine or psychology. And some of those cross-disciplinary connections will prove to be sustainable and valuable, while others will turn out to be mistaken and unfounded, and will hopefully quickly fizzle out.

Fischer (2008) has drawn attention to these features of education, involving periods of rapid development, followed by periods of retrenchment and consolidation where nothing appears to be happening in terms of externally observable improvements in performance. Fischer wishes to underpin this non-linear progress, and the appearance of the Joseph effect and Noah effect, by linking it to the patterns of neuronal development of the brain. As an extension of the metaphor this suggests some interesting possibilities.

In general, such systems that follow a non-random walk exhibit quasi periodicity, appearing to have a natural oscillation, although not one with a perfectly regular period. On the other hand, those oscillations are relatively easily "entrained," falling into the pattern of a nearby but slightly different oscillation. The brain certainly seems to have some of those features in common with non-linear systems, producing quasi-periodic activity when at rest (alpha waves) but that pattern of behaviour rapidly disappears when the brain is active. Similarly, or applying the metaphor slightly differently, mental processes appear to be relatively easily entrained, as when one gets an irritating tune, or "earworm," stuck inside one's head and there is apparently no way to lose it. In this case, as in other cases of obsession, the mind appears to be able to go over the same ground repeatedly, but not find any way out.

I am not absolutely sure whether the previous paragraph offers a metaphor for brain activity, or suggests a mechanism by which it can operate. However that may be, it is clear that explanations at the cellular level of the brain are not necessary to explain these virtuous and vicious cycles of learning. Those effects can be equally well and completely explained at a macro, sociological level, without recourse to brain or biological explanations.

No doubt, the idea that the brain is also a non-linear system suggests some interesting parallels, but engaging with the concept of non-linear systems with quasi-periodicity is going to involve a radical re-imagination of cause and effect, and how we think of interventions that shape the future direction of such systems. Simple patterns of cause and effect, such as are sought by the majority of studies forging links between neuroscience and education (or in many other areas of educational research) are simply not tenable. If we take seriously the idea of the butterfly effect, that events below the threshold of observation can produce massive changes in the system, then identifying the single cause of a single outcome becomes impossible.

It is worth adding that the converse of the butterfly effect also occurs; massive inputs seem to have no lasting effects. Atmospheric tests of nuclear weapons appear to have come and gone without any long-lasting effects on global weather patterns, or even effects at the site of those tests. The atmosphere appears to be able to select those events that will have an effect and those that do not. And people do the same.

Whenever I pick up a saw, whether to cut a branch off a tree or to cut a length of floor board, I am reminded that my mother taught me the first law of sawing, "Saw slowly." (It was a joke, of course, as my father was a carpentry teacher, but my mother had obviously heard the first law of sawing so often that she knew it well.) It seems to me that she gave me this instruction often, although in fact she probably only told me once, or at most twice. However, in effect she has been saying the same thing to me three or four times a year ever since, every time I pick up a saw. We seem to have little choice over which of these educational moments stick with us, become repeated and come to affect our behaviour. Traumatic or emotional events seem to make it more likely that we will remember something, even against our will. But, like the earworm, we appear to collect many memories willy-nilly, reinforcing their effect when they are prompted by scatological connections. We can on occasions, through an act of will, or by repeated drilling, select some of the influences on us, as when we learn our multiplication tables or chant the alphabet, but mostly we seem to accumulate them because they fit in with the way we are, or in some way conform with our sense of self identity.

One of the problems with evidence-based practice in education is that we never know where to look for the evidence, in the same way as we never know where to look for the butterfly. Occasionally I have met a pupil who I taught years before, and they have said, "Do you remember when you told us X? That made a very big difference to me/the way I thought/what I did." And I sadly have no memory at all of telling them X. It sounds the sort of thing that I might have said. I might have said the same thing or something similar on a dozen occasions. But why does this pupil pick it out as a moment of great significance? Why did it pass other members of the class by with no effect? I have no idea at all.

What I do remember, fifty years on, is a geography teacher telling us to open our books at the chapter on Norway, and saying, "It says here that the main exports of Norway are coat hangers and mousetraps. Do not remember that. It is wrong." That is certainly the only thing I learned about Norway in geography that year, and it may even be the sum total of everything I learned in geography that year. So it appears to be an effective teaching method to tell pupils not to remember something because it is wrong, but I have no idea of how to operationalise that for good effect in teaching.

The specific lesson, that coat hangers and mousetraps are not the major exports of Norway, may not have served me very well, but the more general lesson, that not everything that can be found in books is true, has certainly served me better. And it is possible that I was, at just that moment, pre-prepared to accept such a lesson and attach importance to it. In the sense that systems can pick out the influences that will impact them, I can imagine learners preparing themselves to learn, sensitising themselves to those influences that conform with their sense of self-identity, but I can see no corresponding hope that teachers can spot the "butterfly moment" at which their words will have maximum effect.

In much the same way as individuals can go over their own history, picking out those things which will be reinforced and become strong influences, and not picking out those things that will be forgotten, institutions can rewrite their own history, giving particular significance to key points. Chief among such points is the organisation's "creation myth" which tells people, both insiders and outsiders, what kind of an organisation it is.

It is almost impossible to imagine being a committed member of an organisation without acquiring some form of that organisation's creation myth. I attended a school that was founded four hundred years ago to educate the sons of poor members of the local community. I then went on to study at a university which owes its existence to the rebellion of a group of scholars at another, older and more hidebound institution, who left their parent institution to found a radical alternative. I undertook postgraduate study at an institution that had been founded to train teachers for the state school system. And so the major concerns of each institution are encapsulated in a story about why it is there.

In a previous chapter I exemplified this process in the case of the University of South Wales. The institution was founded as a college of mining, and that fact is never very far away, either in terms of the commitment to the concerns of the local communities, or in the importance attached to engineering and practical studies.

Similarly, whole national systems of education have long term memory that picks out moments of specific importance and repeatedly revisits them in a process of reasserting the values of that system. The constitution, key acts of legislation, important court rulings, significant events, all taken together make up the tapestry of the educational system that needs to be understood.

Thus, in the USA, one could hardly understand an educational issue without understanding the Constitution, the protections offered to citizens by the Bill of Rights, the decision in the Brown v. Topeka case, and so on. These form some of the key points in the history of the development of the system that Americans themselves continually refer to in defining their own educational system. Similarly, in the UK, one might pick the 1944 Education Act, the 1988 Education Reform Act, and various other acts of legislation depending upon the specific topic that one was interested in. Or in China, one might refer to the teaching of Confucius, the Revolution, the Great Leap Forward, the Cultural Revolution and the opening of the economic system as key historical reference points that the education system has to be viewed against, and which help to identify the current nature of the system.

But beyond that, there is the background culture which helps to shape the personal identity of all the teachers and administrators involved in making and running the system. I do not suppose that many Russian teachers and administrators have read War and Peace, or that many Spanish teachers and administrators have read El Quijote, any more than the majority of teachers and administrators in England have read Henry V or David Copperfield. But they become part of the background culture that is imbibed without reading, through sayings, quotations and daily practices, and which become part of what it means to be Russian, Spanish or English. In that sense, what a novel says about a fictitious event can be just as true of the actual system as anything that is found in a randomised, controlled trial. Novels record the way that people think, but they also shape the way that people can think, in a way that is exemplified by the non-random walk.

Education is full of examples of the butterfly effect, of those who were inspired to overcome terrible difficulties by events which, without the benefit of hindsight, would seem trivial and insignificant. Such instances occur as one-off events, unpredictable and capricious, chronicled as much by novels and poetry as by scientific papers and large scale studies. But education is equally full of the opposite, of events that fail to happen in spite of massive motivation and earth-shattering events. No amount of privilege guarantees success, just as no amount of privation dooms someone to failure.

But this creates massive difficulties for those involved in education, not least for scholars who are trying to identify what produces positive outcomes in education, and policy makers who need to know what "good practice" is, even before they know what stimulates good practice. In the absence of those criteria which arise from the scientific model, such as validity and reliability, we lack even the simplest of guidance as to where to seek understanding.

What should be clear, however, is that we need the most radical rethink of the idea of causation as it operates in the field of education, in order to take advantage of this view of complexity, as exemplified by the non-random walk.

Complexity has attracted a lot of attention from those who seek to understand modern institutions, and our failure to bring them under control in the way we might once have hoped. Radford (2006), for example, examines the way that complexity theory matches up with holistic approaches to educational planning, and stands in opposition to analytical or reductionist approaches where causes and effects stand in a simple one-to-one relationship with each other.

Apart from the original fields that gave rise to complexity theory, which include meteorology, computing, and chemistry, the concepts of complexity have been applied, more or less effectively, to the fields of economics (Mandelbrot & Hudson, 2005), leadership (Wheatley, 1992) and management (Morgan, 2006). And of course, the study of higher education has not escaped the application of these ideas. Most prominently, Barnett (2000) has presented an image of what complexity means for the idea of the university.

Barnett (2000, p. 7) draws a distinction between complexity, which occurs within a specific frame of reference, and super-complexity which happens when there are competing frames of reference. That is not, however, a distinction that is common in accounts of complexity.

A search for the term "complexity" in the literature on higher education returns hundreds of citations. These cover a range of applications, and more importantly cover a range of meanings attributed to complexity. Some authors even argue that there is no such thing as complexity theory, but rather there is a group or cloud of theories which share a family resemblance (Rosenhead, 1998). Rosenhead (1988) is critical of authors who transfer ideas from the sciences of complexity to other areas (in his case, specifically management of organisations) with more enthusiasm than is warranted. He argues that complexity can only rise to the level of a fully developed analogy, as opposed to a metaphor, if some care is taken to ensure that the assumed parallels between the different fields of application are clearly defined.

What I have been at pains to show in this chapter is that too little attention has been paid to exactly how the concepts of complexity, developed in the physical world of weather, astronomy and chemistry, can be transferred to the sphere of human activity. In that transfer process, a great deal of value has been lost, and the insights that complexity offers dissipated, mainly because complexity has been interpreted in purely mechanical terms. As a result, complexity is confounded with the merely complicated.

There is a strictly defined complexity theory, a theory of the complex. It draws its inspiration from specific work in the fields of science and mathematics, and traces its origins back to the likes of Lorenz (1963) and Mandelbrot (Mandelbrot and Hudson, 2005) or to a secondary literature typified by the expository work of Gleick (1988). In trying to stretch this attractive theory to as many applications as possible, many scholars have succumbed to the temptation to apply it beyond its means, or where it only loosely applies, and have therefore used "complexity" as a blanket term to cover that which is merely complicated or intricate.

I argue that it is important to distinguish between the complex and the complicated. The cost of not honouring that demarcation properly is a blunting of the intellectual tool which complexity theory is.

The most important insight that arises from complexity theory is that we need to rethink, in the most radical way, our notions of causation. Because the complex system has this capacity for self-reinforcing feedback, a very small input can be recycled and recycled through the system until it has a major effect. A teacher says something to me, and it has some minimal impact, but it comes back to me on various occasions. I come to understand it better, to interpret it, to attach importance to it, and to use it with increasing regularity. Eventually it becomes a major plank in the way I understand my discipline. And that can happen even without the teacher intending that I should attach so much importance to it.

This feature is the butterfly effect, the effect of non-linearity, that small inputs can have massive outcomes. And it means that we have to rethink the notion of causation altogether. It is not, and this is crucially important, that causes are difficult to identify, or that there are so many factors involved that it is difficult to isolate the cause. Those accounts of causation would be the case in merely complicated systems. In complex systems, anything that might be considered a possible cause is so vanishingly small that it cannot, in principle, be observed. Because we are dealing with complex, and therefore self-regulating, systems, the supposed cause is not effective on its own. It has to be picked out as appropriate by the pupil himself or herself and integrated into his or her own purposes. That is to say, it is not a cause in the conventional sense of that word; it is neither a necessary nor a sufficient condition to provoke the outcome. It is one influence among many others, which has to interact with those many others in order to produce something, but nobody is quite in control of what.

Our conventional sense of causation has to be discarded, rethought and reconstructed completely, in a way that is not demanded by a consideration of a complicated system. A complicated system is one in which an understanding is beyond our resources (Barnett, 2000, p. 7). A complex system is one in which an understanding is intrinsically beyond anybody's understanding, or perhaps where understanding involves something different from conventional analysis of cause and effect.

And here is a clue as to how to differentiate between those who are really talking about complexity, and those who have picked up the terminology of complexity but are really simply describing the complicated: the retention of any classical notion of causation indicates that we are looking at complicated or intricate systems rather than complex ones.

For example, Morgan describes strange attractors in terms that are strongly reminiscent of small, but perfectly ordinary distractions:

> To understand the significance of an "attractor," engage in the following experiment. Imagine that you are sitting in the early morning sun on an open veranda. Before you there is a scene of complete tranquillity: a perfectly smooth lake reflecting the bright blue sky and the greens of the forest surrounding the lake. Loons are calling. Occasionally they dive and resurface. The scene draws you into a mood of complete peace and harmony.
>
> Now, let your attention drift to the room behind you. You focus on the click, click, click of the electric clock; on the gurgling of a noisy refrigerator. A kitchen tap is also dripping. The sounds pull you out of the tranquil scene. Though your eyes may still be focused on the water, your mind is elsewhere.
>
> In a very elementary sense you are caught between two "attractors" that define the context of two completely different situations. As you get pulled toward the one, the other becomes insignificant. (Morgan, 2006, p. 254)

Contrast this with my earlier description of a strange attractor as involving the whole previous trajectory, and one can see the extent to which Morgan is trapped in a conventional, mechanical model. In contrast with this, Wheatley is much closer to capturing the true meaning of complexity:

> But chaos theory has proved these assumptions [that very small influences can be neglected] false. The world is far more sensitive than we had

> ever thought. We may harbor the hope that we will regain predictability as soon as we can learn how to account for all the variables, but in fact no level of detail can ever satisfy this desire. (Wheatley, 1992, p. 127)

Overturning conventional understandings of causation and struggling with the conceptual and methodological dilemmas that follow from that initial step indicate that we are dealing with complexity in a technical sense. And there certainly are conceptual and methodological dilemmas in applying complexity theory to social settings which, in my opinion, nobody yet has the answers to. But we will not find those answers if we try to embed a notion of causation into complexity theory.

There appears to be a paradox here, in that if the concept of causation as conventionally understood is discarded, it appears that the notions of structure and agency must necessarily collapse along with it. How can we talk about human decisions and actions being shaped by pre-existing structures, unless we incorporate a clear concept of cause and effect, and of outcomes that are constrained and bounded by conditions? Even more damagingly, how can I believe in my own agency, if I cannot think of myself adapting my actions to my intended outcomes, cannot match my present means to my ultimate ends, and, in a word, cause an effect?

I want to argue that structure and agency survive this transformation in the notion of causation surprisingly well, in fact revised and refreshed, in spite of any indications to the contrary. I certainly believe in personal agency. Why would anybody who did not believe in their own agency go to the trouble of writing an academic book? I believe that I am the author of my own words on paper, and I expect those same words on paper to have an impact on readers and to change the way those readers think and ultimately act.

However, in spite of the evident truth conveyed by my words on paper, I do not expect any single reader to leap to attention at the end of this paragraph, and say, "My goodness, the scales have fallen from my eyes, and I can now see the truth clearly." At best, I can hope to plant a seed in the reader's mind which will recur periodically, as the reader talks about this or that, as he or she reflects on new experiences, when he or she reads other papers describing the complex or the complicated, until eventually the more technical distinction between the complex and the complicated becomes a natural way of describing the field and of differentiating between different kinds of settings.

My reader is certainly following a path that is shaped by his or her own, personal, strange attractor, not only with its own childhood experiences and prior learning and skills, but with its future aspirations, need and intentions. And of the infinite number of instants along that strange attractor, past, remembered, misremembered, future and imagined, I can only touch the present instant.

What happens after that depends on the reader. That appears to be a very weak sense of agency, insofar as causing an effect is concerned, but it is all that I have to hand. I am clearly free to control my own actions, but so is each of my readers.

Conversely, I feel at this moment that I am, in that very strong sense, the author of the words that I am putting on paper. But on reflection, I am following my own strange attractor, and am operating under the influence of authors whose work I have read, of conversations I have had recently, and further in the past, not to mention my annual appraisal next year and the future evaluation of research quality in my institution. Again, of the infinite number of instants that make up my strange attractor I am conscious of only a few. Occasionally two, three or more will bubble to the forefront of my mind, and I will have to stop writing while I decide once again what it was that I really wanted to write. I suppose that I might say that it is my strange attractor that is forming the words, and that my agency is undermined by that process. On the other hand, my strange attractor is me, and I am the author of it, so my agency is only partially denied.

While I am on the question, I do not expect any minister of education in any country to read this chapter and say, "I see now why I was making such a mess of policy. The universities are following their own strange attractors, and the budgetary provisions made by my ministry are only one instant in that strange attractor that can influence but cannot determine the outcome. I should stop behaving as though the performance of a university could be controlled as though it was a child who can be distracted by offering it some chocolate." On the other hand, I would not have any objection if, in the long run, something like an improved understanding of the structure and persistence (or anti-persistence) of strange attractors led to a more appropriate form of governance for higher education than we have at present. The concept of a strange attractor is powerful in explaining the subtle interplay of structure and agency, and how they can co-exist without either dominating. At the same time, at certain moments an emphasis on agency may be more relevant, and at others an emphasis on structure more informative.

What this amounts to, in global terms, is that there is only a partial connection between different levels in complex systems. While individuals may act with agency and purpose, the resulting behaviour of the system as a whole is not a simple sum of all of the individual actions.

This feature of complex systems, that there are qualities which are emergent, which are characteristic of larger overviews of the system that cannot be reduced to an understanding of the smaller components of the system, is extremely important in understanding the behaviour of complex systems. It means that it makes sense to talk about the culture or direction of an institution that transcends the individual wishes and actions of the members of the institution, even though it does not make sense to talk of such an institution having wishes or purposes. A university may or may not have a purpose in the sense of having a policy goal, or an aim to satisfy, but it cannot have a purpose in the sense of intending to do something, although all of the members of a university might have purposes in the latter sense.

On the other hand, the different levels within a complex system are not disconnected, or related in purely arbitrary ways. Patterns that occur at one level will occur in similar forms at higher and lower levels, in a structure described as recursive symmetry. If we take a fractal pattern, such as the famous fern leaf, the Mandelbrot set, or the Sierpinski triangle, the fractal has an overall shape at the macro level. If we focus in on a small part of the pattern, we see the same patterns repeated at a lower level. And the same happens if we focus in on a yet smaller section, the same patterns recur.

Of course, "the same" has a particular and interesting meaning in this context, as it did when contemplating the patterns in the Game of Life. The eye, and the human observer, can see that a small part of the fern leaf looks like a part of the whole, but patterns do not repeat in identical form; there are slight variations. This has important methodological implications for the way in which we can study complex systems. Inside complex systems, patterns recur with more or less regularity at different levels. We recognise this also as a feature of educational systems, where trust and autonomy at the top tend to produce virtuous cycles of trust and autonomy throughout the institution, while tight control and lack of trust also seem to be repeated at different levels within an institution.

I hope that in the course of discussion I have made it clear that the various concepts used to describe complex systems are intimately linked, in much the same way as the normal curve, random walks and standard statistical tests have been built into the coherent notion of randomness. The strange attractor is a property of a system which shapes its trajectory through time, where every part of that trajectory exerts an influence on every other part. This interconnectedness of every part of the system with every other produces recursive symmetry so that every part of the system looks (somewhat) like every other part. And the system does not respond to individual agency in a simple cause and effect way, but takes your or my input and responds in the context of its own trajectory, sensitive to outside influence certainly, but always responding within the constraints that are set by being this particular kind of complex system. A complex system cannot be controlled or managed in the way that a classical system can. And it is this property of amplifying the effects that fit with its character and minimising the effects that do not that give complex systems their alternative name, often used interchangeably with the description of complexity, namely self-organising systems. Thousands of students and hundreds of teachers and researchers may pass through the university each year, each contributing in some small or large way to the operation of the system, but the university as a whole remains much the same over decades and centuries, in much the same way as my skin looks much that same as it did a year ago, even though I know that all of the cells that I looked at then have long since gone.

Schools, universities and even national systems of education are self-organising systems, not in the sense that if we ignore the rules and the bureaucracy everything will turn out for the best; they are self-organising in the sense that they have a process that seems to select those influences that are compatible with their self-similar development. Thus, even attempts to introduce systems of management and control, or perhaps especially attempts to introduce systems of management and control, will be resisted if they are not compatible with the overall development of the institution as allowed by its strange attractor.

Some care is necessary when describing organisational characteristics of self-management, which might be taken to imply aims and intentions, when aims and intentions are only properly ascribed to people. I do not think that it makes sense to talk about complex systems having intentions, or choosing, or resisting, or any of those things that we routinely ascribe to people (unless, of course, the complex system in question is a person). It is far too teleological. If even a bowl of inorganic chemicals can exhibit complex behaviour, it would be unwise to align the notion of complexity too closely with any notion of selecting and intending (Morris, 2010). But complex systems do behave in ways that can sometimes look remarkably purposeful, in the sense that they seem to be going their own way, or "have a mind of their own." I do not know how else to express it, but I express myself in those terms with some ambivalence.

Complex systems cannot be managed in a naïve way, providing financial carrots and sticks to encourage or discourage particular lines of work. The UK Government has been singularly unwise to try, over the last forty years, to introduce a system of management of higher education based along such lines. Universities have found ways to play the system, to accept those carrots that suit their purposes and to find ways around the carrots that lead them where they do not wish to go. The result has been that policies to widen access or to encourage growth in student numbers, have sometimes had extraordinary and unintended consequences. Gorard (2006) looked at trends in several areas of education, including widening participation, teacher training, the use of targets and assessment of students, and found that policy interventions rarely had the expected effect, or indeed any discernible effect, in a way that prompted him to ask, Does policy matter in education? The fact that educational systems do not respond to policy interventions may itself be evidence that their behaviour is complex.

However, the fact that providing financial incentives has not always worked is not the root of the lack of wisdom in the policy. The real problem is that running educational systems forty years on the basis of neo-liberal policies, where education is supposed to be made responsive to the needs of the market, has changed the system overall; it has promoted consideration of financial criteria and suppressed consideration of educational criteria, and in the long run this will have a damaging effect on the system as a whole.

If we take these various concepts from complexity theory, they should tell us something about how to manage educational institutions. One possible approach would be simply to manage an institution in such a way as to prevent it from becoming a complex system. Complex systems have all of the characteristics that I have described because they have multiple feedback loops and very many degrees of freedom. Reducing the number of feedback loops, and constraining more of the degrees of freedom would be one way of ensuring that an institution was unlikely to become complex, as opposed to just very complicated. A move from an academic structure of collegiality towards new public management might be interpreted as just such an effort to squeeze complexity out of the system and make universities more manageable.

I have to say that I regard such an approach as fatally flawed, not for any theoretical reasons, but for educational reasons. I do not doubt that it could be done, and that a dictatorship can prevent the emergence of complexity. Indeed, I would regard such a policy as being quite reasonable in terms of an understanding of what complexity is and how it functions. However, as I have noted elsewhere, learning is itself a complex process, involving as it does multiple feedback loops, unpredictable outcomes and developmental paths which nobody seems to be fully in control of (Turner, 2007, pp. 142–143). It is also a process in which every part of what one knows is interconnected with every other part, and learning is not a process of simple addition, but may require radical re-organisation of everything that one thought one knew before.

In the context of comparative education, this consideration has further implications. Pinning down exactly what it means to be a citizen of a particular country, what it means to have a specific national character, is extraordinarily difficult, if not impossible. But, even though the English seem to have little idea of what it means to be English, and the French are similarly unselfconscious of what it means to be French, they have, nevertheless developed school systems that appear to be perfectly designed for the transmission of national culture. How the experiences of individual pupils, influenced by individual teachers in unique classroom settings, add up to the preparation of a whole generation adapted to the culture of the national workplace remains one of the unexplained mysteries of comparative education.

Processes of learning cannot be legislated for or planned and managed in a conventional sense. It is certainly possible (if difficult) to squeeze complexity out of an institution but, because patterns repeat recursively through different levels of the system, what was left would not be an educational institution. In a university (or a school) there have to be possibilities for everybody to learn, or nobody will be able to learn.

This consideration of complex systems should give some guidance as to the sort of thing that can be anticipated to be sociological laws, and they will relate to patterns of behaviour rather than simple linkages of cause and effect. In fact, the most general statement, "Educational institutions behave as complex systems," might be seen, itself, as a sociological law. It implies that we should expect to see many characteristics of complex behaviour in educational institutions. We will expect to see patterns of behaviour mirrored at different levels in the institution, although there will be no obvious mechanism producing that uniformity of patterns. We will expect to see virtuous cycles of development and vicious cycles of decay, the Joseph Effect and the Noah Effect, and these cycles will appear to be affected only marginally, if at all, by external influences. And we will expect extreme events to occur with a higher frequency than would be expected if the responses of the system were normally distributed around the mean.

What an understanding of complex systems should make clear is that sociological laws will not be purely mechanical. We know, for example, that the link between social class and educational outcomes is not directly mechanical. While it may be true to say that educational success is strongly linked with socio-economic status, nevertheless there are children from very poor backgrounds who do outstandingly well in the education system, and children from very privileged backgrounds who do very badly.

Similarly, efforts to express sociological laws in stochastic terms, the average level of educational performance correlates with the average level of socio-economic status, and errors are randomly and normally distributed around those average positions, have not been very successful either. We see bunching of results, and virtuous cycles of success, which are typical of complex systems, but are inexplicable in those more classical terms of statistical analysis.

So I come to the conclusion that, although Holmes was right in suggesting that what we ought to be doing is looking for bold sociological laws that would help to explain what is going on in educational systems, I think that he had not fully internalised the changes that had taken place in the physical sciences in the 20th Century, and therefore was rather simplistic in his ideas as to what those sociological laws should look like.

He was, however, absolutely correct, in my opinion, in emphasising two features of sociological laws. The first is that any attempt to manage an institution in accordance with sociological laws will always have unintended consequences. Actually, that is also a feature of complexity, that any effort to manage a complex system is bound to have unintended consequences. Even in a complex system that is governed by purely mechanical rules that are well understood, it will never be possible to know the present situation of the system with sufficient accuracy to know how it will respond to an intervention; the butterfly of uncertainty will intervene between the actual state of the system and what we think it to be, with possibly large consequences.

The second feature of sociological laws that Holmes emphasised was their provisional character. That caution has much more force in the case of complex organisations. We may hypothesise the nature of a complex organisation, and on that basis will be able to create a model of the organisation, and predict its behaviour. We will then compare its actual behaviour with the predicted behaviour, and will regard ourselves successful if the actual organisation behaves in the "same" way as our model. But the "same" here is the "same" in the sense of the Game of Life, some overall similarity of pattern, but never mathematically precise identity. There will always be some scope for judgement as to whether the two behaviours are the same or not, leaving scope for our decisions and our beliefs to be overturned later.

I will add one last comment here about sociological laws which relates to a recurrent frustration I have found in the public understanding of comparative education. Whenever I say to somebody who is not part of the field that I am a comparative educationist, the first question is normally, "OK, then. Who has the best education system?" I do not think that I can be alone in this experience, because it is clearly the first question that politicians ask when they see the outcomes of the PISA studies.

I have been at pains, for many years now, to explain that this is not a question that is of direct concern to a comparative educationist. What is of more interest to the comparativist is why an educational system of a particular form fits with and supports a society of a particular form. The interesting question is not why Finland scores so well on the PISA tests, but what is it about Finnish society that means that it can support and be nourished by a particular form of education. If an effort were made to introduce an education system modelled on the Finnish system into another country, which features of the Finnish system should be emphasised? And would they survive the transfer, or is there something in the receiving system that would lead to conflict, and ultimately to the rejection of the innovation?

I think that I might now try a more general formulation of that particular response. What interests comparative educationists, or what should interest them, is educational systems as complex systems, which in turn form part of larger complex systems of societies. Moreover, education systems are composed of smaller complex systems of schools, departments, classrooms and individuals. What should interest comparative educationists is the subtle recurrence of similar patterns at different levels within the system, without obvious mechanisms for producing those patterns.

Archer (1995) talks about the tension between structure and agency. In a process which she describes as "upward conflation," the social theorist attributes all the driving forces in society to structure, and suggests that individual agency is illusory. The converse process, "downward conflation," involves the social theorist in attributing all the driving forces in society to agency, and suggest that any resulting structure is illusory. Archer, like any reasonable person (not necessarily including all sociologists), takes an intermediate position in which there is reciprocal influence between individuals and the social structures in which they function; individuals create social organisations and social organisations influence the choices of individuals. Exactly how one balances the influence of each level is a methodological choice that each scholar has to make for himself or herself.

But the links between levels, the links between structure and agency are not intuitively obvious. As a result, this is one of the key areas where sociological laws would be useful. The Game of Life offered a highly idealised perspective on how the actions of the individuals concerned might be aggregated together to produce overall patterns. Each individual has exactly eight neighbours, and the influence of the neighbours is well defined so that, if the choices of the neighbours are known, the behaviour of the central cell is fixed. Having established those idealised relationships, let the system run and observe the large scale patterns that are produced. Nobody would really expect the relationships between individual people to be anything like that simple, and it is remarkable that the patterns that result can give us any insight at all into how groups of living creatures behave when they come together. So now the question is whether such a simple model can tell us anything at all, and in particular whether it tells us how we might try to refine the rules that dictate the game to tell us more about how people actually interact.

If the Game of Life offers some hope, however slight, of understanding how the actions of individuals create a broader society, then the non-random walk offers some insight into the opposite process, of how the structure of the environment can shape the choices and movements of the individual. There may be better, and more precise, models that could help to develop this approach, and with any luck at all, the careful study of systems on the assumption that they are non-random walks will help to develop those models.

This suggests that a fruitful area for the exploration of sociological laws is the link between the behaviour of the system and the behaviour of the individual, at least in part because policy makers seem to have particular difficulty in predicting the responses of individuals to system-level changes in policy.

CHAPTER 8

Revisiting the Field

1   The Field in Conversation

Colleagues at the Comparative and International Education Society (CIES), and at Teachers' College Columbia in particular, have prepared a video record of interviews with former presidents of the Society, and this is an invaluable resource (CIES, 2006). I have used it, towards the end of teaching a course in comparative education, as a way of summarising some of the methodological discussions and dilemmas facing comparative educationists.

I have commented on the views of some of those who feature in the video already, mostly to record my points of disagreement with them. But of all of the points made in the video, I think that I found myself in total agreement with only one, when the former presidents were asked to give their advice to new scholars contemplating a career in comparative education. The person with whom I found myself in agreement is Steve Klees. Klees' advice was the following:

> Understand our debates. Understand that there are no correct positions in those debates. Be clear about what your own position is on those debates. And join the CIES and come to our conferences.

If we pick out some of the key debates in the field, all of which I have touched upon in the course of this book, we might highlight:
– Is comparative education a discipline or a field?
– Is it legitimate for outsiders to formulate theories about the people they study? What role should the conceptual frameworks of those studied play in the analysis?
– Is comparative education a science, or an art?
– Are qualitative research methods or quantitative research methods more appropriate to comparative education?
– What part does the nation state play in the analysis of comparative education?
– To what extent should comparative educationists confine themselves to understanding the impact of policy, and to what extent should they be advocates of specific policies?

I think that it is significant that Klees puts understanding the debates first. None of these debates is simple, and having an answer to the question is less important than understanding what the question represents. Whether comparative education is a discipline or a field would be a completely empty discussion about words, unless it also carried implications about how comparative education students should be taught and prepared to study the field. If it is a discipline we should expect comparative education to be relatively self-sufficient or free standing in terms of its methods, its canon of literature, and its university courses. If it is a field, then we should expect scholars of comparative education to be economists, sociologists, historians or psychologists before they come to study comparative education.

Similarly, each of the questions debated by comparative educationists has a greater significance than merely needing a yes or no answer. "Is comparative education a science?" receives a variety of responses from different scholars in the field, but what is of more interest is what each meant by "science." Understanding the debate involves more than just understanding the words.

Klees follows the suggestion that we should understand the debates by advising us to take a position on the debates. That may be, as it is in my case on the question of whether comparative education is a discipline or a field, a dismissal of the question as irrelevant. I think that the fact that certain studies are accorded the status of "discipline" is a fact of academic politics, and actually tells us nothing of value about either the area of study itself or the methods and content of those areas. At the cutting edge of any field there are those who struggle to incorporate new methods and new insights, and whether we call them fields or disciplines makes no difference.

Of course, that position implies certain other views, not least a denial of the special position of the supposed disciplines as contributors to the study of comparative education. But having a position in any debate does not necessarily mean coming down on one side or the other (if there are only two sides).

On other questions I may be able to take a more well-defined position in the debate. I am quite clear that I think that comparative education is a science. But even that simple statement may be in need of clarification. I understand "science" in the context of late 20th Century science and the development of a science of complexity. Please do not confuse my idea of comparative education as a science with that of Noah and Eckstein, Bereday, Holmes or King. It will take – has taken – a whole book to explain exactly what I mean by saying that comparative education is a science, and there may still be more to be said.

One of the central tenets of 19th Century science was that the future direction and progress of science was assured, and that once the scientific method of induction is adopted, the future addition of empirical evidence and increasing confidence in scientific theories is guaranteed. That faith in induction was severely shaken by changes in science in the early 20th Century, and it would now be more widely accepted that the direction of science is not one of inexorable progress; science is advanced by individual scholars who have bold hunches and who subject them to rigorous testing. In that sense the development of science remains something more of an art.

Probably one of the most difficult methodological choices that faces any social scientist, but which faces comparative educationists in a particularly sharp form, concerns the question of outsider status, and whether an outside observer can legitimately infer what the cultural processes, especially thought processes, are in another culture. Put another way, are the people who are being studied objects of study, or are they active subjects, whose own consciousness must be taken into account? Do the reports of people of their own cultural practices have a special and privileged position in understanding what they are doing?

As with some of the other methodological questions here, I am going to argue that the possible options are not the clear-cut dichotomy that they originally appear. I want to argue the case that I can, as an outsider, legitimately impose my own framework of understanding on other people. When I say that a school is a complex system, I mean that I am going to use my model of a complex system to understand the interactions in that school, and that I will be justified in doing that, irrespective of whether that is how the teachers and pupils in the school understand their behaviours. I want to argue that you are following a non-random walk, and selecting the influences that shape your life-path, whether or not that is how you conceptualise your experiences. That is to say, I am asserting the methodological legitimacy of the outsider choosing a theoretical framework for understanding the culture and people that they are studying.

At the same time, it seems to me that it would be incredibly stupid to try to construct my understanding of what happens in a school without any reference to what the teachers and pupils think they are doing. The categories which the participants use to understand their world are likely to have an important, and possibly a crucial, role in how events unfold. Similarly, if I argue that you are on a non-random walk and are capable of picking out the influences that will influence you, I would be foolish to try to anticipate your actions without reflecting on what those stimuli mean to you, and how you interpret them. Since the meaning of stimuli to you is likely to play a major part in your decision to be affected by them or not, it would not be wise to ignore that meaning.

I think that there has been a growing tendency, and in society more generally than just in comparative education, to grant special privilege to the insider view of culture. You have to be a woman to understand the woman's perspective. You have to come from the minority group to understand what it means to be a member of it (and to represent it politically). You have to come from this oppressed group in order to be a suitable role model for the young people of the group.

In the field of comparative education this attitude has led to an excessive reverence for the views of the insider. Only insiders can legitimately describe the operations of the local culture. Indigenous knowledge should be respected. It is not just that I think that such approaches are mistaken; I think that they are profoundly misleading. If anything, the outsider needs theoretical models and rational structures much more than the insider, who may be able to grasp his or her own culture more intuitively. Of course, one would be foolish to ignore the opinions of the members of a culture if one is trying to understand it. But it seems to me that we have gone too far in believing that only the members of a culture are in a position to hold informed opinions about it.

I have been brought up to believe in the efficacy of Western medicine. And I live some of the time in a country where most people have been brought up to believe in the efficacy of traditional Chinese medicine. How should I deal with any tensions that arise between the two? How should I react to the suggestions my friends make to me about my health? It certainly will not be appropriate to defer to traditional Chinese medicine on the grounds that it is indigenous knowledge, although it certainly is. Nor will it be showing proper respect to another culture to dismiss all the provisions of traditional Chinese medicine as nonsense, or as primitive understanding, any more than it would show proper respect to accept traditional Chinese medicine if, and only if, there is support for its conclusions in Western medicine. It is certainly the case that I find it easier to understand traditional Chinese medicine when its findings agree with Western medicine, but that is a question of my personal psychology, rather than an appropriate methodological choice for approaching the truth.

As a believer in and user of Western medicine, I nevertheless have a healthy cynicism about the financial interests of large pharmaceutical corporations. Should I not have a corresponding cynicism about a lucrative trade in wild animal products that play a part in traditional Chinese medicine, and threaten the extinction of a number of species? Bringing about a cross cultural understanding is much harder work than simply standing back and asserting that each culture is sovereign in its own sphere. And drawing a boundary between what is legitimate for the insider and what for the outsider is likely to be fruitless, since both perspectives are essential components of comparative analysis.

The most difficult area where this occurs in comparative education, however, is undoubtedly at the methodological level, where some forms of analysis are claimed to be "indigenous," when they are clearly imports or strongly influenced by external sources.

The point of following through these debates in some detail, however, is not to argue for one side or the other, nor indeed to suggest that a compromise between two extremes is necessary. The real priority here is to understand that, in the absence of debate, the issues have become flattened, and many of the contentions have been simplified to the point of non-existence. Whether comparative education is an art or a science, or whether it is objective or subjective, or, indeed, whether it is a discipline or a field, is less important than understanding the implications of each of these choices for other methodological choices, and how these various options come together to form an integrated approach.

To a distressing extent, these methodological debates have been ignored, and somewhat simplified. Thus we can see scholars (and not only PhD candidates by any means) asserting that they are using quantitative methods, or qualitative methods, as though that was all there was to be said on the matter. Worse still, they may claim to be using "mixed methods" because they are combining a quantitative method with a qualitative method, as though there were only one qualitative method and only one quantitative method. For my part, I prefer an approach that I would call "qualitative mathematics," the sort of approach which involves qualitative judgements on proofs, as can be found in geometry or topology. Or perhaps I might add that complexity theory is, itself, an exercise in qualitative mathematics. But qualitative mathematics has the additional advantage of opening up questions about what it means to be qualitative/quantitative, and whether quantitative methods equate with objectivity and positivism.

But first and foremost, throughout this book I have been arguing for the need to reintroduce the concept of national character. This is not to say that comparative studies can only be at the national level. Nor is it to argue that the operation of multi-national or transnational organisations should be ignored. But it is to say that, quite pragmatically, most of the legislative framework that governs the running of educational systems around the world is passed at national level, and most of the influences on the culture that people are inducted into arise in the context of national systems of education, nationally managed. Attempted "simplifications," such as that offered by Hofstede, really do not add anything at all, and need ultimately to be supplemented by a knowledge of the national character.

Nor would I want to suggest that "nation" is an uncontested and unambiguous term. Nationhood in China, with people of Chinese heritage scattered across many political jurisdictions, some but not all of which are deemed to be part of one nation, is quite different from nationhood in France or Scotland. And many groups which have a common culture and sense of nationhood straddle political boundaries that do not recognise their existence as a nation.

So I would hardly be advocating the adoption of the nation as the main basis for comparison on the grounds of simplicity. But it seems to me that we lose a great deal in comparative analysis if we cannot recognise that national differences are of prime importance.

And then I come to the question of the extent to which comparative educationists should confine themselves to understanding the impact of policy, and to what extent should they be advocates of specific policies. I confess that I have found this one of the most difficult questions. As a comparative educationist, I have seen it as my academic function to draw attention to the fact that different policies are different because they are found in different contexts and are responses to different situations. But in other parts of my professional career I have been involved in staff development, encouraging teachers at all levels to use student centred approaches which engage them in actively constructing their new knowledge as they acquire it. What then do I do with the claim that Chinese students are used to learning things by rote, are passive learners and do not respond well to teaching methods imported from the west?

This, in another guise, is the old question of whether we think we are in possession generalities that describe the behaviour of all people, or whether what we know is specific to the culture in which we observe it. Well, as the reader will doubtless by now expect, my answer to this question is that it is a bit of both. We share, as human beings, in a common physiology and neurology, and so, at bottom, there will be common processes that are common to all learning. But as soon as we start learning, what we learn is specific to the culture in which we are being brought up.

For example, if we believe that babies learn by imitating those around them, then that will be the common basis for all learning. However, once babies start imitating, what they learn will be what the people around them are doing, and that may vary widely around the globe. So I believe that there are common grounds for a psychology of learning, and there are cultural specificities that are built on that common foundation. But I think it is the duty of the comparative educationist to emphasise that which is culturally specific over that which is common to everybody.

Incidentally, I do not believe that babies start to learn by imitating those around them. There is a television programme called Copycats, where members of a family have to mime an action, play a tune, or draw a picture. Each member of the family repeats the procedure, passing the performance onto the next, points being available for how far along the line the message is transmitted before it is lost. What is very clear from watching this programme, or any similar performance, is that a person can only copy an action if they have understood its meaning. The idea that babies learn by copying and somehow come to understand meaning by repeated copying makes no sense to me at all. So, I am inclined to believe that meaning, and therefore cultural difference, enters into the process of personality development at a very early stage.

On the other hand, if meaning cannot be transmitted mechanically, but new knowledge has to be reconstructed and remade by each person as they acquire it – if each person is on a non-random walk and has to integrate new knowledge into the path they were already travelling on – then learning processes may have quite a lot in common, even over a broad array of content.

So now what do I make of my Chinese students who prefer rote learning? Well, I have to say that I am in awe of anybody who has to remember over two thousand distinct characters in order to be able to read. And I recognise that if that was one's first experience of formal learning, one might well develop habits and skills which predisposed one to learning by rote. But I also recognise that my purpose in teaching is to encourage students to go beyond what I have taught them and to develop their own positions and understandings, and that can never be achieved by stopping at the stage of learning by rote. I can only conclude that, if my students continue to learn only by rote, I am using the wrong teaching methods for my expressed purpose.

I hope that some of the opinions I have expressed in the preceding pages will be controversial, because I think that the debate in the field of comparative education is precisely what makes it vital. I think that the field was never more vital than the 1960s and 1970s, when methodological debate stimulated development, together with care in expressing oneself and openness to challenge. I think that the field has suffered a decline to the extent that debate has been left on one side, certain orthodoxies have taken root, and simplistic analysis and description have become dominant.

But what is clear is that comparative education cannot be advanced by a simple description of the debates. "X said this, but Y said that," does nothing to move us forward. Actually, it rather damages the study of comparative education, because it suggests that any of our predecessors can be summarised in a simple and unchanging format. What I hope is clear from what has gone before is that earlier scholars did not so much contribute a view to the debate, as take part in the debate, with all that implies for give and take.

Vygotsky (1997) says that children do not learn an opinion and then take part in a discussion to express their inner feelings. They take part in a discussion in order to formulate their views. Perhaps the same is true of scholars at all stages of development; one only becomes fully aware of one's views when confronted with a different view and one is forced to defend one's position. In the process, what that position is becomes clear to everybody involved, but not least to the person whose position it is.

Which brings us to Klees' third point, which he makes with a smile, as though caught out acting as a marketer for the CIES, rather than as a scholar and former president. It is important to join the CIES, or any other comparative education society, or many comparative education societies, in order to be part of the community that is engaged in the debate. If there is something that I regret about the last forty years in comparative education it is that those debates have become increasingly muted, and presentations at CIES have become less ambitious in terms of the scope they provide for comparison.

Being a comparative educationist crucially means locating one's insights in the context of scholars who have made up the study of comparative education, and being part of that community. But I think that there is something further to be said here, about the convoluted nature of comparative education as a way of thinking. Once one has started thinking about national systems of education in comparative terms, suspending judgement about which is the best, then before long one is thinking about competing groups of scholars in similar terms, and before you know it, everything is comparative. The study of comparative education itself becomes a complex activity, so that understanding the debates, properly understanding the debates, eventually becomes an obstacle to having a clear-cut position on the debates. That is, or ought to be, a corrective to an excessive certainty over advocating any specific policy.

I do not think that I can leave this review of the field of comparative education without reference to three threats, I would say major threats, to the future health and well-being of the study of comparative education. These threats arise as the converse of Klees' advice, from not attaching sufficiently to the current debates in the field, from excessive partisanship in debates that are not well understood, and from not being part of the community of comparative education.

To take the last point first, in the last fifty years there has been a dramatic increase in the number of scholars who have international experience. This is perhaps most true in Europe, where there have been explicit efforts to increase student mobility and to develop academic links at an international level, but there have been similar trends worldwide. This means that there is a growing number of scholars who have international experience and who therefore believe that they have an inside track on comparative education.

I think this is a threat to comparative education. Although I have not tried to offer an explicit definition of comparative education in terms of either content or methods, I do want to assert that mere international involvement does not make comparative education as I understand it. To me comparative education starts from an intention and a conscientious effort to understand the conceptual framework and ways of reasoning of others. It involves what

I have described as comparative intelligence, the ability to hold in mind two contradictory frames of reference without being paralysed. And it involves a hope that one might be able to understand how other people interpret what we see as obvious. Simply travelling does not guarantee a comparative sensitivity. Believing that it is possible to transfer a policy across national boundaries without further reflection stands diametrically opposed to comparative sensitivity.

We face a situation now, and which is likely only to increase in the future, where there is a growing group of scholars (and others, possibly including politicians) who believe that comparative insight is an automatic consequence of international experience. International experience may help, by stimulating insights, and triggering the beginning of comparative sensitivity, but unless we are quite clear about the difference between intellectual engagement in transnational phenomena and physical engagement, those naïve comparativists will remain a threat to the field.

The second major threat to the field is the disappearance of the nation state and national character from analysis. Of course, this has not been complete, and there are still plenty of scholars who make studies of single nations, or who use the nation as an important dimension of analysis. However, there are also those who argue that national identity is becoming irrelevant for comparative study.

There are two prongs to this argument. The first is that the rise of international organisations, and the influence of international capitalism and transnational corporations makes the nation state less and less important, as policies promoted by the IMF and World Bank have an impact in many countries, and the activities of major publishers influence curricula around the world. This makes discussion of global trends in policy more important than national political debates, and the study of globalisation is more important than any local considerations.

The second line of argument is that there are certain cultural trends, possibly driven by capitalism initially, but now taking on a life of their own, which means that Hollywood, consumerism and brands that are recognised around the world are coming to dominate and destroy local cultures. This makes it possible to talk about a "world culture," rather than being concerned with different national cultures.

Now, I think that the trend marked by these two lines of intellectual argument is a threat to comparative education because it leads to accounts of educational systems in global terms, a kind of global sociology of education. And this belief that a single formulation can apply to all situations is as opposed to comparative sensitivity as the idea that a single policy can work in multiple settings. But I also believe that the two lines of argument that lead to this conclusion are profoundly wrong.

First, from the institutional perspective, national governments still pass laws, issue decrees and set regulations for the running of schools in their territories. Even if there are international trends, which of course there are, promoted by UNESCO or the World Bank, these still have to be interpreted through national legislatures in order to have an effect in educational institutions. One of the great interests of comparative studies that I have already referred to is the link between detailed regulation and the general aim of policy. This link is tenuous at best, and the study of how far specific regulations contribute to the overall explicit goals of those same policies is an empirical question open to comparative study. This question does not disappear simply because the overall goals of policy are included in the terms of an agreement with the IMF.

Second, from the cultural perspective, national cultural identity (which does not always, or even ever, exactly coincide with the physical boundaries of a nation state) paradoxically grows in importance with the increasing commercial domination of Hollywood or Bollywood. I have argued elsewhere (Turner, 2007) that far from thinking that the same conditions will always give rise to the same outcomes, as, for example, we might imagine identical quintuplets being completely indistinguishable, one of the major drives of human beings is to distinguish themselves. Identical quintuplets will, therefore, be making every effort to make sure that they are seen as different. In much the same way, even as we all sit watching the same films in cinemas and watching American crime dramas on the television, there is a resurgence of national pride among the Welsh, Scots, Bretons, Basques, Catalans...

National cultures are complex systems and consequently embody their entire history, which is necessarily unique, and which fashions the response to external stimuli. I think that it is profoundly mistaken to think that we will all soon be mixed together in one giant melting pot.

And the third threat to comparative education is an excessive certainty in response to the question of whether comparative education is a science, or indeed whether any study is a science. As widely interpreted, this is coming to mean the acceptance of the randomised controlled trial as the gold standard for research. That means all research including educational research.

In my view the randomised controlled trial should not be taken as the gold standard for all research. I do not believe that such trials give access to privileged results in education, for a number of reasons. Perhaps I should start by rejecting the most common reason given for not believing that randomised controlled trials can be of value in the field of education. That reason is that social conditions are so complicated, and there are so many factors involved, that one could never be sure of including all the relevant factors in the trial. I think that I need only stress here that this is an appeal to the complications of the system, and I want to talk about its complexity.

In a complex system, even if one could pick out two identical samples on every possible factor (for example two classrooms with pupils matched on every conceivable variable) the samples would subsequently interact (the pupils would interact) to produce group effects (each classroom would develop its own culture). Since these group effects are emergent effects that cannot be reduced to a simple sum of the component parts, they are in principle unpredictable, and therefore not capable of being controlled in the way necessary to meet the requirements of a randomised controlled trial.

I have argued implicitly, if not explicitly, that anecdotal evidence, and even evidence from fiction, can be as valuable in some enquiries as results from randomised controlled trials. Methodologically, I think that this is extremely important, and that we need to be absolutely clear of the importance of the professional knowledge of teachers, much of it anecdotal or arising from unrepeatable instances, in all fields of education, including comparative education.

However, we are beset by the onslaught of the randomised controlled trial, if not from all directions, then at least from two directions. The first is from the large scale survey of performance or attitudes, of the kind represented by PISA and PURLS. I do not wish to assert that such studies can never be useful, but if we admit that they are all that is useful, if we accept that the randomised controlled trial is the gold standard for educational research, then education will be seriously damaged. Any innovation will be possible only after extensive trials to show that it is beneficial, and teachers will increasingly be constrained not to exercise their professional judgement. Faced with reading scores that are consistently statistically reliable, it will become impossible to ask whether "reading" means the same thing for a Chinese reader as for an English, Arabic or Hebrew reader, or whether an expert reader does the same thing when "reading" as a novice reader. In short, if we accept that the randomised controlled trial is the gold standard of research, any kind of comparative enquiry will become completely impossible.

The other direction from which comparative education faces an onslaught from the randomised controlled trial is from the increasing medicalisation of education. Medicine, after all, is the area where the randomised controlled trial has the broadest acceptance, probably with considerable justification. But if we accept the randomised controlled trial as the gold standard of research, then medical researchers will have the last word on all educational issues, and teachers and educators will be excluded. We see this already in the field of learning disabilities, where a growing number of conditions are described in medical terms, and dyslexics are contrasted with "healthy people." But that will seem like rather a mild intervention if the neuroscientists have their way.

The idea that learning can be equated with rewiring the synapses of the brain removes any kind of cultural importance from anything that might be learned, and implies a kind of universalism which is the antithesis of the comparative sensitivity. Neuroscientific studies of educational issues presuppose that when a task is given to several people, they will perform the same mental function, and therefore have the same brain activity, which can be studied empirically. So, for example, it is assumed that when several people are given a long multiplication to perform, they will all perform the same mental functions, which can be described as "multiplying." We can then look for the areas of the brain that are involved in "multiplying." What teachers know, but apparently medics do not, is that some of those people will be multiplying, while others are mentally adding up long columns of numbers and yet others are mentally counting on their fingers and toes.

We have a tendency to reify things that we can categorise under a single heading and name. Reading, writing, driving, singing or performing calculations are all complex functions that not only involve many sub-activities, but also change according to our purposes and experience. If we wanted to know what mental operations were involved in driving a car, we might take measurements from the scalp of a number of people to see which parts of the brain control driving. But why it should be assumed that I, who have spent years studying engineering and my formative years under cars, should be thinking the same thing as somebody who has learned to drive but knows nothing about the machinery involved, is a mystery known only to neuroscientists.

At the present time, the hubris of neuroscientists in asserting that they have just discovered that it is a good idea to get some exercise in between long sessions sitting still, or that a person should be given both the big picture and attention to detail in order to learn, may be amusing. But if we accept that the method that they employ is appropriate for studying educational issues, even in principle, then comparative studies of education are doomed. It is important for us to argue, and to argue vociferously, that teachers understand something about education that is of value, which does not come from randomised controlled trials and which neuroscientists need to take into account.

Quite apart from anything else, the randomised controlled trial is based upon the conventional notion of causation, and that good policy will necessarily cause good outcomes. Not the least among the bad effects of adopting the randomised controlled trial as the standard to which research should aspire is that it will hinder the re-examination of the concept of "cause" that is necessary for developing a sense of complexity, and which I have advocated.

So I think that there are some serious threats, both practical and theoretical, to the future of a healthy comparative education, and the field will only continue in good health if we confront those explicitly. Most importantly, we do need to maintain a reflective contact with our past, not in a deferential way, but with an awareness of where our discipline comes from. I think that some of this sense of the past has been lost, at least in part because scholars now are in too much of a hurry just to get on and make comparisons. This also implies an attitude to what counts as research that I think is somewhat unfortunate. Research, and that is often "Research" with a capital "R," is seen as something active. It involves going somewhere – in the case of comparative research, going overseas – or interviewing somebody, or at the very least handing out a questionnaire. The reflective, contemplative, theoretical aspects of research get ignored, with the damaging result that assumptions are made, and by implication one side of our debates is presumed to be in the right. This seems to me to be very far from the comparative approach.

2   Conclusions

What I have tried to do here is to give a personal reflection on the field, discipline, area or study of comparative education. When I first studied comparative education, normal academic conventions required that writing should be impersonal. We went to extraordinary lengths to avoid writing "I." In the opinion of the author of this book, that was a mistake, and, largely thanks to the efforts of feminist theorists, we have been liberated from that rather stiff form of expression, at the same time as we have been encouraged to locate the research in the context of the personal experience of the researcher.

That general position suits my purposes rather well, as I have been at pains to stress the importance of the one-off experience and the anecdotal as the basis of sound professional knowledge. So I offer this account of how my own, one-off and unrepeatable experience creates my understanding of comparative education, a field of study that I obviously regard as important in both theoretical and practical terms.

But this is more than a mere change in writing style, or academic conventions. It goes hand in hand with a recognition that the observer is important in framing the description of events that we receive. The 19th Century goal of producing accounts that were independent of the observer were wrong, in the sense that they aspired to a neutral objectivity. From where I view theoretical discussions, the publication of the special theory of relativity in the early years of the 20th Century changed all that, but not in the way that is commonly supposed. Ironically, the theory of relativity is not a theory of relativism, that everything depends on the viewpoint of the observer. On the contrary, Einstein's assertion was that relativity involves a methodological preference for statements that are true for any observer, whatever his or her frame of reference. That means that the goal of relativity is not a science that ignores the observer, but one that recognises the subjectivity of each observer, and then looks for what they have that can be described in universal ways.

I think that is a reasonable metaphor for what I hope we aim for in comparative education; a recognition of cultural specificity coupled with an ambition to overcome it and to understand how cross-cultural dialogue is possible. I do not expect that ambition to be easily achieved, but I am sure that it can only be achieved through a process of self-reflection and self-awareness.

I came to the study of comparative education in the late 1970s. The 1960s had seen a burgeoning of theoretical reflection on the nature of comparative education, and had produced such seminal works as the major works of Bereday, Holmes, King, Mallinson, Noah and Eckstein, among others. In addition, the institutional base of societies of comparative education and the organs of UNESCO and the IBE had been established. By the 1970s, much of that explicit debate had been spent, although some of the personal animosities lingered on and one could not help being aware of some of the tensions.

At a personal level, I found that atmosphere very uncomfortable. I do not like conflict, and will go to considerable lengths to avoid it. But in methodological terms that period seems to me to have been extraordinarily productive. It has been superseded by the present situation, where methodological reflection seems to be seen as superfluous. There is a spirit abroad that we can forget about the thorny questions of how one does comparative education, and can, or should, just get on and do it. At best, the result is an anodyne set of comparisons which more or less reflect Bereday's vision of the field, normally not progressing far beyond juxtaposition. At worst, the products of comparison resemble the output of the CIA World Factbook (CIA, 2014), providing a series of statistics about the land, the population and the country's resources, but very little that is a serious attempt to understand another culture.

When I launched into the field of comparative education, there was a serious shortage of data. Finding out the simplest facts about a foreign educational system was difficult, and frequently involved travel, which was also difficult. Today, the situation has changed radically. Anybody can go to the website of the UNESCO Institute for Statistics and download more data than can reasonably be imagined. After that he or she can go to the OECD website and download the data from "Education at a Glance," and details of PISA and PURLS. Any further shortage of data can be made good by the World Bank, and that is before starting to trawl the internet for the websites of national ministries of education. The major difficulty with conducting studies in comparative education is no longer the lack of data. Nor, would I say, is it the surfeit of data, although trying to deal with all the data that is available could certainly produce a nasty case of indigestion.

The real threat to comparative education is that we take all that data as, well, "data" or "given." Data should be our starting point for reflection and interrogation, not the end point. The fact that we can find data on literacy rates in 180 countries should not blind us to the recognition that what it means to read, what it means to be literate, is itself problematic. What level of literacy counts as "being literate"? What is this literacy for? Is it just about converting symbols on paper into sounds, filling in application forms and following the news, important though those things may be, or is it about something more? Does reading have a special place in this culture, or in that?

Of course, it is better to start that reflection from the data, as one can today, than to start without it. Reflection and analysis can get further, have a keener edge today, than it could forty years ago, when one could only speculate about what the data were likely to show. But data is always collected for a purpose, and that purpose may shape the data that is available. Critical questioning is always needed as well.

There is the serious danger that comparative education allows its agenda to be driven by the needs of policy makers. While policy makers are important, and have always been an important element in the mix that is comparative education, they are not the sole reason for the existence of the field of study.

We see a great deal of interest focused, at the moment, on the notion of "world class universities," with a corresponding concern over league tables and ranking systems. I have an interest in that field myself, and have written about the arbitrariness of such rankings. However, standing back from the mechanics of rankings, the concept of world class universities is driven by a policy imperative, that governments around the world have decided that they cannot afford to fund all universities on the same basis as they have been funded in the past. This leads to a discourse around the need to focus resources in "centres of excellence," and the need to produce a "critical mass" of researchers in any subject area. It may, in some circumstances, make sense to focus resources in cryogenics or particle physics in one or two centres of excellence, but whether this is a model that should be applied to all disciplines should at least be open to question. There is plenty for comparative educationists to be interested in here; should the same policies be applied to all areas of scientific endeavour? Is there evidence that the concept of a critical mass applies in all areas of knowledge? And if it does, how big is it? And are there other considerations, especially in the fields of education and health care, which speak to the need to have resources distributed across the country, rather than concentrated in specific centres of excellence?

That is to say, university rankings and the concept of the world class university may well be important topics for comparative education, but we should not allow ourselves to take the question as posed by policy makers as definitive for the field. What is needed are studies that critically examine the underpinnings of the problem, the way that the problem has been made, from every possible angle. And that can only be done in a spirit of self-awareness and critical examination.

I have already mentioned the idea of complexity, and suggested that it is in the fractal nature of complexity, in the fact that as one focuses in closer, more detail is revealed, that complexity incorporates the notion of super-complexity. I have also suggested that the study of education has this fractal nature also, in the sense that what we learn about education has ramifications at the individual level, the institutional level and the societal level. If that is true of the study of education in general, it must be much more evidently the case of comparative education. Deciding what to compare does not only relate to the matter that is to be compared, but also the method of comparison to be employed. Before one has gone very far one is in a labyrinth of comparative comparative education – a Holmsean analysis leads this way while a Bereday analysis leads that; the Chinese view this phenomenon in this way, the French in that. Comparative education is not to be exhaustively described in terms of its content matter or its methods; it is the dynamic interplay of content and methods, and the transformation that is wrought by turning any method back upon itself that leads to the endless fascination, and that means there will always be something more to learn.

In the public understanding of education, a number of simplistic and mechanical models of education are prevalent. Politicians and policy makers frequently talk about education in terms that can best be described as a transmission model; education is driven by teachers, who transmit knowledge, while learners are passive receivers.

In actual fact, this vision of education as some kind of mechanical process influences educational research far beyond the confines of comparative education. Most educational research has been on the basis of identifying prior causes of educational outcomes, in the old fashioned sense of causation described by Mill. But in the very nature of education, much of the focus of educational activity is on the future. This is one reason for stressing that the notion of causation embodied in the strange attractor, whatever it is (and I have to say again here that I think that there is some serious theoretical rethinking that needs to be done to be sure what that is), involves attraction to all points along the future strange attractor as well as all points of the past. What we will become is as important for understanding education as antecedent causes.

In comparative education this obsession with antecedent causes has led to an emphasis on identifying the prior causes of success in the PISA process, and by implication of identifying those evidence-based policies which can be relied upon in all circumstances, and irrespective of cultural context, to produce the desired results. Although there has been some criticism of such evidence-based approaches in the literature, or focusing on what works, this has not yet been linked with the corresponding critique of method, and the need for a radical re-evaluation of what we understand by causation, which I hope that I have pointed to here.

The programme of re-evaluation that I am indicating here is by no means going to be easy. All of those models that we have used unthinkingly will need to be re-examined. A first step, but only a first step, is the recognition that we are still very heavily reliant on those mechanical models, especially when it comes to framing questions about the psychology of learning. It is a relatively small leap from the thought that all learning must in some way be embodied, to the thought that it must be embodied in all people in the same way, and that therefore we can go and look for the embodiment of processes in brain scans.

The dominant metaphor in education has moved from the machinery of the steam engine to the computer, but it is still the metaphor of machinery to most researchers. The idea that the brain can be understood by analogy to the computer seems not to include the idea that different brands of computer can perform very similar looking functions with very diverse underlying mechanisms. One of the fascinations of cross-cultural study is the recognition that people may be doing something that I recognise as familiar, but that their reasoning about that performance is completely alien, or, mutatis mutandis, that they do something very strange, but for reasons that I recognise as familiar.

We live, and we think, for the most part with a heritage that comes to us from the 20th Century and includes such mechanical approaches as behaviourism. A major element in this thinking is the idea that people can learn by a process of imitation. In this scheme of things, we are presumed to learn actions first, and attach meaning and significance to them later. That this is patent nonsense can be seen in simple children's games. One such game is presented as a television games show called "Copycats," which I mentioned before. What is evident from even the most cursory viewing of these activities is that a person can only copy a picture or an action to the extent that they understand what it means.

This is not a particularly new thought. Vygotsky (1997) pointed out that the problem of a theory of learning by imitation is that it does not explain the selection and construction of what is to be imitated. In order to imitate, the imitator must already know, or must decide, which aspects are fundamental and which are merely accidental. Burgess (2002) notes that the word "pedagogy" derives from the word for the slave employed to take children to school in ancient Greece. It was, he adds, common practice to make the slave drunk and to laugh at the foolish actions of one intoxicated, which ought, as Burgess notes, disabuse anybody who thinks that teaching by example can be effective.

Reflecting on these various points must lead to the conclusion that learning and education, far from being a mechanical process of transmission involve the learner in a complex process of selecting the influences which will influence him or her. And that, in turn, implies that culture, far from being something that is absorbed through learning, plays an active role in selecting what is learned and how it is learned. I hope that even that brief description will conjure up an image of a strange attractor and a system that responds to stimuli at the level of the flap of a butterfly's wing.

The task of re-imagining educational research on the basis of that underlying metaphor will require a great deal of further effort. It will involve thinking "outside the box," to use a cliché which is now firmly established inside the box. And it has been the fascination, as well as the challenge, of comparative education that it has required constant effort to try to move beyond the limitations of the ideas that we hold at any specific moment.

In the concluding paragraphs of this book, I cannot offer a simple recipe for doing comparative education research well, or for escaping from the discussions and debates that I have alluded to throughout this volume. In the early 1990s there was a fascinating debate in the pages of *Evaluation and Research in Education*, between Harvey Goldstein and Anand Desai about the use of data envelope analysis (DEA) in the social sciences. In terms of their general positions, Desai was in favour of using it for exploratory and indicative investigation, while Goldstein was against its use, preferring the multi-level statistical analysis methods he had done so much to develop. For the most part the two protagonists talk past each other without developing a better understanding.

I should perhaps add that I have used DEA, and have found it useful, and I am generally disposed to accept Desai's argument. However, in the course of the argument, or in summing up the argument, Goldstein says something that I find extremely significant:

> The difficulty with DEA is that it cannot by itself establish the nature of the true relationship between the output and input variables. (Goldstein, 1992, p. 43)

In other words, for Goldstein there is no doubt that there is a "true relationship" between variables that is out there in the world waiting to be discovered.

For Desai, however, that is exactly the question that is open to doubt, and which can be explored through DEA. Their disagreement cuts through all of the ways in which they view social phenomena, because they start from different assumptions.

As a corrective to this difficulty, I have argued that what we need to do is to use more explicit modelling of educational processes. This is not, on its own, a complete solution. Goldstein's explicit models (and he is very committed to explicit models) incorporate his assumptions, as Desai's explicit models incorporate his, and my explicit models incorporate mine. We cannot reason about education at all without making some assumptions. But by using explicit modelling we may hope to make those assumptions more visible, and more open to examination.

And herein lies the difficulty. In order to study anything, but especially anything in education, one has to make certain assumptions about what one can see and how one can interpret it. And those assumptions will have a direct impact on what one can see and how one interprets it. There is no way out of this bind, but one has always to proceed with the thought at the back of one's mind that those initial assumptions may be wrong. Philosophical and methodological decisions have to be made, but one may always find, at the end of a long study, that all one is seeing is the implications of those assumptions in practical terms.

And so, if I end up where I started, the reason that it is so difficult to offer a definition of comparative education is because an inescapable element of comparative education is a commitment to problematise comparison, and a resistance to reification, which, taken together, make a simple definition of comparative education impossible.

References

Al-Nasser, N. A. (2012, May 3). *The Middle East and North Africa at the Dawn of the 21st Century: Challenges and hopes*. Address of the President to the 66th Session of the General Assembly of the United Nations. Retrieved February 27, 2015, from http://www.un.org/en/ga/president/66/statements/middleeast_northafrica_hopes030512.shtml

Archer, M. S. (1979). *Social origins of educational systems*. Cambridge University Press.

Archer, M. S. (1995). *Realist social theory: The morphogenetic approach*. Cambridge University Press.

Ariely, D. (2009). *Predictably irrational: The hidden forces that shape our decisions*. Harper.

Barnett, R. (2000). *Realizing the university in an age of supercomplexity*. SRHE and Open University Press.

Beer, S. (2009). *Think before you think*. Wavestone Press.

Bereday, G. Z. F. (1964). *Comparative method in education*. Holt, Rinehart and Winston.

Bodie, Z., Kane, A., & Marcus, A. J. (2008). *Investments* (7th ed.). McGraw-Hill.

Borges, J. L. (1970). *Labyrinths: Selected stories and other writings*. Penguin Books.

Burgess, T. (2002). *The devil's dictionary of education*. Continuum.

Checkland, P., & Scholes, J. (1999). *Soft systems methodology in action*. Wiley.

CIA. (2014). *The CIA world factbook*. CIA. Retrieved February 27, 2015, from https://www.cia.gov/library/publications/the-world-factbook/

CIES. (2006). *Comparatively speaking: An oral history of the first 50 years of the Comparative & International Education Society. Columbia University*. Retrieved February 27, 2015, from https://www.youtube.com/watch?v=RZXKr7lSOnY

Davenport, W. (1960). Jamaican fishing: A game theory analysis. In S. W. Mitz (Ed.), *Papers in Caribbean anthropology* (pp. 3–11). Yale University.

Delamont, S. (2005). Four great gates: Dilemmas, directions and distractions in educational research. *Research Papers in Education, 20*(1), 85–100.

Derrida, J. (2001). Structure, sign and play in the discourse of the human sciences. In *Writing and difference* (A. Bass, Trans., pp. 351–370). Routledge.

Dewey, J. (1910). *How we think*. Heath and Co.

Eckstein, M. A. (1970). Toward a strategy of urban-educational study. In J. A. Lauwerys & D. Scanlon (Eds.), *World year book of education 1970*. Evans.

Eckstein, M. A. (1983). The comparative mind: Metaphor in comparative education. *Comparative Education Review, 27*, 311–323.

Epstein, E. H. (1983). Currents left and right: Ideology in comparative education. *Comparative Education Review, 27*(1), 3–29.

Fischer, K. W. (2008). Dynamic cycles of cognitive and brain development: Measuring growth in mind, brain, and education. In A. M. Battro, K. W. Fischer, & P. Léna (Eds.), *The educated brain* (pp. 127–150). Cambridge University Press.

Fowler, M. (2008). *Brownian motion*. Retrieved February 27, 2014, from http://galileo.phys.virginia.edu/classes/152.mf1i.spring02/BrownianMotion.htm

Gardner, M. (1970). Mathematical games – The fantastic combinations of John Conway's new solitaire game "life." *Scientific American, 223*, 120–123.

Glaser, B., & Strauss, A. (1967). *The discovery of grounded theory: Strategies for qualitative research*. Aldine.

Gleick, J. (1988). *Chaos: Making a new science*. Penguin.

Gorard, S. (2006). Does policy matter in education? *International Journal of Research and Method in Education, 29*(1), 5–21.

Gu, M. (2013). *Cultural foundations of Chinese education*. Brill.

Hannaford, I. (1996). *Race: The history of an idea in the West*. Johns Hopkins University Press.

Hans, N. (1967). *Comparative education: A study of educational factors and tradition*. Routledge.

Heidegger, M. (1971). *Poetry, language, thought*. HarperCollins.

Hilder, T. (1995). The viable system model. Cavendish Software. Retrieved February 27, 2015, from http://www.flowmap.com/documents/vsm.pdf

Hofstede, G. H. (2001). *Cultures consequences: Comparing values, behaviours, institutions and organizations across nations* (2nd ed.). Sage Publications.

Hume, D. (1969). *A treatise of human nature*. Penguin Books. (Original work published 1739)

Hurst, H. E. (1951). Long-term storage capacity of reservoirs. *Transactions of the American Society of Civil Engineers, 116*, 770–799.

Kant, I. (2007). *Critique of pure reason*. Penguin Books. (Original work published in German in 1781)

Kuhn, T. S. (1962). *The structure of scientific revolutions*. University of Chicago Press.

Lee, H. (1963). *To kill a mockingbird*. Penguin.

Lee, Y. K., & Hoon, K. (1995). Brownian motion: The research goes on...." *Surprise 95, 4*. Retrieved February 27, 2015, from http://www.doc.ic.ac.uk/~nd/surprise_95/journal/vol4/ykl/report.html

Libet, B., Gleason, C. A., Wright, E. W., & Pearl, D. K. (1983). Time of conscious intention to act in relation to onset of cerebral activity (readiness-potential) – The unconscious initiation of a freely voluntary act. *Brain, 106*, 623–642.

Lorenz, E. N. (1963). Deterministic nonperiodic flow. *Journal of the Atmospheric Sciences, 20*, 130–141.

McDowell, J. (1994). *Mind and world*. Harvard University Press.

McIntyre, D. (2013). *On equal terms*. University of South Wales.

REFERENCES

McLean, M. (1981). *Joseph A. Lauwerys: A festschrift.* University of London, Institute of Education Library.

Mallinson, V. (1966). *An introduction to the study of comparative education.* Heinemann.

Mandelbrot, B. B., & Hudson, R. L. (2004). *The mis-behaviour of markets: A fractal view of risk, ruin and reward.* Profile Books.

Martin, E. (2010). *John Conway's game of life.* Retrieved February 27, 2015, from http://www.bitstorm.org/gameoflife/

Mason, M. (2007). Comparing cultures. In M. Bray, B. Adamson, & M. Mason (Eds.), *Comparative education research: Approaches and methods* (pp. 165–196). Comparative Education research Centre, University of Hong Kong/Springer.

Merriam, C. E. (1966). *The making of citizens.* Teachers College Press.

Mill, J. S. (2012). *A system of logic, ratiocinative and inductive: Being a connected view of the principles of evidence, and the methods of scientific investigation.* (Cambridge: Cambridge University Press. (Original work published 1843)

Morgan, G. (2006). *Images of organization.* Sage.

Morris, S. (2010). *The Belousov Zhabotinsky reaction* [Video]. Vimeo. Retrieved February 27, 2015, from http://vimeo.com/17094664

Myrdal, G. (1944). *An American dilemma.* Harper and Row.

Noah, H. J. (1974). Fast-fish and loose-fish in comparative education. *Comparative Education Review, 18*(3), 341–347.

OECD. (2014). *PISA 2012 Financial literacy questions and answers.* OECD. Retrieved April 5, 2016, from http://www.oecd.org/pisa/pisaproducts/PISA-2012-FINANCIAL-LITERACY-QUESTIONS-AND-ANSWERS.pdf

Paulston, R. G. (1999). Mapping comparative education after postmodernity. *Comparative Education Review, 43*(4), 438–463.

Peaker, G. F. (1975). *An empirical study in twenty one countries: A technical report.* John Wiley and Sons.

Perkinson, H. J. (1995). *The imperfect panacea.* McGraw-Hill.

Pink, D. (2010). *Drive: The surprising truth about what motivates us.* Canongate Books.

Popper, K. R. (1957). *The poverty of historicism.* Routledge and Kegan Paul.

Popper, K. R. (1959). *The logic of scientific discovery.* Hutchinson Education.

Quality Assurance Agency for Higher Education (QAA). (2011). *The UK quality code for higher education: Part B: Assuring and enhancing academic quality* (Chapter B8: Programme monitoring and review). QAA. Retrieved February 27, 2015, from http://www.qaa.ac.uk/assuring-standards-and-quality/the-quality-code

Quality Assurance Agency for Higher Education (QAA). (2012). *Glossary.* QAA. Retrieved February 27, 2015, from http://www.qaa.ac.uk/Pages/GlossaryEN.aspx#39

Radford, M. (2006). Researching classrooms: Complexity and chaos. *British Educational Research Journal, 32*(2), 177–190.

Reynolds, C. W. (1987). Flocks, herds, and schools: A distributed behavioral model. *Computer Graphics, 21*(4), 25–34 (SIGGRAPH '87 conference proceedings). Retrieved December 6, 2017, from http://www.red3d.com/cwr/index.html

Robbins, D. (1988). *The rise of independent study*. Open University Press.

Robinson, K. (2010). *Changing paradigms* [Video]. Royal Society for the Encouragement of Arts, Manufactures and Commerce. Retrieved December 6, 2017, from https://www.thersa.org/discover/videos/rsa-animate/2010/10/rsa-animate---changing-paradigms

Rosenhead, J. (1998). Complexity theory and management practice. *Human Nature Review*. Retrieved February 27, 2015, from http://human-nature.com/science-as-culture/rosenhead.html

Sadler, M. (1900). How far can we learn anything of practical value from the study of foreign systems of education? [Lecture]. Reprinted 1979 in J. H. Higginson (Ed.), *Selections from Michael Sadler: Studies in world citizenship*. Dejall and Meyorre.

Sellars, W. (1953). Inference and meaning. *Mind, 62*, 313–338.

Tey, J. (2009). *The daughter of time* (reprint ed.). Arrow.

Tolstoy, L. (2007). *War and peace: Penguin classics*. Penguin Books.

Turner, D. A. (2004). *Theory of education*. Continuum.

Turner, D. A. (2007). *Theory and practice ef Education*. Continuum.

Turner, D. A. (2010). *Using the medical model in education: Can pills make you clever?* Continuum.

Turner, D. A. (2017). Comparison as an approach to the experimental method. *Compare: A Journal of Comparative and International Education, 47*(3), 406–415.

Turner, D. A. (2018). Teaching (some) basic concepts of comparative education using the game of life. *World Studies in Education, 18*(2), 43–60.

Turner, D. A. (2019). What is comparative education? In A. W. Wiseman (Ed.), *Annual review of comparative and international education 2018* (International Perspectives on Education and Society, Vol. 37, pp. 99–114). Emerald Publishing.

Turner, R. H. (1960). Sponsored and contest mobility and the school system. *American Sociological Review, 25*(6), 855–867.

Vygotsky, L. (1978). *Mind and society*. Harvard University Press.

Vygotsky, L. (1997). *The collected works of L.S. Vygotsky: Volume 4. The history of the development of higher mental functions* (R. W. Rieber, Ed.). Plenum.

Waldow, F., & Steiner-Khamsi, G. (Eds.). (2019). *Understanding PISA's attractiveness: Critical analyses of comparative policy studies*. Bloomsbury.

Wheatley, M. J. (1992). *Leadership and the new science: Learning about organization from an orderly universe*. Berrett-Koehler.

Wiener, N. (1954). *The human use of human beings: Cybernetics and society*. Houghton Mifflin.

WinLife32. (n.d.). Webpage. Retrieved February 27, 2015, from http://www.winlife32.com/

Printed in the United States
by Baker & Taylor Publisher Services